Illuminate Publishing

WJEC/Eduqas
GCSE PE

Matthew Penny

Published in 2022 by Illuminate Publishing Limited, an imprint of Hodder Education, an Hachette UK Company, Carmelite House, 50 Victoria Embankment, London EC4Y 0DZ

Orders: Please visit www.illuminatepublishing.com

or email sales@illuminatepublishing.com

© Matthew Penny

The moral rights of the author have been asserted.

All rights reserved. No part of this book may be reprinted, reproduced or utilised in any form or by any electronic, mechanical, or other means, now known or hereafter invented, including photocopying and recording, or in any information storage and retrieval system, without permission in writing from the publishers.

British Library Cataloguing in Publication Data

A catalogue record for this book is available from the British Library

ISBN 978-1-913963-10-1

04/22

Printed by: Cambrian Printers Ltd.

The publisher's policy is to use papers that are natural, renewable and recyclable products made from wood grown in sustainable forests. The logging and manufacturing processes are expected to conform to the environmental regulations of the country of origin.

Every effort has been made to contact copyright holders of material reproduced in this book. If notified, the publishers will be pleased to rectify any errors or omissions at the earliest opportunity.

Editor: Haremi Ltd., Cheltenham

Design: EMC Design Ltd, Bedford

Cover Design: Neil Sutton, Cambridge Design Consultants

Typeset by York Publishing Solutions Pvt Ltd, India

Cover photograph: © dolomite-summits / Shutterstock.com

Please note: The specification information in this book is correct at the time of going to press. It is, however, important to check with your examination board (WJEC or Eduqas) to view their current specification and assessment information.

Contents

How to Use This Book	4
1 Health, Training and Exercise	14
2 Exercise Physiology	56
3 Movement Analysis	90
4 Psychology of Sport and Physical Activity	130
5 Socio-Cultural Issues in Physical Activity and Sport	160
Glossary	184

Mark Schemes

Chapter 1	190
Chapter 2	192
Chapter 3	194
Chapter 4	196
Chapter 5	200

Appendices

Chapter 1	202
Chapter 2	206
Chapter 3	209
Chapter 4	210
Chapter 5	212

Index	214
Acknowledgements	220

How to Use This Book

This book is for the **WJEC** and **WJEC Eduqas GCSE** in **Physical Education**. It has been written specifically to cover the written assessment part of these specifications: **Unit 1: Introduction to Physical Education (WJEC)** or **Component 1: Introduction to Physical Education (Eduqas)**.

The book covers each section of the Unit 1/ Component 1 specification content. It includes stimulus questions covering the assessment objectives, theoretical information, practical investigations, top tips, quick checks and topic tests. All of these combined provide a comprehensive resource to build up and then check your knowledge and understanding.

What Is Unit 1 / Component 1?

Unit 1 / Component 1: Introduction to Physical Education is the theoretical part of the specification, tested via a written assessment. You will be assessed through a range of short-answer and extended-answer questions. (For WJEC you will also encounter questions based on audio-visual stimuli and sources.)

How the Book Is Organised

The book is designed to use creative and innovative content to support your learning and stimulate your curiosity. My teaching experience has shown me that this curiosity for learning often accompanies exam success. I aim to offer a range of different learning approaches that you can use both independently and in the classroom.

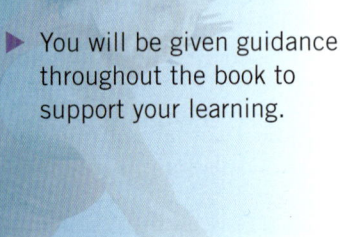

▶ You will be given guidance throughout the book to support your learning.

How to Use This Book

Unit 1 / Component 1 includes five content areas. Each chapter in this book focuses on one area:

- Chapter 1: Health, Training and Exercise
- Chapter 2: Exercise Physiology
- Chapter 3: Movement Analysis
- Chapter 4: Psychology of Sport and Physical Activity
- Chapter 5: Socio-Cultural Issues in Sport and Physical Activity

Use the tables on the next few pages to get a basic understanding of the GCSE specification and see how each chapter listed above corresponds to a specific part of the course. The column labelled 'Content' in each table lists the topics in the five content areas.

Go online to find the full specification for your exam board and find the tables of Unit 1 / Component 1 content. The tables in the full specifications also have a column called 'Amplification', which gives you more detail on what you need to know for each sub-topic. You can find the full information for your exam board on the exam board's website:

WJEC   https://www.wjec.co.uk/qualifications/physical-education-gcse/

Eduqas   https://www.eduqas.co.uk/qualifications/physical-education-gcse/

From time to time specifications are updated by awarding bodies, so do make sure you are working with the most recent version available. Each chapter of the book will cover the specification in a clear, concise and learner-friendly way to help you build your knowledge and understanding. You need to understand all the content for each key area in some depth. It's also important to understand that questions in the exams might cover more than one key area of the specification. Some questions may have parts covering two or three key areas.

◀ We will be considering a wide range of sporting activities.

How to Use This Book

▶ You will learn about the relationship between health, fitness and wellbeing.

Key area	Content
1. Health, training and exercise	Health, fitness and wellbeing
	The contribution which physical activity makes to health and fitness
	Consequences of a sedentary lifestyle
	Diet and nutrition
	Components of fitness
	Measuring health and fitness
	Methods of training
	Training zones (WJEC)
	Training zone graphs and analysing data (Eduqas)
	Principles of training and exercising
	Warm-up and cool-down
	Data analysis

Author Notes

For this key area, you will need to understand the relationship between **health, fitness and wellbeing**, as well as knowing the definition of each of these terms. Making links between **sedentary lifestyles, physical activity** and **diet and nutrition** is also important.

I also suggest you really understand the energy balance equation and the functions of nutrients. I recommend you gather a sound knowledge and understanding of **components of fitness** and their definitions, understand **measuring health and fitness** by knowing tests and test protocols for each component of fitness, and know the different **methods of training** that will improve each component of fitness. It is important to know the difference between a test and a method of training; this is where candidates often make mistakes.

Finally, you'll need to understand the three phases of a **warm-up** and a **cool-down**, as well as how to apply the **principles of training (SPOV)**, and **progressive overload (FID)**. Make sure you know all about **training zones**.

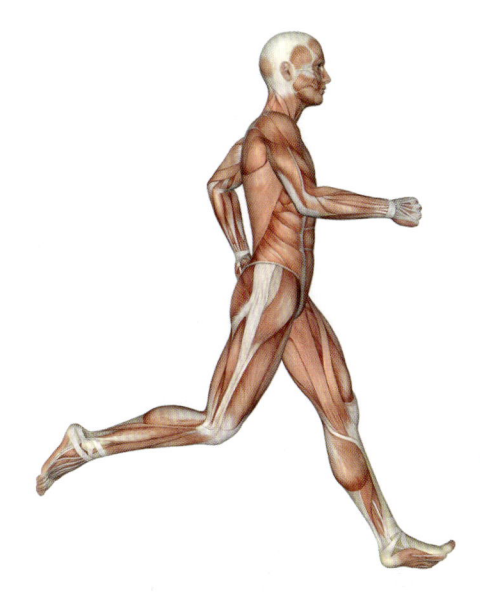

◀ Understanding the structure of the body will help you understand the impact that exercise has upon it.

Key area	Content
2. Exercise physiology	Muscular-skeletal system
	Cardio-respiratory and vascular system
	Aerobic and anaerobic exercise
	Short-term and long-term effects of exercise
	Data analysis

Author Notes

To help you get to grips with this key area, think about it in three sections:

1. The **muscular-skeletal system** content requires knowledge and understanding of the **structure and function** of both the skeletal system and the muscular system. You will need to know the major muscles, including the **characteristics of muscle fibres** and how they function within a variety of sports. You'll also need to know about bones, including the production of blood cells as well as their roles in producing different types of movement, alongside the roles of **tendons** and **ligaments**.

2. The **cardio-respiratory system** content requires that you know about the **structure and function** of both the cardiac system *and* the respiratory system. Make sure you can correctly label a diagram of the heart and lungs, and explain how nutrients, oxygen and waste products are **transported**, as well as understanding **cardiac values** and **lung volumes**.

3. You need to know about the **effects of exercise** on the body. You will need a good overview of both **aerobic and anaerobic exercise** as well as the characteristics and factors that affect both aerobic *and* anaerobic exercise. You'll need to know about how different nutrients link to different intensities of exercise. Exercise **intensity** and **duration** will affect both **short-term and long-term exercise**, so you need to understand these links. Can you link them to cardiac and lung volumes? Knowing your body's long-term **adaptations** after a lengthy period of training is also key. There is also a clear link to key area 1 in this chapter as you need to understand the effects of exercise on physical, social and mental well-being.

▶ Analysing the movement of the body will help you identify areas for improvement to maximise performance.

Key area	Content
3. Movement analysis	Muscle contractions
	Lever system
	Planes of and axes of movement
	Sports technology
	Data analysis

Author Notes

This key area starts by looking at **muscle contractions** and can be linked to the content on the muscular and skeletal systems in key area 2. You need to know the two types of muscle contractions, as well as the relationship between pairs of **antagonistic muscle contractions** and how they work together to produce movement. Muscles, joints, and the skeletal system work together to produce the three types of **lever systems**, which create movement. You need to know the **classification of levers** as well as identifying their **mechanical advantage or disadvantage**.

Some learners find **planes and axes of movement** a difficult concept to grasp. At their core is an understanding of the three planes of movement (**sagittal, frontal** and **transverse**) and the three axes of rotation (**sagittal, frontal** and **vertical**). What I've found really helps reinforce knowledge of these is applying them to sporting examples. This topic can be linked to key area 1, where you looked at movement of the muscular and skeletal systems.

The final part of this chapter is about **sports technology**. You will need to understand the role technology plays in analysing movement and how it can be used to improve performance. Technology can also play a role in coaching (developing performance) and officiating (making decisions). This topic might be linked to an AO3 question in which you **discuss** the positive and negative effects of its use in sport.

How to Use This Book

◀ Technology can be used to track performance targets.

Key area	Content
4. Psychology of sport and physical activity	Goal-setting
	Information processing
	Guidance
	Mental preparation
	Motivation
	Characteristics of a skilled performance
	Classifications of skills
	Types of practice
	Data analysis

Author Notes

In the exam this key area might be linked to AO2 and AO3 questions. **Goal setting** and setting **SMART targets** are areas you will also cover and apply when you set targets for your personal fitness programme (performance analysis and evaluation), so this is an opportunity to use the knowledge and experience you gain carrying out your coursework.

This key area also looks at how you learn different skills through different **types of practice** and **guidance**. These skills all have a **classification** and can be placed on skills continua. To excel in sport, you need to identify the **characteristics of a skilled performer**, and how they may look different from those of an unskilled performer.

When performing in sport, performers use a range of **mental preparation** techniques to improve **motivation** and performance. Sources of motivation can be **intrinsic** and **extrinsic**, so you will need to understand these and be able to apply them to a sporting context.

How to Use This Book

▶ It is important to understand the factors that influence participation in exercise.

Key area	Content
5. Socio-cultural issues in sport and physical activity	Participation
	Strategies to improve participation in sport and physical activity (this is a heading for WJEC, but also covered within the Eduqas specification)
	Provision
	Performance
	Data analysis

Author Notes

This chapter might be one linked to AO3 questions in which a knowledge and understanding of **factors that contribute to participation, provision and performance** is essential. The curriculum in **physical education** and what influence it has on your participation, as well as **physical literacy** in sport, is something I would advise you understand and reflect on as you work through this topic.

For an understanding of **strategies to improve participation in sport and activity**, I recommend you spend time researching campaigns that have been used to encourage participation, provision and performance (focusing on **race**, **gender** and **disability**). Listening to sports news may also help you to understand these issues and develop your own opinions to help you support your answers to AO3 questions. Watching sport can also help you to understand and create opinions on the **commercialisation of sport** and the role of the **media, advertising** and **globalisation**.

Sport also comes with the added pressure of winning, so you will need to understand the difference between **gamesmanship** and **sportsmanship** as well as knowing about **deviance** in sport.

Features of This Book

Big Question

One of the main ideas I've used when creating this textbook is to have a 'Big Question' running through each content area. You will see this each time you move from one chapter to the next. I've found the Big Question a very helpful way of providing a focus point for the learning that follows. Giving a real-life sporting example as the context for the knowledge and understanding that follows makes it easier to relate theory to an actual sporting event, movement or routine.

The theoretical knowledge still needs to be there underneath, but experience suggests that students find it easier to recall and apply that knowledge if they have the chance to use it in a real-world sporting context.

You'll see that at the end of each chapter we recap on the Big Question again. This is to help you consolidate your learning and check your knowledge and understanding. By the time you get to the end of the chapter and revisit the Big Question, you should have a good idea of how you'd answer it yourself.

THE BIG QUESTION

A Now that you have developed a knowledge and understanding of health, fitness and wellbeing, it's time to have a go at part 1 of the Big Question.

1. Describe one possible impact of a sedentary lifestyle. (2 marks)

Within each Big Question I've tried to put theory into a sporting context, making it easier for you to understand and recall.

Key Terms

A list of key terms is included at the start of each chapter. As you work through each chapter you need to develop your understanding of these key terms. This will help to demonstrate your knowledge and understanding when answering questions in your exam. Don't worry if you're not sure about the meaning of a key term – look it up in the glossary of all the key terms at the back of the book.

Key Terms

Aerobic training zone	Anaerobic training zone	Atherosclerosis	Calorie
Component of fitness	Continuous training	Dehydration	Diabetes
Exercise	Fitness	Fitness test	Health
Hydration	Hypertension	Insomnia	Interval training
Physical adaptations	Plateauing	Reliable	Reversibility
Sedentary	Tedium	Test protocol	Valid

Key terms have been picked out in blue so any time you see blue phrases, you'll know it is terminology you ought to try and learn.

Topic Test

A topic test with marks at the end of each topic gives you an example of an exam-style question that could be asked in this area of study. I have used this to show you how questions are broken down into component parts: a command word, topic, and qualifying word or phrase. These components are colour-coded in each topic test, so you can begin to build an insight into what the examiners are looking for when marking.

How to Use This Book

If you really grasp these colour codes and can learn to look for the component parts of a question, you'll give yourself the very best chance of writing a good answer.

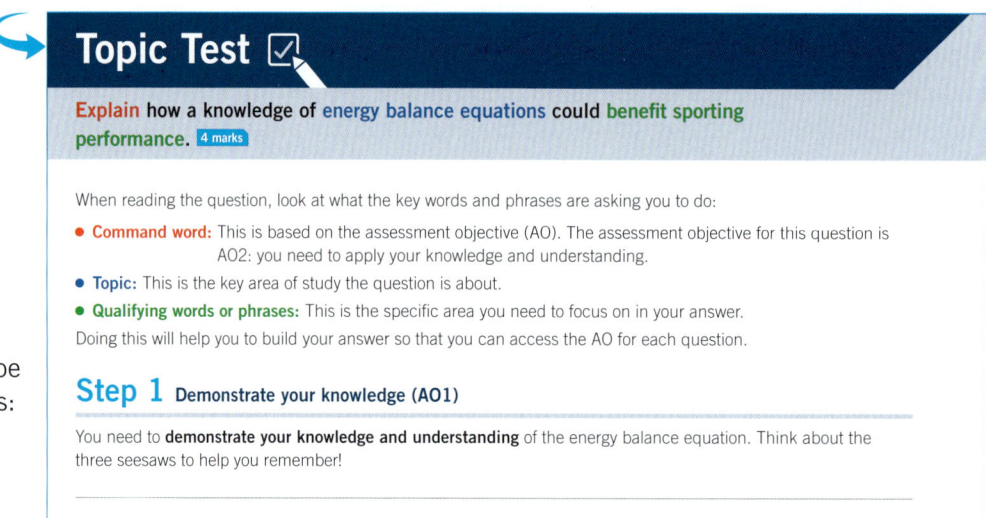

Topic Test ☑

Explain how a knowledge of energy balance equations could benefit sporting performance. **4 marks**

When reading the question, look at what the key words and phrases are asking you to do:
- **Command word:** This is based on the assessment objective (AO). The assessment objective for this question is AO2: you need to apply your knowledge and understanding.
- **Topic:** This is the key area of study the question is about.
- **Qualifying words or phrases:** This is the specific area you need to focus on in your answer.

Doing this will help you to build your answer so that you can access the AO for each question.

Step 1 Demonstrate your knowledge (AO1)

You need to **demonstrate your knowledge and understanding** of the energy balance equation. Think about the three seesaws to help you remember!

▶ Note the colours, they'll be the same in all topic tests:

red = command word

blue = topic area

green = qualifying words

Practical Investigation

Practical Investigation

Equipment

You will need the following:
> a range of sporting equipment linked to your chosen exercise/sporting activity
> a camera to capture the images of your chosen activities
> a pencil and paper to sketch the class of lever shown and record your results.

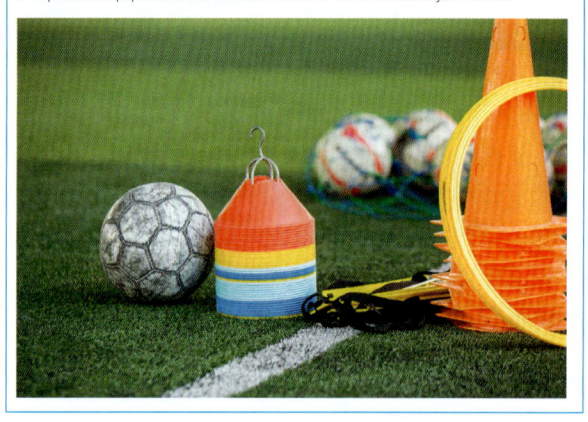

The practical investigations throughout the book give you opportunities to apply your knowledge. They include a range of research tasks, investigations and ideas to develop revision resources to help stimulate your curiosity for learning.

◀ Generally speaking, you can secure knowledge in your memory better with active learning: these practicals are perfect ways to try this out.

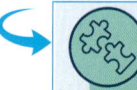

Extension

Extension

Using the principles of training, how can you make a training activity more demanding?

Extension tasks are there to encourage your curiosity about the topics covered and to stretch and challenge your understanding of them.

◀ Extension tasks are there to develop your understanding further.

How to Use This Book

Links to Assessment Objectives

One of the best ways you can prepare yourself for the exam is understanding what an assessment objective (AO) is and what it means. This helps you know what sort of question you're looking at and therefore what sort of exam skills you need to deploy in your answer. Links to the different AOs are included throughout each chapter.

These are the AOs for the WJEC and Eduqas GCSE PE specifications. In Unit 1 / Component 1, you will need to meet AO1, AO2 and AO3.

AO1: Demonstrate knowledge and understanding of the factors that underpin performance and involvement in physical activity and sport

AO2: Apply knowledge and understanding of the factors that underpin performance and involvement in physical activity and sport

AO3: Analyse and evaluate the factors that underpin performance and involvement in physical activity and sport

> **AO2**
> You will need to be able to apply your knowledge of which bones work together to produce movement at the major joints of the body.

◀ We always flag up the Assessment Objective involved – get used to identifying them.

Quick Check

These quick-fire questions throughout the book will help you regularly assess your understanding of each topic.

> **Quick Check**
> Identify the main function of carbohydrates. **AO1**

◀ These questions appear on the page very close to the text that you have just worked through; there's no excuse for not having a go and seeing how much information has sunk in!

Knowledge Check

Knowledge Checks allow you to check your understanding of topics in more depth and test your memory recall.

> **? Knowledge Check**
> Answer the following questions using your knowledge about this topic.
> 1. Which of the following fitness tests can be used to test cardiovascular endurance? **AO1**

◀ Knowledge Checks are designed so you can test your own knowledge independently.

Top Tips

Look for top tips, which provide helpful advice and support as you work through each chapter.

> **Top Tip**
> In a balanced diet:
> 55–60% of calories should be from carbohydrates
> 25–30% of calories should be from fats
> 15–20% of calories should be from proteins.

▶ These tips can cover anything, from key information you really should learn, to revision ideas, to how to answer certain sorts of questions.

13

CHAPTER 1

Health, Training and Exercise

The choices you make have an immediate and long-term impact on your lifestyle. Knowing about health, training and exercise will help you to understand the importance of making healthy lifestyle choices that influence not only your health and fitness but also your physical, social and psychological wellbeing.

THE BIG QUESTION

Whether you are looking to maintain a healthy lifestyle, develop your fitness by following an exercise programme or train for a competitive event, it is important to understand the relationship between health and exercise and to do the right exercise for you. As you complete this chapter, you will develop the knowledge, understanding and skills you need to understand this and to answer the Big Question.

These are the topics you'll need to answer the Big Question:

A **Health, fitness and wellbeing:** What are the risks of a sedentary lifestyle?

B **Diet and nutrition:** What diet would you need as a marathon runner? And as a 100 m sprinter?

C **Components of fitness and measuring health and fitness:** What components of fitness would a downhill mountain biker need, and how could you test them?

D **Methods of training and training zones:** What method of training might an athlete use to develop the speed they need to excel in an activity like football? What percentage of their maximum heart rate would they expect to work at while sprinting down the pitch?

E **Principles of training and exercise:** How can overload be used to make training sessions demanding?

F **Warm-up and cool-down:** What are the benefits of cooling down after a training session?

As you work through this chapter, we will identify all the skills and knowledge you'll need to be able to answer the Big Question. If you can do that, you will have brilliant AO1 and AO2 skills ready to use in your GCSE.

In this chapter you will learn about:

› the relationships between health, fitness and wellbeing
› the function of nutrients and the consequences of a sedentary lifestyle
› the components of fitness specific to sporting activities and the importance of measuring health and fitness
› different methods of training and the suitability of each method to the individual and the activity
› the principles of training and their application to developing health and fitness
› the benefits of warming up and cooling down.

In this chapter you will be using the following key terms. You can look up the meaning of these terms in the Glossary (page 184 onwards).

Key Terms

Aerobic training zone	Anaerobic training zone	Atherosclerosis	Calorie
Component of fitness	Continuous training	Dehydration	Diabetes
Exercise	Fitness	Fitness test	Health
Hydration	Hypertension	Insomnia	Interval training
Physical adaptations	Plateauing	Reliable	Reversibility
Sedentary	Tedium	Test protocol	Valid

1A Health, Fitness and Wellbeing

This is the question we're going to be working towards answering at the end of this topic.

> **1. Describe one possible impact of a sedentary lifestyle.**
>
> **AO1 – 2 marks**

There is a clear relationship between **health**, **fitness** and **exercise**. It is important that we are aware of the various factors that contribute to health. Being deemed 'healthy' can be based on three factors:

> physical wellbeing
> social wellbeing
> mental wellbeing.

You can define health as having full physical, social and mental wellbeing and being free from disease.

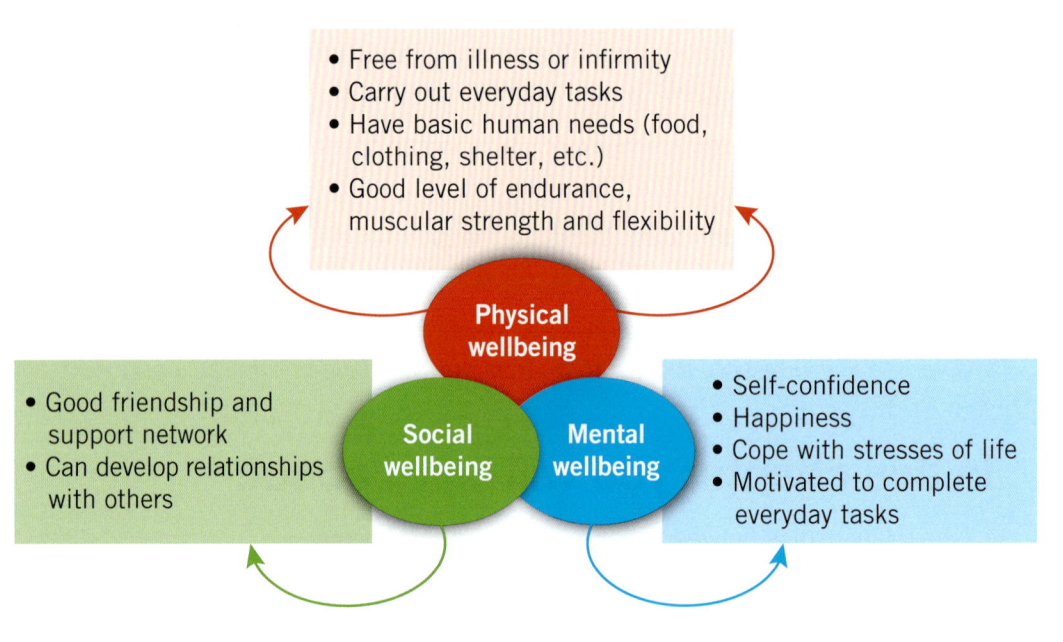

AO2

You will need to apply your knowledge of the three factors that contribute to a person's health.

- Free from illness or infirmity
- Carry out everyday tasks
- Have basic human needs (food, clothing, shelter, etc.)
- Good level of endurance, muscular strength and flexibility

Physical wellbeing

- Good friendship and support network
- Can develop relationships with others

Social wellbeing

Mental wellbeing

- Self-confidence
- Happiness
- Cope with stresses of life
- Motivated to complete everyday tasks

Top Tip

Use this diagram to help you describe the three factors that contribute to a person's health. This will help you with your AO1 knowledge.

Top Tip

Make sure you know the definitions of 'health', 'fitness' and 'exercise'. This will help you with your AO1 knowledge.

Exercise will have an impact on overall fitness. Fitness can be defined as an ability to meet the demands of your environment.

The effects of exercise on fitness depend on duration, intensity and type of exercise performed. Developing fitness through exercise is key to performing everyday tasks. A person carrying out an office job will have a different physical fitness requirement from that of a professional footballer. Therefore, everyday fitness is relative and based on the individual and their specific needs.

Wellbeing is the state of being comfortable and happy. The relationship between health and fitness can have an impact on wellbeing. The choices we make have a long-term effect on health, fitness and wellbeing. Some of these choices relate to our individual circumstances such as education, social relationships, nutrition and exercise.

Lifestyle Choices

Making positive lifestyle choices has many benefits for physical, social and mental health. Some considerations for positive lifestyles choices are:

> regular exercise
> eating a balanced diet
> having sufficient sleep
> balancing school/work and social commitments.

We make many choices in life but we don't often think about the positive and negative impacts they have on our lives. Both positive and negative lifestyle choices have an impact on our physical, social and mental wellbeing.

Positive choices like adhering to a training programme or taking part in regular exercise help with reducing body fat, which improves physical health. This may also help with mental and social health by leading to improved confidence and social interaction with like-minded people.

Negative choices such as leading a sedentary lifestyle, along with poor diet, smoking and misuse of drugs, can all contribute to a lack of self-confidence along with issues such as obesity, diabetes and hypertension.

Benefits of positive lifestyle choices include the following.

Physical	Social	Mental
> Reduces body fat > Strengthens muscles including the heart > Improves function of body's major systems, e.g. cardiovascular and respiratory systems > Allows you to complete daily physical tasks with ease > Reduces chances of developing some diseases, e.g. diabetes	> Helps you have the confidence to socialise and meet new friends > Helps you have the ability to deal with emotions > Helps deal with success and failure > Develops confidence to communicate > Develops confidence to work as a team – interaction with others	> Improves self-confidence > Improves motivation to complete daily tasks > Helps to deal with stress > Develops the ability to deal with emotions > Improves confidence > Exercise in particular will release serotonin, a 'feel-good' hormone

Quick Check

1. Identify three benefits of being physically active. **A01**
2. What is the definition of health? **A01**

Consequences of a Sedentary Lifestyle

It is important to reflect on any negative lifestyle choices you make so you can re-evaluate them and apply strategies to put things right. Negative lifestyle choices may include:

> a sedentary lifestyle
> poor diet

1A Health, Fitness and Wellbeing

> smoking

> alcohol

> misuse of drugs.

A sedentary lifestyle is one that involves little or no physical activity. This decision will have a big impact on the health and wellbeing of an individual. Potential consequences of a sedentary lifestyle are shown in the table.

Physical	Social	Mental
Increased risk of diseases such as: > diabetes > cancer > **atherosclerosis** > **obesity** > hypertension > **insomnia**	> increased feeling of isolation > feeling of loneliness > decreased motivation to socialise	> increase in stress levels > reduced motivation (giving up too easily, dropping out of activities, clubs, etc.) > poor self-esteem > poor body image > lack of self-confidence

Top Tip

Making positive lifestyle choices will have many benefits for your physical, social and mental health.

▶ Making careful, considered, healthy dietary choices helps promote health and wellbeing.

Taking part in sport and exercise not only benefits our physical health (by reducing the risk of disease, lowering blood pressure and making us physically strong), it also provides us with other benefits, such as improved motivation and the development of friendships. This interaction with others improves your mental and social health by creating a feeling of belonging which, in turn, will improve self-confidence and emotional happiness.

Practical Investigation

It is important that we make good choices in life. Create a poster identifying the **benefits of a healthy lifestyle**, which can be used to inform students about these choices.

Equipment

You will need the following:

> computer, tablet or other device with suitable software to create a poster

or

> A4 paper
> coloured pens or pencils.

Method

Create an information poster. You may wish to include:

> the heading 'Benefits of a healthy lifestyle'
> a definition of 'health'
> a range of positive choices under the headings of: physical, social and mental wellbeing
> effective use of graphics, colours and fonts
> text which is clear and to the point.

This practical investigation is designed to get you thinking about the benefits of a healthy lifestyle. As you reflect on your findings, think about the following question:

Is there anything that you could change about the lifestyle choices you make that might benefit your health?

Extension Activity

Create an information poster identifying the consequences of a sedentary lifestyle. Think carefully about the headings that you will include and how you will present your information in a clear and concise way.

1A Health, Fitness and Wellbeing

Topic Test

Our health will have an impact on our wellbeing as well as on our performance in sport. Identify two factors that contribute to a person's health. `2 marks`

When reading the question, look at what the key words and phrases are asking you to do:

- **Command word:** This is based on the assessment objective (AO). The assessment objective for this question is AO1: you need to demonstrate your knowledge and understanding.
- **Topic:** This is the key area of study the question is about.
- **Qualifying words or phrases:** This is the specific area you need to focus on in your answer.

Doing this will help you to build your answer so that you can access the AO for each question.

Demonstrate your knowledge (AO1)

You need to **demonstrate your knowledge and understanding** of health by **identifying** two factors that can contribute to it. Think about the definition of health.

_____
_____
_____
_____

Use the terms in the tick list of terminology to help you plan your answer to meet AO1. Look at how many marks are available to help you decide how much detail to include:

- ☐ Physical
- ☐ Social
- ☐ Mental
- ☐ Wellbeing
- ☐ Illness
- ☐ Injury

20

Chapter 1 Health, Training and Exercise

THE BIG QUESTION

RECAP

A Now that you have developed a knowledge and understanding of health, fitness and wellbeing, it's time to have a go at part 1 of the Big Question.

1. Describe one possible impact of a sedentary lifestyle. (2 marks)

What does the term 'sedentary' mean?

Identify **one** risk.

What impact might this risk have?

21

1B Diet and Nutrition

This is the question we're going to be working towards answering at the end of this topic.

> 2. Compare the diets of a typical marathon runner and a typical 100 m sprinter during the build-up to a race.
>
> AO2 – 4 marks

Energy Balance

This is the relationship between food going into the body to provide energy and the amount of energy (**calories**) used during exercise (or simply, nutrients + exercise = energy balance). It is also important to make links with exercise intensity and energy expenditure. For example, the more intense the exercise, the more energy you will use. This can also be applied to duration: the longer the activity, the more energy is used up.

With this in mind, there are three main outcomes:

Energy Balance

The amount of energy taken in through food equals the amount used in exercise and other activities. This means weight will stay the same.

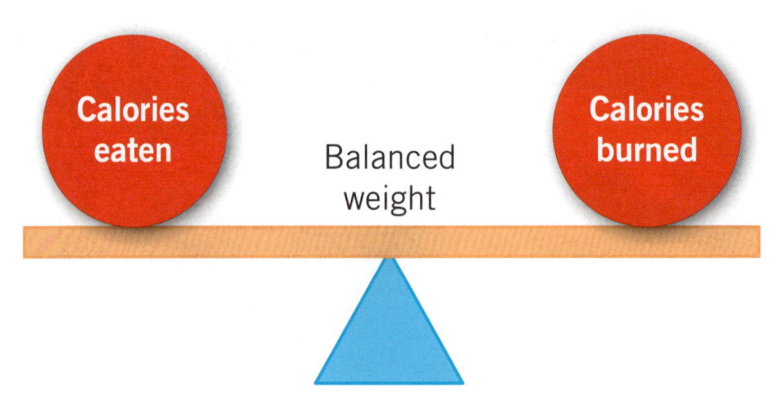

Calories eaten — Balanced weight — Calories burned

Positive Energy Balance

The amount of energy taken in through food is greater than the amount used. This means there will be a weight gain.

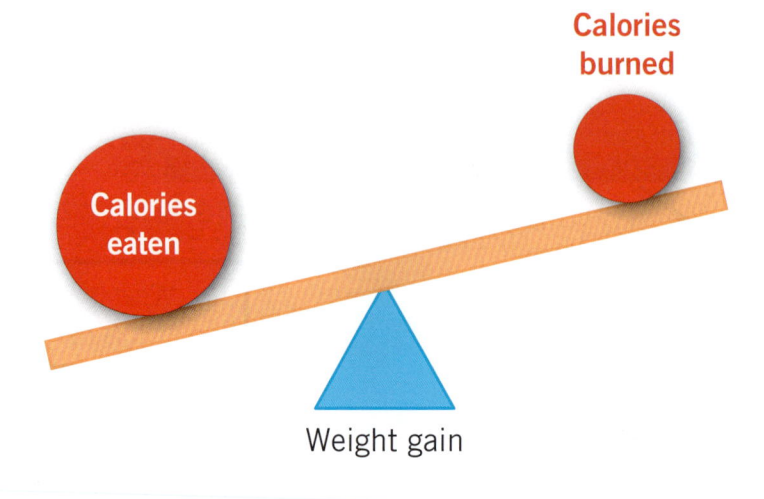

Calories eaten / Calories burned — Weight gain

AO2

You will need to apply your knowledge of the three factors that contribute to a person's health.

Top Tip

Use these diagrams to help you describe the three factors that contribute to a person's health. This will help you with your AO1 knowledge.

Negative Energy Balance

The amount of energy taken in through food is less than the amount used. Therefore, there is weight loss.

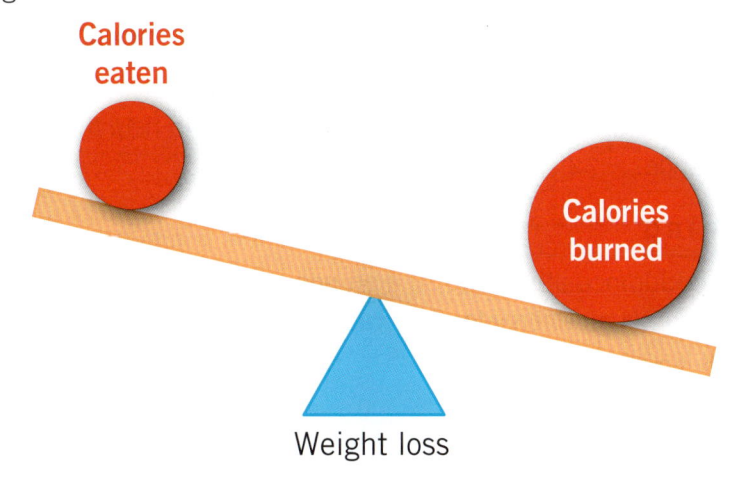

Calories eaten

Calories burned

Weight loss

Function of Nutrients

The energy our body needs comes from the calories we consume. Our calorie intake should come from a balanced diet consisting of carbohydrates, fats, protein, vitamins and minerals as well as water.

When each nutrient is consumed and broken down in the body, it is used to perform a specific function, as shown in the table.

Nutrient	Function
Carbohydrates	The main source of energy
	Simple carbohydrates (sugars) – provide a quick release of energy
	Complex carbohydrates (starches) – provide a slow release of energy
	Used for medium- to high-intensity activities
Fats	A source of energy
	Used for insulation
	Includes both saturated fats (such as animal fats) and unsaturated fats (such as vegetable oils)
	Used in low-intensity activities
Proteins	For tissue growth and repair
	Can be used for energy in extreme circumstances
Vitamins	Involved in bone growth and general health
	Help to maintain and regulate bodily functions
Minerals	Essential for bone growth
	Help to maintain and regulate bodily functions
Water	Essential for hydration
	Essential for all body functioning

Quick Check

Identify the main function of carbohydrates. **A01**

Top Tip

In a balanced diet:

55–60% of calories should be from carbohydrates

25–30% of calories should be from fats

15–20% of calories should be from proteins.

1B Diet and Nutrition

Nutrition and Physical Activity

When you become more active, your body requires more energy so it is important you eat the right nutrients to maintain an energy balance. Athletes consume more nutrients than non-athletes due to the energy demands (intensity and duration) of their sport or training programme.

Athletes may use nutritional strategies like the ones below to help them achieve their desired performance.

Carbo-loading

This is used by endurance athletes to take on board more carbohydrate, which will provide them with enough energy for their race. They eat more starchy carbohydrate during the week leading up to the race.

Protein Intake

Protein is used for growth and repair so athletes looking to increase their muscle strength or mass follow a high-protein diet alongside their specific training programme.

Hydration

Hydration is important for all athletes as it helps to maintain their athletic performance. Insufficient water in the body will result in **dehydration**, which reduces reaction time, decision-making ability and overall performance.

> **AO2**
> You will need to apply your knowledge of specific nutrients and their functions to examples in sport.

> **Top Tip**
> The recommended calorie intake is 2500 calories per day for an average adult male and 2000 calories per day for an average adult female. Athletes consume considerably more depending on the intensity and duration of their sport and/or training programme.

▶ A healthy, balanced diet will include a range of types of food. For example, the foods shown here are good sources of protein.

> **Quick Check**
>
> Match the nutrient to its function. **AO1**
>
> | Carbohydrate | Used for insulation |
> | Fat | Required for growth and repair |
> | Protein | Main source of energy |

It is important to consume the right nutrients to fuel your body for physical activity.

Chapter 1 Health, Training and Exercise

Practical Investigation

Print the revision mat in Appendix 1.1 in A3 size or copy out the headers onto a large sheet of paper leaving space for your answers.

Method

Fill in the answers to the questions about macronutrients and micronutrients to show your knowledge and understanding of the main components of a balanced diet.

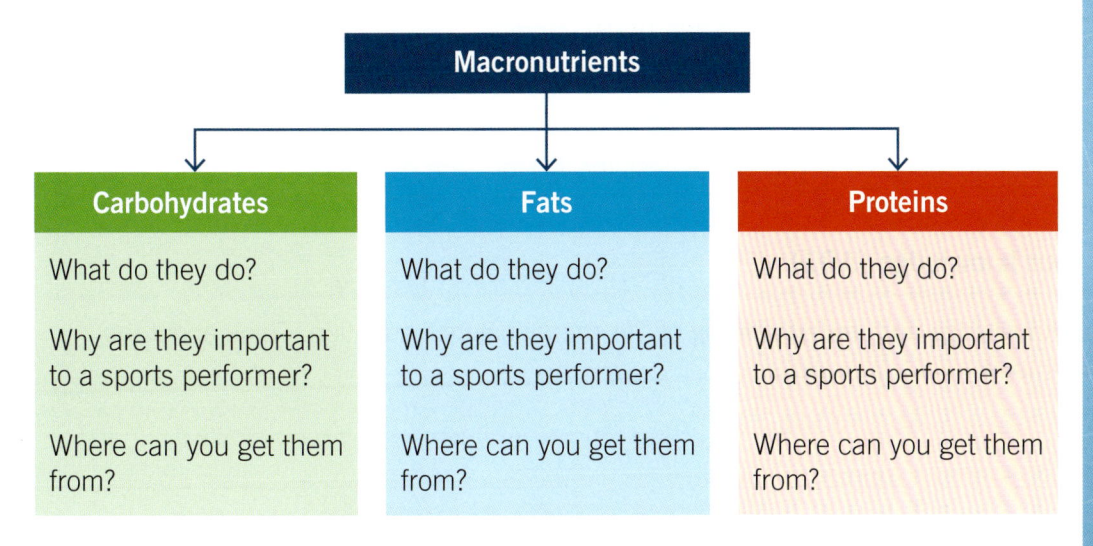

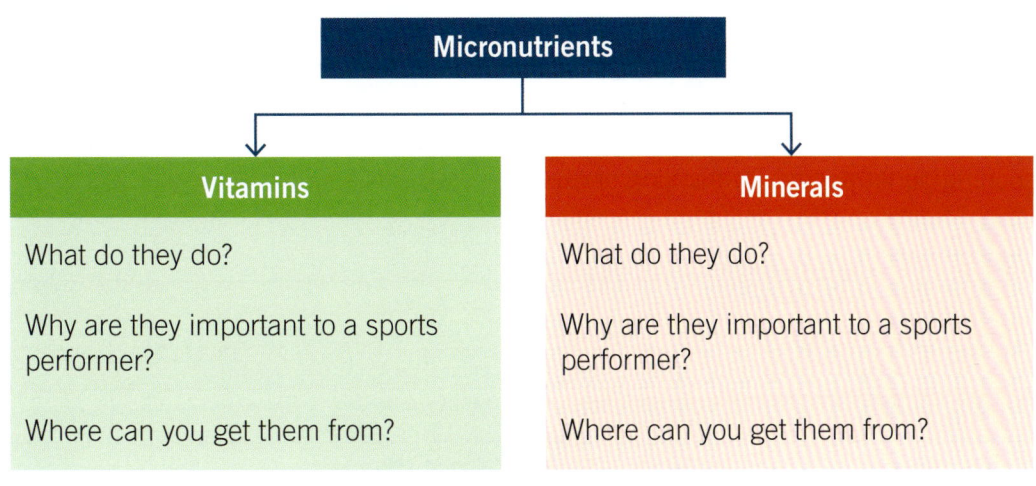

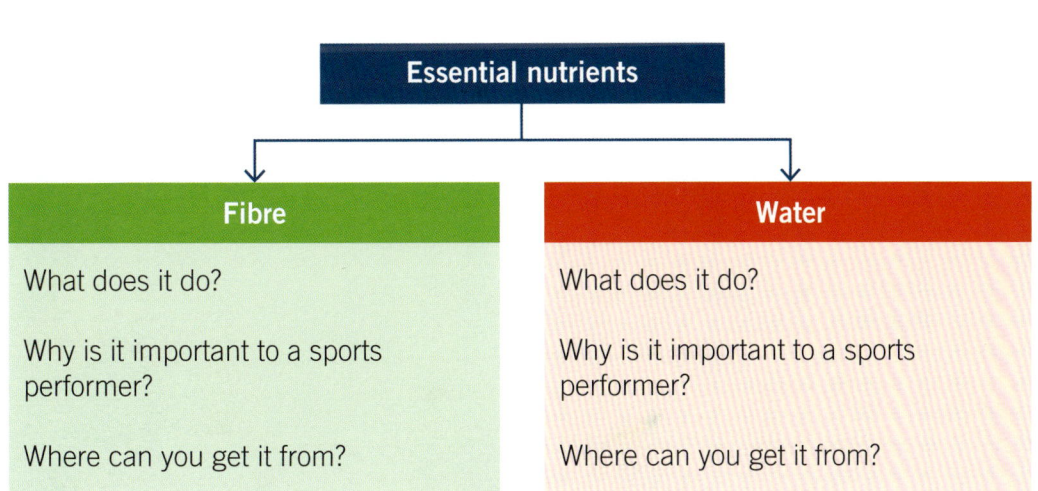

Macronutrients

Carbohydrates
What do they do?
Why are they important to a sports performer?
Where can you get them from?

Fats
What do they do?
Why are they important to a sports performer?
Where can you get them from?

Proteins
What do they do?
Why are they important to a sports performer?
Where can you get them from?

Micronutrients

Vitamins
What do they do?
Why are they important to a sports performer?
Where can you get them from?

Minerals
What do they do?
Why are they important to a sports performer?
Where can you get them from?

Essential nutrients

Fibre
What does it do?
Why is it important to a sports performer?
Where can you get it from?

Water
What does it do?
Why is it important to a sports performer?
Where can you get it from?

Extension

Conduct further research online to develop your knowledge and understanding of the importance of fibre and water in our diets. Fill in the answers to the questions about fibre and water on the revision mat.

1B Diet and Nutrition

Topic Test

Explain how a knowledge of **energy balance equations** could *benefit sporting performance*. **4 marks**

When reading the question, look at what the key words and phrases are asking you to do:

- **Command word:** This is based on the assessment objective (AO). The assessment objective for this question is AO2: you need to apply your knowledge and understanding.
- **Topic:** This is the key area of study the question is about.
- **Qualifying words or phrases:** This is the specific area you need to focus on in your answer.

Doing this will help you to build your answer so that you can access the AO for each question.

Step 1 Demonstrate your knowledge (AO1)

You need to **demonstrate your knowledge and understanding** of the energy balance equation. Think about the three seesaws to help you remember!

_____
_____
_____

Step 2 Apply your knowledge and understanding (AO2)

You need to **apply your knowledge and understanding** of the energy balance equation in order to **explain** how understanding it could benefit sporting performance. Try thinking of examples, such as sports that require you to meet a weight criterion.

_____
_____
_____
_____

Use the terms in the tick list of terminology to help you plan your answer to meet AO2. Look at how many marks are available to help you decide how much detail to include:

- ☐ Calories eaten
- ☐ Calories burned
- ☐ Weight gain
- ☐ Weight loss
- ☐ Energy balance

Chapter 1 Health, Training and Exercise

THE BIG QUESTION

B Now that you have developed a knowledge and understanding of diet and nutrition, it's time to have a go at part 2 of the Big Question.

2. Compare the diets of a typical marathon runner and a typical 100 m sprinter during the build-up to a race. (4 marks)

Remember that the question asks about comparing the diets. Look at the prompts below and apply your knowledge to how they influence the type of diet needed by each type of athlete.

RECAP

Top Tip

Annotate the question **topic**, **command word** and **qualifying words/ phrases** in the Big Question.

- Long duration activity
- Will need energy release over a long period
- Short duration activity
- Will need quick release of energy
- Will need muscle growth to help generate speed and power

1C Components of Fitness and Measuring Health and Fitness

This is the question we're going to be working towards answering at the end of this section.

> 3. A downhill mountain biker needs to contract her leg muscles quickly and apply force to the pedal in an explosive act to generate speed and complete the course in the fastest time possible.
>
> a) Other than speed, identify one component of fitness the mountain biker requires. (1 mark)
>
> b) Outline a definition of the component of fitness you identified in part a). (1 mark)
>
> c) Identify a fitness test that can be used to test the component of fitness you named in part a). (1 mark)
>
> AO1 – 3 marks

There are 11 **components of fitness**. You will need to:

> know the definition of each component of fitness and apply it to a sporting example

> measure health and fitness using tests and understand **test protocols**.

Components of fitness can be classified into 'skill-related' and 'health-related' components. The tables below show the classification, definition and an example for each of the 11 components of fitness.

Skill-related components of fitness:

Skill-related component of fitness	Definition	Example in sport	Lifestyle example
Agility	Ability to change direction at speed	A rugby player side-stepping a defender	Changing direction when walking in a busy street
Balance	Ability to hold your centre of mass over a base of support	A gymnast holding a handstand	Standing on tiptoes to reach an item on a shelf
Coordination	Ability to use two or more body parts at the same time	A tennis serve	Catching an object

Top Tip

To help you remember the skill-related components, use **ABC S**mart **P**eople **R**ead:

Agility

Balance

Coordination

Speed

Power

Reaction time

Chapter 1 Health, Training and Exercise

Skill-related component of fitness	Definition	Example in sport	Lifestyle example
Speed	Moving body parts or changing location as quickly as possible	100 m sprint in athletics	Running to school
Power	Strength × speed. Moving a mass quickly	Shot put; a basketball player jumping to slam-dunk	Jumping over a puddle
Reaction time	The time taken to react to a stimulus	An athlete reacting to a starting pistol; a wicketkeeper in cricket reacting to catch a ball	Playing a computer game

Health-related components of fitness:

Health-related component of fitness	Definition	Example in sport	Lifestyle example
Body composition	Body shape. The percentage of body weight that is fat, muscle and bone	A 100 m sprinter would have more muscle mass than a marathon runner	People who are less physically active are less likely to have a healthy body composition
Flexibility	The range of movement at a joint	A gymnast performing the splits	Bending down to pick up an item
Muscular strength	A force a muscle can produce to overcome a resistance	A rugby player pushing in a scrum	Carrying a suitcase
Muscular endurance	The ability for a group of muscles to work continuously over a period of time	A cyclist continuously using the muscles in the legs to pedal the bike	Using leg muscles to walk up a flight of stairs
Cardiovascular endurance	The ability for the body to exercise continuously for a period of time	A marathon runner continuously working the body for the duration of the race	Walking to school

Top Tip

To help you remember the health-related components of fitness, use **B**ig **F**unny **M**en **M**unch **C**ookies:

Body composition

Flexibility

Muscular strength

Muscular endurance

Cardiovascular endurance

Quick Check

Identify the definition of flexibility. **A01**

Explain why a football player needs to use speed during a match. **A02**

29

1C Components of Fitness...

Measuring Health and Fitness

Measuring health and fitness using a range of **fitness tests** can be useful in many ways.

| Identify base level of fitness | Identify strengths and weaknesses | Monitor developments | Compare fitness levels | Motivation by seeing progress |

It is a good idea to test:

> **before a training programme:** this will identify the baseline as well as strengths and weaknesses so you can set specific goals

> **during a training programme:** for example, if you are following an eight-week training programme, testing after four weeks will allow you to monitor your progress. Data from your tests will allow you to make appropriate adjustments to your programme

> **after a training programme:** this will allow you to compare your fitness before the programme to your fitness afterwards to evaluate your progress, as well as comparing your results with others.

Each component of fitness must be tested using a suitable test (for some components, there is more than one type of test). For the test results to be both **valid** and **reliable** it is important to follow the correct test protocol. The ability to track progress over time depends on the reliability of the test. Tests could be inaccurate if carried out inconsistently or using the wrong protocol, or could be measuring something irrelevant to the performer or their activity if not valid.

The tables below show the component, test and a summary of the test protocol.

Skill-related component of fitness	Test	Summary of protocol
Agility	Illinois agility run	> Use cones to set out the standard course for the test, using exact measurements > Start by lying face down on the start line > Complete course following the route through the cones as fast as possible > Time how long it takes
Balance	Stork balance test	> Stand with your hands on your hips > Place one foot on the inside knee of the opposite leg > Raise the heel of the standing foot and hold the balance for as long as possible > Time how long you can hold the balance
Coordination	Alternate hand throw	> Stand 2 m from a wall with a flat surface > Throw a tennis ball against the wall with one hand and then catch it with the other > Repeat the process and count the number of successful catches in 30 seconds

Chapter 1 Health, Training and Exercise

Skill-related component of fitness	Test	Summary of protocol
Speed	30 m (or 50 m) sprint test	› Find an even surface and mark out a distance of 30 m (or 50 m) › Using a rolling/flying start, sprint as fast as you can to the finish › Time how long it takes
Power	Vertical jump	› Find a wall and stand side on from it › With the arm closest to the wall, reach up keeping both feet flat on the floor. Mark the height you can reach using chalk › From a standing position, jump as high as you can, making a mark on the wall at the highest point › Measure the distance between the two points in cm
Reaction time	Ruler drop test	› An assistant holds a 30 cm ruler vertically at the 0 cm point above your index finger › The assistant releases the ruler without warning › Catch the ruler › Measure the distance the ruler has dropped. This is the measurement on the ruler at the top of your thumb and index finger

Health-related component of fitness	Test	Summary of protocol
Body composition	Skinfold callipers test (body fat/body density test)	› Take four measurements: biceps, triceps, back and hips › Convert readings to body fat percentage
Flexibility	Sit and reach	› Remove shoes › Sit on the floor with knees locked and feet against a sit and reach box › With one hand on top of the other, reach forward and push the slider forwards as far as possible › Record the distance
Muscular endurance	One-minute press-up test	› Perform a press-up in which the arm moves from a straight position to an angle of 90 degrees at the elbow › Perform as many press-ups as possible in 60 seconds
	Abdominal curl test	› Lie on the mat with feet flat on the floor and knees bent › A partner supports your ankles › Sit up on the bleep and then down on the bleep › Stay in time with the bleeps (progressive test) › Record how many sit-ups completed

1C Components of Fitness...

Health-related component of fitness	Test	Summary of protocol
Muscular strength	Hand grip dynamometer	› Hold the hand grip dynamometer with your dominant hand › Squeeze with maximum effort and record result › Repeat the test three times and record the best score
	One rep max test	› Select the body part that is to be tested and a suitable lift, e.g. pectorals – bench press › Conduct an appropriate warm-up › Lift a weight that is more than your training weight › Rest for five to ten minutes › Repeat the process but add weight in suitable increments › Test ends when weight cannot be lifted using the correct technique › Record the last weight lifted correctly
Cardiovascular endurance	Multi-stage fitness test	› Measure a course of 20 m and set up equipment to play a recording of the bleeps at the correct intervals › Run the 20 m course in time with the bleeps › The time between the bleeps will decrease as you move up through the levels › Keep running until exhaustion prevents you from reaching the distance on the bleep › Record the level and shuttle you reach
	Cooper's 12-minute run	› Cover as much distance as you can in 12 minutes (running or swimming) › Ideally carry out the test on a running track or an area where you can clearly calculate the distance travelled during the time

? Knowledge Check

Answer the following questions using your knowledge about this topic.

1. Which of the following fitness tests can be used to test cardiovascular endurance? **A01**

   ☐ Abdominal curl test
   ☐ 12-minute Cooper run
   ☐ Sit and reach test

2. Fill in the blanks using the words in the box. **A01**

   | measure   accurate   valid   reliable |

   A fitness test needs to be valid and _____. A/an _____ test will _____ what it is supposed to measure. A reliable test will be _____ and precise.

Chapter 1 Health, Training and Exercise

Data Analysis

Below is a table of fitness results from a group of GCSE PE candidates. The graph shows results for three candidates who carried out the following tests: one rep max, 12-minute Cooper run and the 30m sprint test.

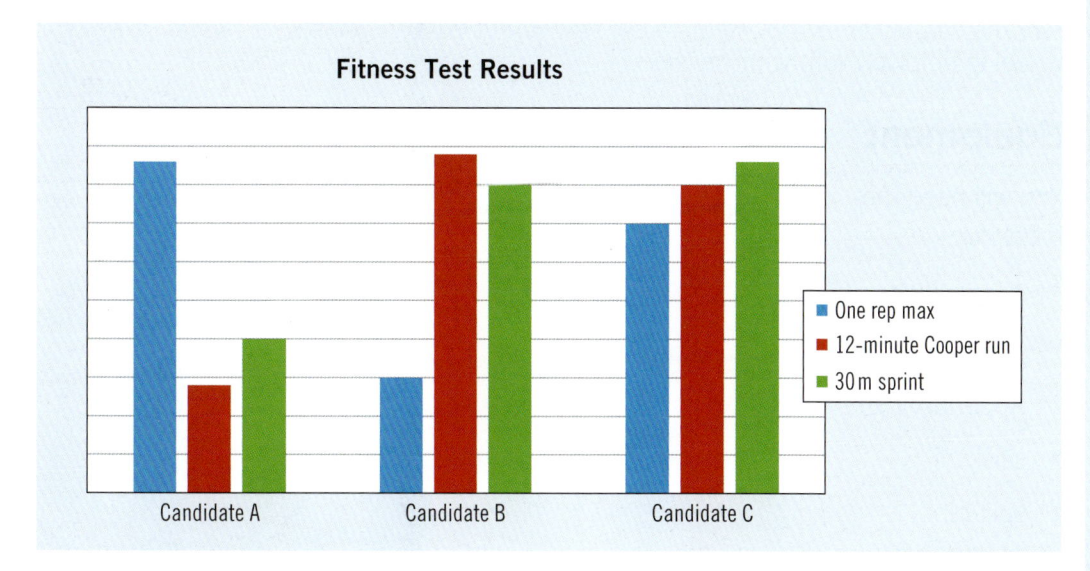

Fitness Test Results

(Bar graph showing results for Candidate A, Candidate B, and Candidate C across three tests: One rep max (blue), 12-minute Cooper run (red), 30m sprint (green).)

1. Candidate B has the highest score in the 12-minute Cooper run test. Explain the protocol for this test.
2. Candidate C is a team games player. Explain why strength and speed are important components of fitness in team games.

As well as testing, there are other tools for measuring health and fitness:

Health questionnaire or a physical activity readiness questionnaire (PAR-Q) – often used as part of an induction if you are joining a fitness gym; employers may use them to establish if an employee is fit and healthy enough to work.

Screening methods – heart rate monitors, blood pressure readers and calorie trackers for the amount of energy spent exercising and taken in through food. These can be used for monitoring and to assess if there are any potential problems.

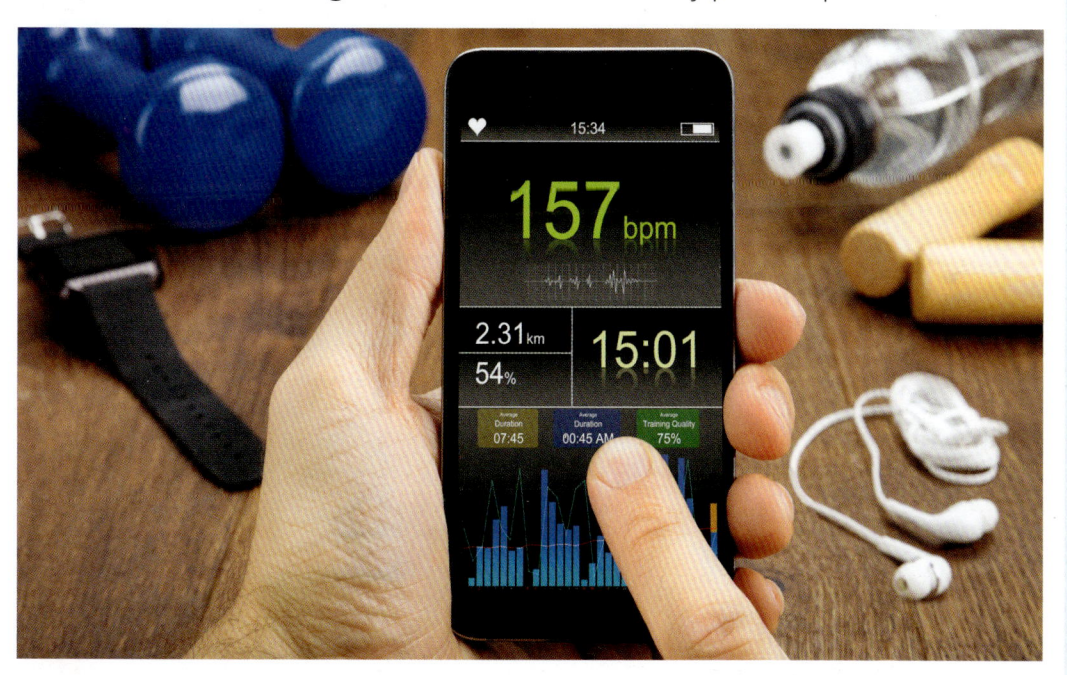

Top Tip
Test results can be compared to national norms – you can look these up online.

AO2
You will need to know the protocol for each test as well as understanding the terms validity and reliability.

Quick Check
Identify the recognised tests for:

cardiovascular endurance: _____

agility: _____ **AO1**

◀ Technology has made it easier for people to monitor their health whilst exercising.

33

1C Components of Fitness...

Practical investigation

Revision Wheel

You will need to know the definition of each component of fitness. Create a revision wheel to help you with your revision.

Equipment

You will need the following:

> a photocopy of the revision wheel task (see Appendix 1.2)
> scissors
> split pin.

Method

1. Using the photocopy of the revision wheel task, carefully cut out each template so that you have two discs.

2. Take the blue disc and carefully cut out a window along the dotted lines.

3. Fold in the tab on the blue disc.

4. Using the split pin, carefully pierce the centre of the blue disc. Push the split pin through the hole.

5. Place the gold disc behind the blue disc. Pierce the centre with the split pin.

6. Open up the split pin and carefully enlarge the holes if necessary, making sure the wheel can turn smoothly.

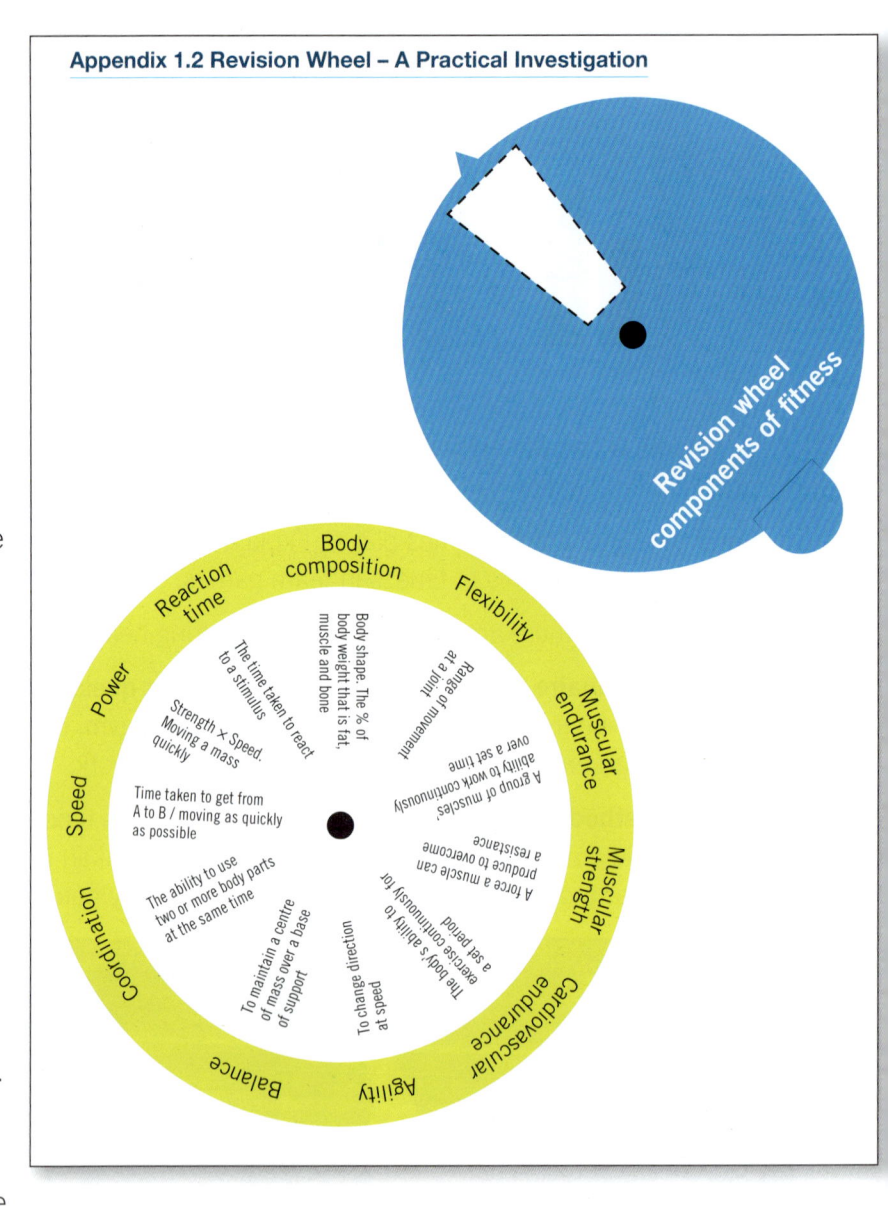

Appendix 1.2 Revision Wheel – A Practical Investigation

Chapter 1 Health, Training and Exercise

How to Use the Wheel

Line up the arrow with one of the components of fitness to see its definition within the 'definition window'.

Use the revision wheel to test yourself and your peers until you can recall all 11 definitions for the components of fitness.

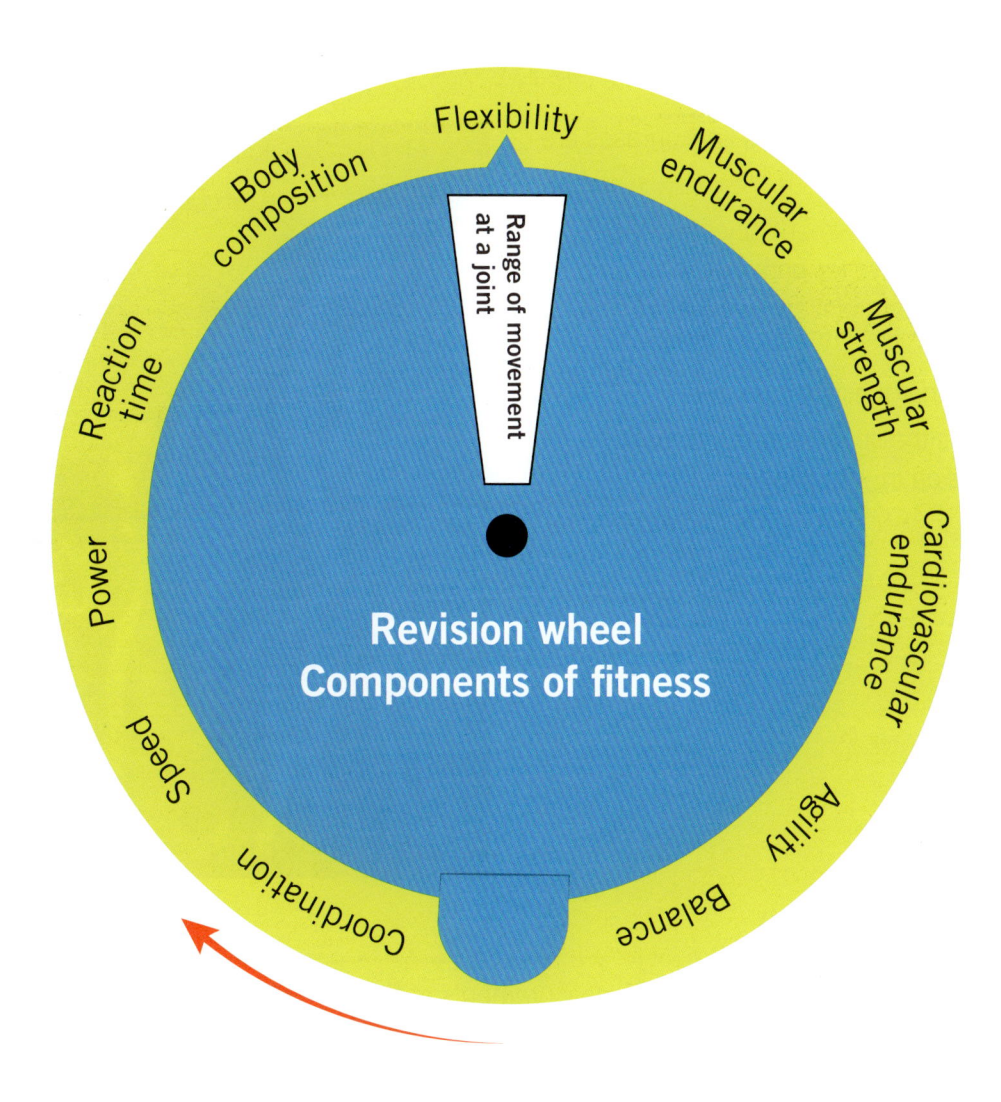

**Revision wheel
Components of fitness**

Components around the wheel: Flexibility, Muscular endurance, Muscular strength, Cardiovascular endurance, Agility, Balance, Coordination, Speed, Power, Reaction time, Body composition.

Definition window: Range of movement at a joint

Extension Activity

Can you create your own revision wheel for fitness testing?

Use the same components of fitness as shown on the wheel above. Replace each definition with the fitness test used to test that particular component of fitness. You can use the tests from the table on pages 30–32 but remember some components may have more than one test!

35

1C Components of Fitness...

Topic Test

A netball player needs to use agility to receive a pass by changing direction at speed and beating an opposing player into space.

a) **Identify** a **test** for **agility**. `1 mark`

b) **Describe** the **test protocol** for **agility**. `3 marks`

When reading the question, look at what the key words and phrases are asking you to do:

- **Command word:** This is based on the assessment objective (AO). The assessment objective for both question parts is AO1: you need to demonstrate knowledge and understanding.
- **Topic:** This is the key area of study the question is about.
- **Qualifying words or phrases:** This is the specific area you need to focus on in your answer.

Doing this will help you to build your answer so that you can access the AO for each question.

Step 1 Demonstrate your knowledge (AO1)

You need to **demonstrate your knowledge and understanding** of measurements of fitness by **identifying** an appropriate test to answer part a).

The test for agility is: _____

Step 2 Demonstrate your knowledge (AO1)

You need to **demonstrate your knowledge and understanding** of test protocols by **describing** the appropriate protocol to answer part b). Remember, a protocol is a set of clear instructions about how a test should be completed.

The test protocol for this agility test is:

_____
_____
_____
_____
_____

Chapter 1 Health, Training and Exercise

THE BIG QUESTION

RECAP

C You are starting to build the knowledge and understanding you need to answer the Big Question. You have already answered parts 1 and 2; now it's time to answer part 3 and apply your knowledge and understanding.

3. A downhill mountain biker needs to contract her leg muscles quickly and apply force to the pedal in an explosive act to generate speed and complete the course in the fastest time possible.

a) Other than speed, identify one component of fitness the mountain biker requires. (1 mark)

b) Outline a definition of the component of fitness you identified in part a). (1 mark)

c) Identify a fitness test that can be used to test the component of fitness you named in part a). (1 mark)

What components of fitness will help you ride a bike?

If you don't know anything about mountain biking, just think about riding a bike in general.

What component will help you to produce an explosive movement that is not speed?

What is the definition of this component of fitness?

How would you test this component?

37

1D Methods of Training and Training Zones

This is the question we're going to be working towards answering at the end of this section.

> 4. Football players need to develop speed to help them cover the pitch.
> a) Identify a method of training that a centre forward in football could use to develop their speed. (1 mark)
> b) Speed relies on the anaerobic energy system. What percentage of a player's maximum heart rate are they likely to be working at when sprinting down the pitch? (1 mark)
>
> AO1 – *2 marks*

When choosing a method of training, it is important to consider the component of fitness you want to develop, as well as how appropriate it is to you as an individual and to your activity. You should also consider how the methods of training fit into a training session, which should also include an appropriate warm-up and cool-down.

This topic will help you to understand:

› the different methods of training
› the suitability of each method of training, depending on the context
› the importance of a warm-up and a cool-down.

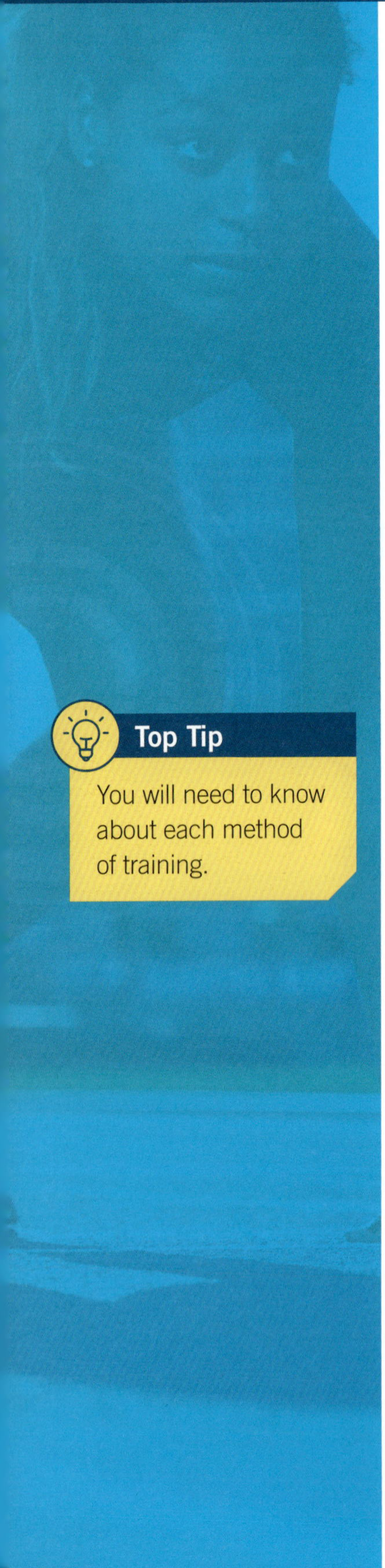

There are two main methods of training: **interval training** and **continuous training**.

The diagram gives information on the two methods of training along with examples and the recommended intensity and duration for each method.

Top Tip

You will need to know about each method of training.

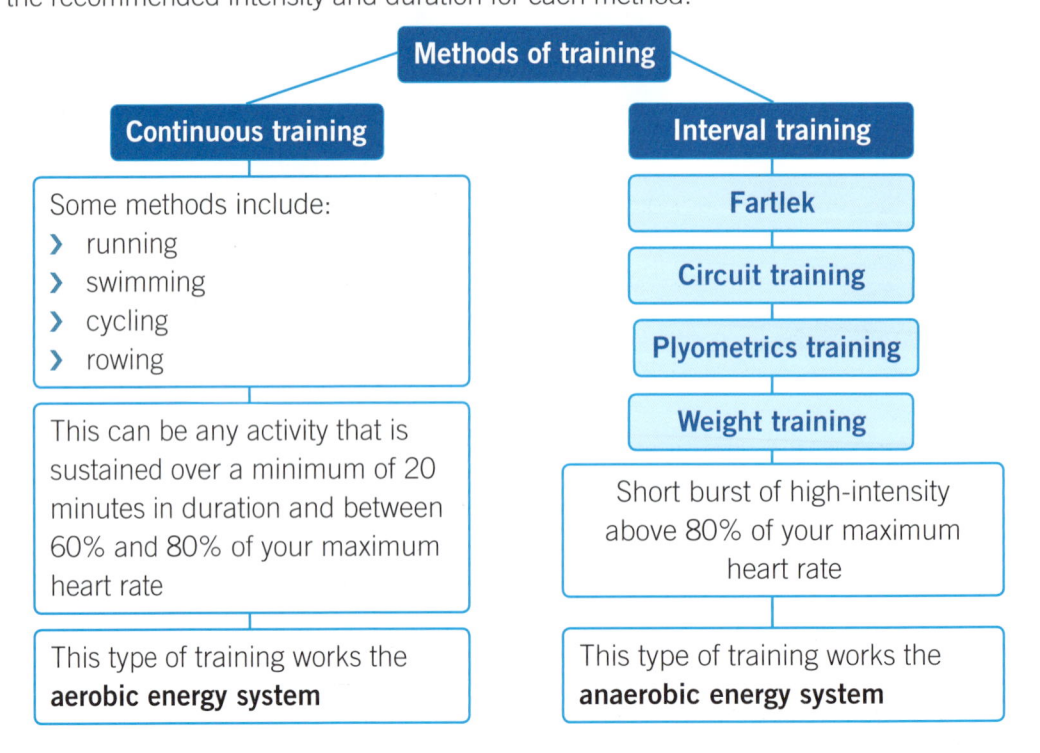

Methods of training

Continuous training

Some methods include:
› running
› swimming
› cycling
› rowing

This can be any activity that is sustained over a minimum of 20 minutes in duration and between 60% and 80% of your maximum heart rate

This type of training works the **aerobic energy system**

Interval training

- Fartlek
- Circuit training
- Plyometrics training
- Weight training

Short burst of high-intensity above 80% of your maximum heart rate

This type of training works the **anaerobic energy system**

Continuous training is exercise maintained without rest over 20 minutes or more, while working in the range of 60% to 80% of maximum heart rate. This method of training develops components of fitness that require endurance and involves work in the aerobic training zone. A sport that requires cardiovascular endurance can benefit from continuous training. Examples of continuous training methods include:

- running
- walking
- cycling
- swimming
- rowing.

Interval training is exercise at an intensity of 80% of your maximum heart rate and above. This intensity can only be sustained for short periods of time, which are followed by periods of rest. Each of these short periods of exercise is known as a set, and each time you repeat an exercise within that period is known as a rep. This method of training develops explosive components of fitness, such as speed, power and strength. It involves working in the anaerobic training zone.

The following are methods of interval training:

Fartlek training (or speed play) is an interval type training where there are intervals of work at different intensities and over different terrains. An example of this would be a walk, jog or sprint at different gradients and terrain to add intensity. This type of training is best done in parks with a variety of terrain.

Circuit training involves a series of exercise organised at stations. Each station has an exercise which is specific to the performer's needs. A station can focus on specific components of fitness, working different muscle groups and body parts. Completion of work at a station can be timed or can consist of a set number of reps. Completion of a series of stations is a circuit.

> **Top Tip**
>
> You can calculate an estimate of your maximum heart rate using this rule:
>
> maximum heart rate = 220 − your age

◀ Fartlek training should be carried out on a variety of different terrains.

◀ Performers need to carry out a set number of reps at each training station.

It is important that performers use correct techniques and that the energy demands and intensity are suitable to their needs.

Flexibility training can be performed as a circuit, part of a training session or a stand-alone flexibility/mobility session. This involves increasing the range of movement at a joint through a range of stretching techniques.

- **Static stretching:** This is where a stretch is held in a static position using resistance from the floor, wall, a partner or another part of your body, e.g. standing and holding the foot to stretch the quadriceps muscle. It involves holding the position for up to 30 seconds and is the most common type of stretching.

- **Active stretching:** This is carried out while moving, for example heel flicks, lunges and arm circles. This type of stretch requires movement rather than holding a position. It is often carried out in a warm-up but can also be used in a cool-down.

- **Passive stretching:** This is where another person or an object is used to help with the stretch, for example lying on your back with your leg in the air and a partner holding your ankle to stretch the hamstrings.

1D Methods of Training and Training...

> **PNF stretching (proprioceptive neuromuscular facilitation):** This requires a partner to provide a resistance. The performer stretches the muscles and a partner helps them to hold the stretch for around ten seconds. This is followed by a relaxed phase before the partner slowly applies pressure to extend the stretch outside the typical range.

Plyometric training is used to increase power. It involves movement such as bounding, hopping and jumping. It can be performed using equipment such as boxes, hurdles, jump ropes and medicine balls. When bounding and jumping, these movements encourage a rebound technique where the muscle controlling the movement lengthens rather than shortens.

Plyometric training can put a lot of strain on joints so it is vital that the correct techniques are used.

Weight training involves using resistance to develop muscle strength and endurance. Lifting weights involves using free weights or machine/resistance weights. Each time a weight is lifted is called a repetition (rep) and a series of repetitions is called a set, for example 3 × 10 (3 sets of 10 repetitions). Depending on the desired goal, the range of sets and reps may vary. For example, to gain:

▲ Plyometric training exercises can add strain to joints.

> muscle strength, perform repetitions in the range of 2–6 and sets of 3–5

> muscle endurance, increase the reps in the range of 12–15 and reduce the sets to 3–4.

When lifting weights, it is important that the correct techniques are used. When using free weights, it is recommended that a 'spotter' is used for safety reasons. A spotter is a training partner who may support the lift if the performer is having difficulty, especially when lifting heavy weights.

Extension

Use the following equation to answer the questions about maximum heart rate (MHR):

MHR = 220 − Age

1. Calculate your maximum heart rate.
2. Calculate 60% of your maximum heart rate.
3. Calculate 80% of your maximum heart rate.

▶ A coach can help you learn the correct techniques to avoid injury.

Chapter 1 Health, Training and Exercise

Training Zones

When planning a training session, you need to take into account the training needs of the performer and the specific component of fitness they want to develop. Understanding training zones will help you to do this.

The training zone you are working in depends on your exertion, which is measured by the percentage of your maximum heart rate that you reach during a session. The following table shows each training zone.

Training zone	Maximum heart rate percentage	Example
Light	50–60%	This is light intensity work, which would benefit beginners
		The upper range of this zone helps to burn body fat and promote cardiac health
		This can be used for beginners (sedentary people) getting back into shape
Aerobic	60–80%	This is light to moderate intensity exercise, which develops cardiac health, cardiovascular endurance and aerobic fitness
		This zone can be used for conditioning activities
		Working towards the lower range of this zone will help to burn body fat, increase endurance and improve heart health
Anaerobic	80–100%	This is high-intensity training, which helps to develop speed, power and strength as well as anaerobic fitness (the lactic acid system)
		This zone helps with conditioning and competitive training (game-/event-specific training)

The graph identifies training zones. Performers need to measure their heart rate to monitor which zone they are in.

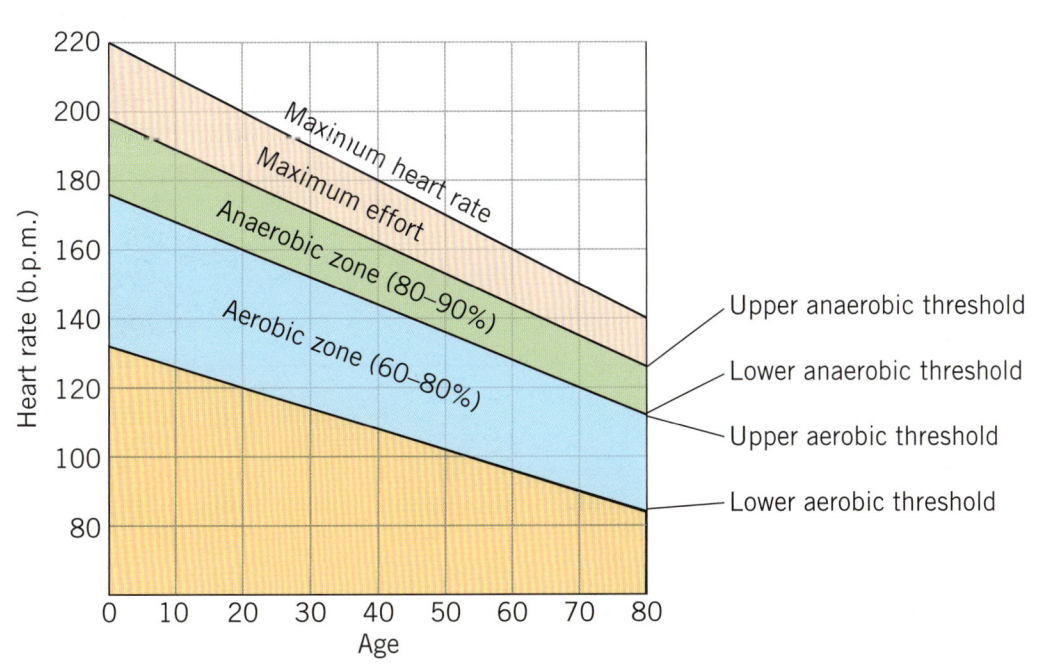

Extension

Which of these athletes is likely to train between 80–90% of their MHR for the majority of their training load?

a) A 100 m sprinter

b) A goalkeeper in football

c) A marathon runner

41

1D Methods of Training and Training...

Practical investigation

Taking part in a practical training session for each method of training will allow you to gain an understanding of each training method and how you can relate each method to specific activities, intensities of exercise and movements.

Preparation

Make five copies of the table in Appendix 1.3. Research these methods of training and make notes in the tables:

> continuous training
> circuit training
> fartlek training
> plyometric training
> weight training.

Choose a few different types of exercise to use in your investigation that are suitable for these training methods. Decide which exercises you will carry out in your training session for each method and write them in the table.

Equipment

Make a list of the equipment you will need and write it in the table for each method.

Make sure you know about any risks involved in the exercises you have chosen and that you know how to avoid injury. Remember to warm up and cool down at the start and end of each session (look at Topic 1F if you need more information about this).

Training type:	
About this training method:	
My exercise(s):	
Equipment:	

Chapter 1 Health, Training and Exercise

Training type:	
Description of session: What did you do? Was it mostly aerobic or anaerobic? Which component of fitness did you develop?	
Advantages of this training method:	
Disadvantages of this training method:	
Sport or activity this is suitable for:	

Method

With supervision from a teacher or coach, carry out each of the training sessions you have planned and record your experiences.

The description of your session should include:

- what the session included
- the intensity of the session (including whether exercise was mostly in the aerobic training zone at 60–80% of your maximum heart rate, or the anaerobic training zone at more than 80%)
- the component of fitness developed.

Advantages and disadvantages of the training method should include:

- accessibility to different people – for example, is it suitable for all levels of fitness? Is it expensive?
- specialist equipment needed
- the recommended sport or activity this method of training will help to develop fitness for.

Quick Check

What methods of training are described below?

1. Exercising at a steady rate for a sustained period of time without rest.
2. A series of exercises performed one after the other with short rest periods between each exercise.
3. An activity which may include three sets of 10 repetitions. **A01**

Extension

After completing your sessions explain how each session could be made more demanding. Think about applying the principle of overload (frequency, intensity and duration).

1D Methods of Training and Training...

Topic Test

Explain why an athlete might use **weight training** to **improve their performance**. `3 marks`

When reading the question, look at what the key words and phrases are asking you to do:

- **Command word:** This is based on the assessment objective (AO). The assessment objective for this question is AO2: you need to apply your knowledge and understanding.
- **Topic:** This is the key area of study the question is about.
- **Qualifying words or phrases:** This is the specific area you need to focus on in your answer.

Doing this will help you to build your answer so that you can access the AO for each question.

Step 1 Demonstrate your knowledge (AO1)

You need to **demonstrate your knowledge and understanding** of the methods of training. Which components of fitness will weight training develop?

_____
_____
_____

Step 2 Apply your knowledge and understanding (AO2)

You need to **apply your knowledge and understanding** of weight training in order to **explain** how it might benefit an athlete. Think of a type of athlete who might use the components of fitness you identified. How will weight training improve their performance?

_____
_____
_____
_____

Use the terms in the tick list of terminology to help you plan your answer to meet AO1 and AO2 in Steps 1 and 2. Look at how many marks are available to help you decide how much detail to include:

- ☐ Strength
- ☐ Power
- ☐ Speed
- ☐ Repetitions
- ☐ Sets
- ☐ Interval
- ☐ Explosive

Chapter 1 Health, Training and Exercise

THE BIG QUESTION

RECAP

D Now that you have developed a knowledge and understanding of methods of training and training zones, it's time to have a go at part 4 of the Big Question.

> 4. Football players need to develop speed to help them cover the pitch.
> a) Identify a method of training that a centre forward in football could use to develop their speed. (1 mark)
> b) Speed relies on the anaerobic energy system. What percentage of a player's maximum heart rate are they likely to be working at when sprinting down the pitch? (1 mark)

This question is trying to find out what you know about methods of training. You don't need to know anything about football.

What method will help to develop speed?

Is anaerobic exercise high intensity or low?

Knowing the intensity of the activity will help you to identify the percentage of maximum heart rate the footballer is likely to be working at.

45

1E Principles of Training

This is the question we're going to be working towards answering at the end of this section.

> **5.** Explain how an athlete can use the principles of training to improve their performance.
>
> **AO2 – 4 marks**

The principles of training are theories behind designing an effective training and exercise programme. There are **four** main principles that need to be applied to a training programme.

1. **S**pecificity	The training method must be specific to the individual and the activity. It is important to consider the movement and intensity required for performance.
2. **P**rogression	This refers to the gradual increase in training frequency, intensity and duration.
3. **O**verload	This is challenging the body to push beyond its normal limits to avoid *plateauing*.
4. **V**ariance	This is the change in training to maintain motivation and reduce boredom or *tedium*.

It is also important to remember the principle of 'progressive overload'.

Frequency	Making training more demanding by increasing the number of training sessions per week, e.g. two, three or four times per week.
Intensity	This is how hard the training session is. You can increase the intensity by lifting heavier weights, increasing reps, running faster, running for longer or reducing rest.
Duration	This is the length of the training activity – for example, whether you are actively training for 20 minutes, 40 minutes or longer during a session.

Top Tip

Remember the acronyms:

Principles of training = **SPOV**

Progressive overload = **FID**

Rest is an important consideration when planning a training programme. Rest is important for **physical adaptations** to occur. This is supported by replenishing nutrients and drinking enough water.

> **Extension**
>
> Using the principles of training, how can you make a training activity more demanding?

◀ Ensuring that you have enough rest, water and nutrients is important for physical adaptations to occur.

Injuries often occur during a training programme. When athletes stop training, they can lose the gains in fitness they have made – this is called **reversibility**. This means it is important to maintain fitness during this time by exploring alternative training methods. Swimming is very low impact, so it can often be used to maintain fitness while recovering from injury.

◀ Low impact activities, such as swimming, can help maintain fitness whilst recovering from an injury.

1E Principles of Training

Topic Test

Using the principles of training, explain how you could use overload to make a training session more demanding. `3 marks`

When reading the question, look at what the key words and phrases are asking you to do:

- **Command word:** This is based on the assessment objective (AO). The assessment objective for this question is AO2: you need to apply your knowledge and understanding.
- **Topic:** This is the key area of study the question is about.
- **Qualifying words or phrases:** This is the specific area you need to focus on in your answer.

Doing this will help you to build your answer so that you can access the AO for each question.

Step 1 Demonstrate your knowledge (AO1)

You need to **demonstrate your knowledge and understanding** of the principles of training. Remember the SPOV acronym to help you.

_____
_____
_____
_____

Use the terms in the tick list of terminology to help you plan your answer to meet AO1. Look at how many marks are available to help you decide how much detail to include:

- ☐ Specificity
- ☐ Overload
- ☐ Frequency
- ☐ Duration
- ☐ Progression
- ☐ Variance
- ☐ Intensity

Step 2 Apply your knowledge and understanding (AO2)

You need to **apply your knowledge and understanding** of the principles of training in order to **explain** how overload can be used to increase demand within a session. Remember the FID acronym to help you.

_____
_____
_____
_____

Use the terms in the tick list of terminology to help you plan your answer to meet AO2. Look at how many marks are available to help you decide how much detail to include.

- ☐ Progression
- ☐ Frequency
- ☐ Duration
- ☐ Reduce rest
- ☐ Overload
- ☐ Intensity
- ☐ Increase weight
- ☐ Work for longer

48

Chapter 1 Health, Training and Exercise

THE BIG QUESTION

RECAP

E Now that you have developed principles of training, it's time to have a go at part 5 of the Big Question.

5. Explain how an athlete can use the principles of training to improve their performance. (4 marks)

A long jumper may focus on the following components of fitness: speed, power and flexibility.

What specific training methods could the athlete use in their training programme?

How could their training progress throughout the duration of their plan?

How could overload be applied to make training sessions more challenging?

What variety could be added to maintain focus and motivation?

1F Warm-up and Cool-down

This is the question we're going to be working towards answering at the end of this section.

> 6. Describe one benefit of cooling down after completing a training session.
>
> AO1 – 2 marks

Warm-up

Preparation for exercise is vitally important to prepare the body physically and mentally for a training session or competition. The benefits of a warm-up include:

> increasing body temperature and heart rate ready for exercise
> increasing range of movement at joints and stretching muscles
> reducing the risk of injury
> psychological preparation increases focus, confidence and motivation, and being 'in the zone'.

A warm-up consists of three phases:

Top Tip

You will need to know the three phases of a warm-up and the order in which they occur.

Phase 1

Heart raiser

This activity will increase the heart rate to provide working muscles with oxygen as well as raising body temperature to allow the performer to safely stretch muscles and mobilise joints. Intensity should increase gradually.

Phase 2

Stretching and mobility

This increases mobility at joints as well as stretching out major muscles to increase their elasticity and avoid the risk of pulling or straining them. Stretching can be performed through static, active, passive or dynamic stretching or through proprioceptive neuromuscular facilitation (PNF).

Phase 3

Game-specific activity

This includes performing specific skills, drills and movements to help you prepare mentally for the activity you are about to do.

▶ Warming-up before exercise reduces the risk of injury.

50

Chapter 1 Health, Training and Exercise

Cool-down

A cool-down is often overlooked but is an important process as it's the start of the recovery process. The benefits of a cool-down are:

- reducing body temperature and heart rate
- removal of waste products
- reducing delayed onset of muscle soreness (DOMS)
- speeding up recovery
- rehydrating and replacing lost nutrients.

A cool-down consists of three phases:

Top Tip
You will need to know the three phases of a cool-down and the order in which they occur.

Phase 1 → **Phase 2** → **Phase 3**

Heart reducer

Active recovery is low-intensity exercise at this stage of a cool-down. This helps to gradually reduce the heart rate, which in turn helps to remove lactic acids that have built up in the muscles as well as replacing oxygen.

Stretching and mobility

This allows you to return muscles to their normal length after continuous contractions after exercise. Some performers also use ice baths and massage to speed up recovery.

Refuelling

This is when you replace lost fluids to prevent dehydration as well as replacing lost nutrients such as carbohydrates. Protein intake also helps with repair of muscle tissues.

Quick Check
Describe why refuelling is an important phase of a cool-down. **A01**

◀ Cooling down after exercise is an important part of the recovery process.

51

1F Warm-up and Cool-down

Practical Investigation

Plan a specific warm-up for an activity of your choice using the template in Appendix 1.4.

Equipment

You will need the following:

> a photocopy of the warm-up table in Appendix 1.4.

Activity-specific equipment, e.g. for a netball warm-up you may need:

> netballs
> cones
> bibs
> whistle
> stopwatch.

Heart raiser	
Example	**Why?**
A heart raiser for netball may start with some light jogging to slowly increase heart rate. (Add details about what you do in your example warm-up activity, and for how long.)	I will feel an increase in heart rate and breathing rate. (Explain what impact this will have in preparing you for your activity.)

Method

For each phase of the warm-up:

> provide an example (make sure your examples are specific to your chosen activity)

> explain why you have provided these examples and what impact you feel this will have on preparing you for your chosen activity.

Summary of Findings

You should summarise the benefits of your warm-up in the table below. Think carefully about your chosen activity.

Benefits of your warm-up:

Body temperature:
Mobility:
Psychological:
Injury:

◀ Warm-ups and cool-downs are important in football in order to maximise performance and reduce the risk of injury.

Extension Activity

Explain the benefits of the warm-up. Make sure your explanations are specific to your chosen activity.

1F Warm-up and Cool-down

Topic Test

Identify three reasons why it is important to warm up before taking part in physical activity. **2 marks**

When reading the question, look at what the key words and phrases are asking you to do:
- **Command word:** This is based on the assessment objective (AO). The assessment objective for this question is AO1: you need to demonstrate knowledge and understanding.
- **Topic:** This is the key area of study the question is about.
- **Qualifying words or phrases:** This is the specific area you need to focus on in your answer.

Doing this will help you to build your answer so that you can access the AO for each question.

Step 1 Demonstrate your knowledge (AO1)

You need to **demonstrate your knowledge and understanding** of warming up. Remember, there are three phases to a warm-up.

_____
_____
_____
_____

Step 2 Demonstrate your knowledge (AO1)

For each phase of the warm-up, you need to provide an example of what impact it may have on preparing your body for physical activity.

_____
_____
_____
_____
_____
_____
_____

Chapter 1 Health, Training and Exercise

THE BIG QUESTION

RECAP

F Now that you have demonstrated your knowledge and understanding of the benefits of the cool-down, it's time to have a go at part 6 of the Big Question.

6. Describe one benefit of cooling down after completing a training session.
(2 marks)

Remember there are three phases of cool-down.

Heart rate reducer: what is the role of oxygen?

Stretch/mobility: think about muscle contractions.

Refuel: think about the role of food and water in recovery.

55

CHAPTER 2

Exercise Physiology

Understanding exercise physiology is an essential part of understanding health, training and exercise. To train effectively, you'll need to know about the body's responses to physical exercise as well as how the body will adapt to exercise over time. And to achieve this, you will also need to know about the systems of the body and their function.

THE BIG QUESTION

How does your body work and what does this tell us about how it can perform at its best? As you complete this chapter, you will develop the knowledge, understanding and skills you need to relate physiology to different types of exercise and to answer the Big Question. By the end of each topic in this chapter you should be able to answer one of the question parts outlined below.

These are the topics you'll need to answer the Big Question:

A **Muscular-skeletal system:** Which bones articulate at the elbow joint as a javelin thrower prepares to release the javelin? Which muscle fibre type is used to generate speed and power in the run-up?

B **Cardio-respiratory and vascular system:** What are the main parts of the heart? How does gaseous exchange take place in the lungs?

C **Aerobic and anaerobic exercise:** Different activities will require the use of different energy systems. Which is the dominant energy system in a 100m race? What are its characteristics?

D **Short- and long-term effects of exercise:** Describe the long-term effects of a cardiovascular training programme on the body.

As you work through this chapter, we will identify all the skills and knowledge you'll need to be able to answer the Big Question. If you can do that, you'll have brilliant AO1 and AO2 skills ready to use in your GCSE.

In this chapter you will learn about:

> the structure and function of the muscular and skeletal systems
> the structure and function of the cardiovascular, respiratory and vascular systems
> the characteristics and factors affecting aerobic and anaerobic exercise
> the short- and long-term effects of exercise.

In this chapter you will be using the following key terms. You can look up the meaning of these terms in the Glossary (page 184 onwards).

Key Terms

Abduction	Adduction	Aerobic exercise	Anaerobic exercise
Cardiovascular system	Circumduction	Creatine phosphate system (ATP-CP system)	Diffusion
Duration	Exhale		Extension
Flexion	Glycolysis	Expiration	Inspiration
Intensity	Lactic acid	Inhale	Oxygen debt
Pulmonary circulatory system	Respiration	Lactic acid system	Systemic circulatory system
Vasoconstriction	Vasodilation	Rotation	

2A

Muscular-skeletal System

This is the question we're going to be working towards answering at the end of this section.

> 1. A javelin thrower needs to generate speed and power to throw the javelin in a competition.
>   a) Identify the bones that articulate at the elbow joint as the thrower prepares to release the javelin. (2 marks)
>   b) Identify and explain which muscle fibre type is most likely to be used in the run-up. (2 marks)
>
> AO1 – 4 marks

The muscular-skeletal system has two parts – the muscular system and the skeletal system. Both systems work together to bring about movement. To understand this complete system, we will first look at the parts of the system individually.

Muscular System

The muscular system is responsible for producing movement through muscle contractions.

There are two different types of muscles in the human body:

> **Involuntary muscles** whose contractions are not under conscious control. Involuntary muscles include:
> - **smooth muscle**, which is found in the walls of internal organs and helps to maintain bodily functions
> - **cardiac muscle**, which is the muscle in the walls of the heart.
>
> **Voluntary muscles** whose contractions are under conscious control. The muscles are also known as skeletal muscles. We can control the intensity and duration of each contraction.

Skeletal Muscles

The muscular system works together with the skeletal system to produce movement. Muscles can only produce movement by **contracting** (shortening). When muscles contract, they pull on skeletal bones to produce movement at a joint.

The following image shows the major skeletal muscles of the body along with the movements they are responsible for. Some muscles work together to perform a function. For example, the deltoids, trapezius, latissimus, biceps and triceps all work in conjunction to perform circumduction at the shoulder joint.

AO2

You will need to be able to apply your knowledge about the major muscles of the body.

Top Tip

There are over 650 muscles in the human body.

Top Tip

Skeletal muscles contract to produce movement at a joint.

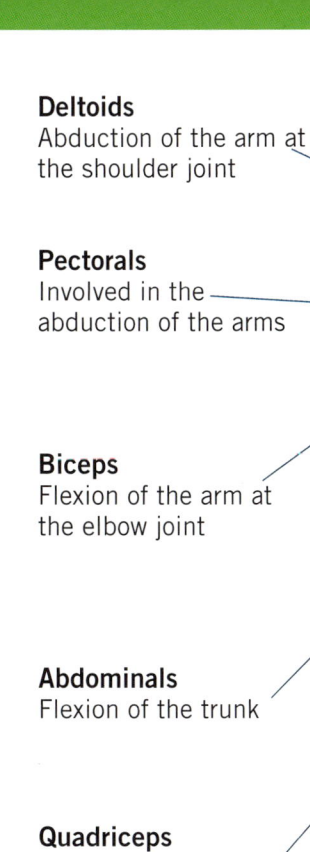

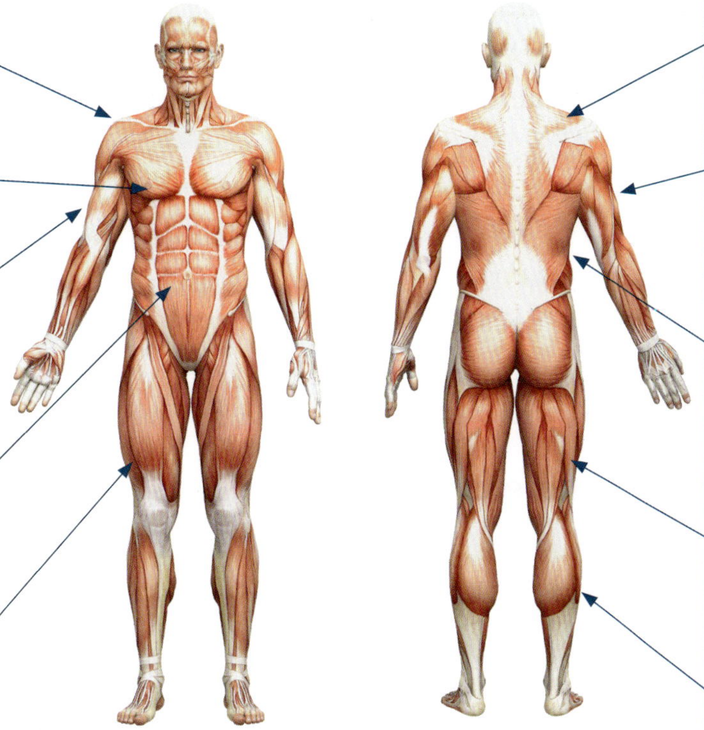

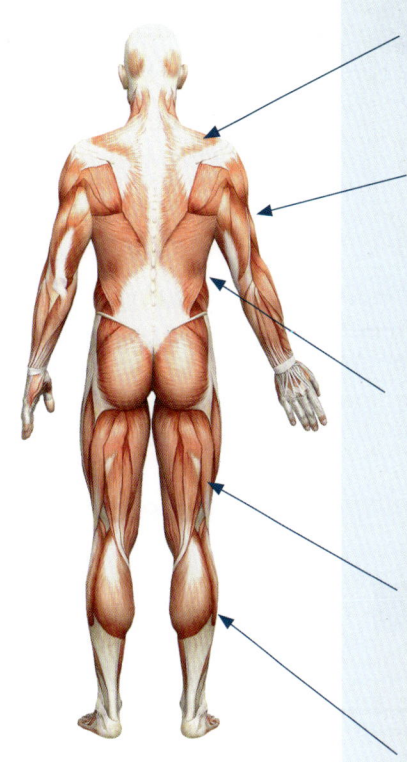

Chapter 2 Exercise Physiology

Deltoids
Abduction of the arm at the shoulder joint

Pectorals
Involved in the abduction of the arms

Biceps
Flexion of the arm at the elbow joint

Abdominals
Flexion of the trunk

Quadriceps
Extension of the leg at the knee joint

Trapezius
Rotation of the shoulder

Triceps
Extension of the arm at the elbow joint

Latissimus dorsi
Adduction of arm movement at the shoulder

Hamstrings
Flexion of the leg at the knee joint

Gastrocnemius
Extension at the ankle

Muscle Fibres

Each skeletal muscle is made up of fibres. There are two types of muscle fibre:

› slow twitch (Type I) fibres
› fast twitch (Type II) fibres.

It is important for you to know the characteristics for each type of fibre.

Characteristic	Slow twitch (Type I)	Fast twitch (Type II)
Colour	Red	White
Energy system	Aerobic	Anaerobic
Fatigue resistance	High	Low
Speed of contraction	Slow	Fast

Data Analysis

The percentages of fast and slow twitch fibres in the muscles of three athletes were analysed. The table shows the results.

Athlete	Fast twitch fibres	Slow twitch fibres
A	45%	55%
B	65%	35%
C	30%	70%

1. Identify which athlete is most likely to be a marathon runner.
2. Explain your answer to question 1.

AO2

You will need to apply your knowledge of the characteristics of slow and fast twitch fibre types.

Quick Check

A 100m sprinter will principally use their fast twitch muscle fibres in a race.

Identify which muscle fibre is likely to be used by a marathon runner. **AO1**

Identify two other sporting activities that may use each fibre type. **AO1**

2A Muscular-skeletal System

A02

You will need to apply your knowledge of the functions of the skeleton.

Top Tip

You will need to know the major bones of the skeleton shown in this diagram.

Quick Check

Identify three bones that articulate at the elbow joint. **A01**

Skeletal System

The skeletal system has four main functions:

> **Movement**. The bones of the skeleton act as levers and produce movement at a joint when they are pulled on by muscles.

> **Support**. The skeleton forms the structure of the body. The muscles that are attached to the skeleton give the body its shape.

> **Protection**. The skeleton protects vital organs like the brain and the cardio-respiratory system.

> **Production of blood cells**. Both red and white blood cells are produced by the bone marrow of the long bones of the skeleton.

The Skeleton

The adult skeletal system consists of 206 bones. The skeleton provides a framework for muscle to attach to via **tendons**, which gives the body its shape. The main bones involved in movement are shown below.

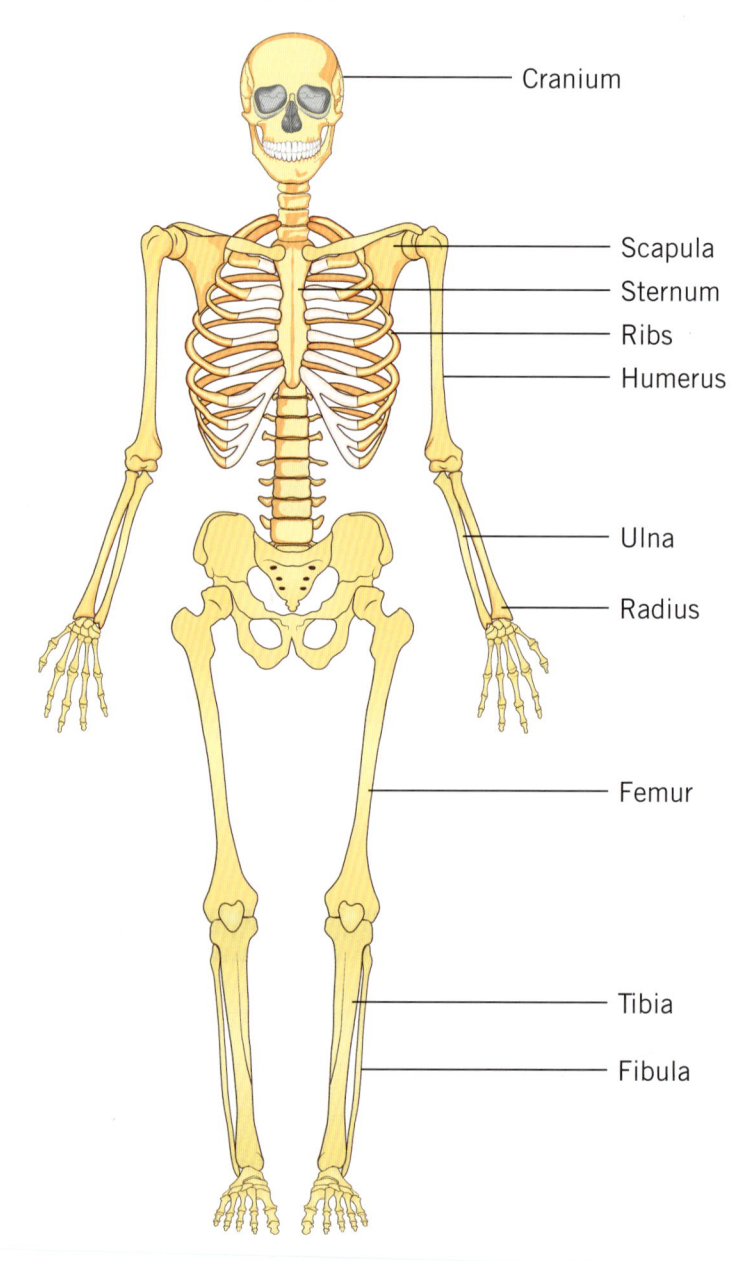

- Cranium
- Scapula
- Sternum
- Ribs
- Humerus
- Ulna
- Radius
- Femur
- Tibia
- Fibula

Types of Bones

There are four main types of bones that make up the skeleton.

Type	Example	Description
Long	Femur and ulna	These are found in the limbs and are cylindrical in shape. The main function is to act as levers for movement.
Short	Carpals and tarsals	These can be found in the wrist and ankle and are designed for strength and weight bearing due to their small and compact nature.
Flat	Cranium, sternum, scapula and ribs	These have flat surfaces. Their function is mainly for protection of the internal organs. (You need to know about flat bones for protection if you are studying for Eduqas.)
Irregular	Vertebrae	Individually shaped, these bones have the function of protection and muscle attachment.

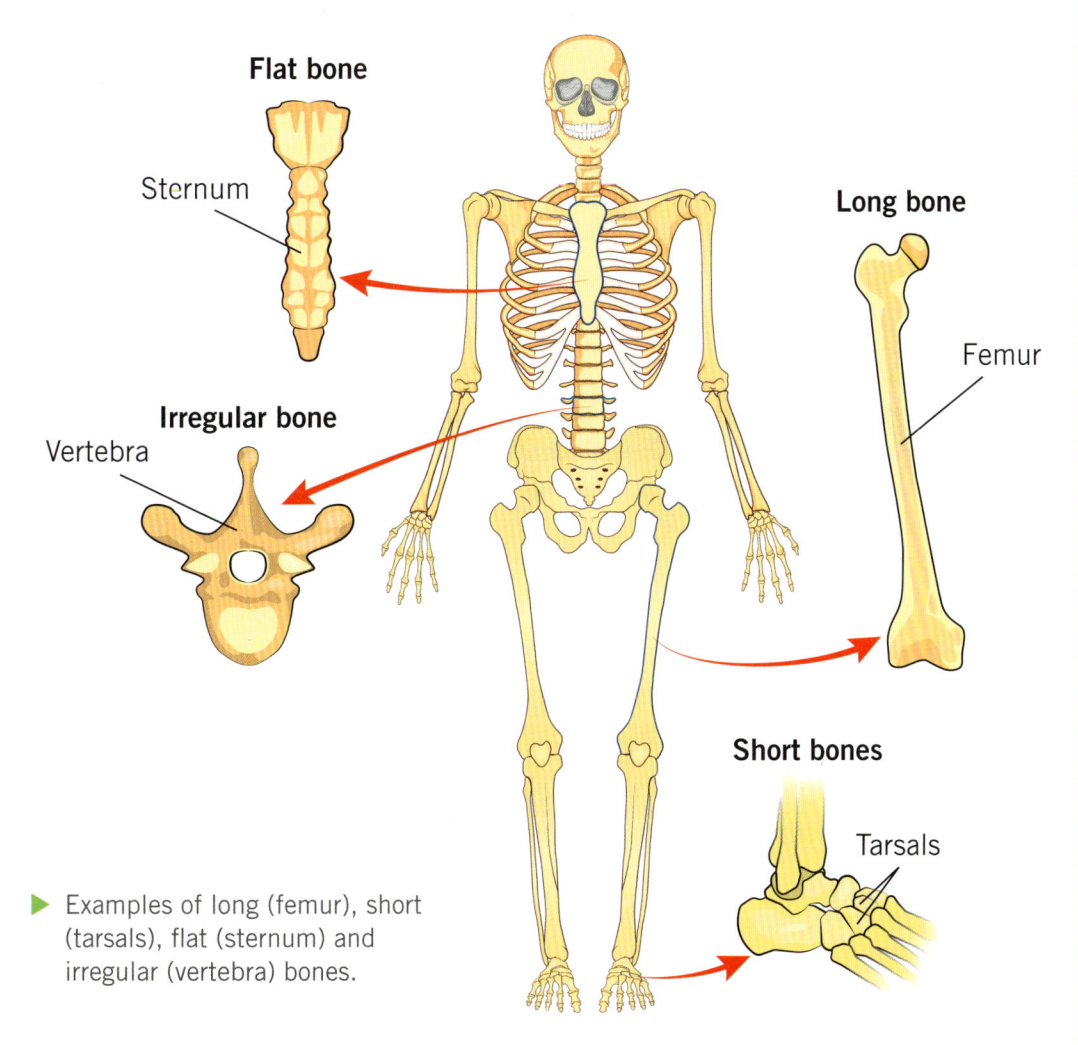

▶ Examples of long (femur), short (tarsals), flat (sternum) and irregular (vertebra) bones.

A02
You will need to be able to apply your knowledge of which bones work together to produce movement at the major joints of the body.

Quick Check
Identify the four functions of the skeleton. A01

Chapter 2 Exercise Physiology

61

2A Muscular-skeletal System

Movement of the Muscular-skeletal System

The muscular system and the skeletal system work together to produce movement. Muscles are attached to bones by tendons to help produce movement. Bones are attached to other bones by **ligaments** to give joint stability.

Movement occurs at joints, which are where two or more bones meet (or articulate). Joints where movement takes place are called **synovial joints**.

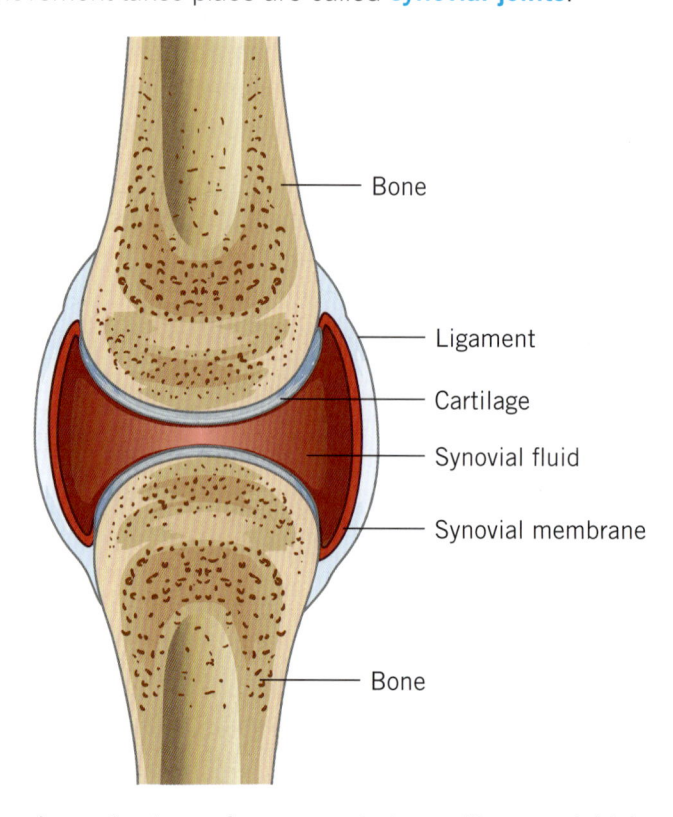

Labels on diagram: Bone, Ligament, Cartilage, Synovial fluid, Synovial membrane, Bone

A02
You will need to be able to apply your knowledge of joints and their locations as well as the type of movement that occurs at that joint.

The table below shows the type of movement at specific synovial joints:

Joint type	Examples	Movement types
Ball and socket	Shoulder	**Flexion** and **extension**
	Hip	**Abduction** and **adduction**
		Rotation
		Circumduction
Hinge	Knee	Flexion and extension
	Elbow	
Pivot	Neck	Rotation

Quick Check
Identify the type of joint at the elbow. A01

Chapter 2 Exercise Physiology

Practical Investigation

Equipment

You will need the following:

> a photocopy of the skeleton worksheet in Appendix 2.1 (you may choose to enlarge this to A3 to make cutting out easier)

> eight split pins

> a glue stick

> coloured pencils (or pens)

> scissors.

Appendix 2.1 Skeletal System – A Practical Investigation

Method

1. Photocopy the skeleton worksheet. Carefully cut around each of the images.

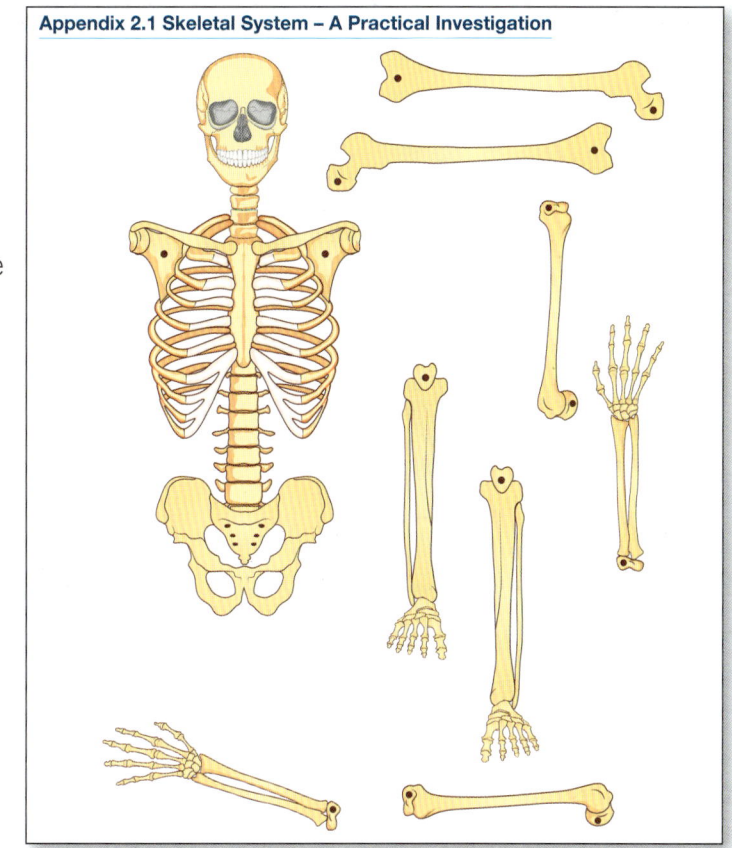

2. Identify the radius, ulna, humerus, femur, tibia and fibula and write the names of the bones on the images.

3. Use the split pins to attach the bones together to build your skeleton.

4. Apply glue to the back of the main body of the skeleton and stick it on to a new page of your workbook or a blank piece of paper. Around the skeleton, label each joint and describe the movement that takes place there.

Extension Activity

Now that you have completed your skeleton and identified all the major bones explore the skeleton further by completing the table below.

Identify:

> the bones
> the joints
> the muscles that move the bones at each joint.

Bone or bones	Joint	Muscles
Scapula		Deltoid and trapezius
Radius and ulna		
	Knee	

Extension

Can you identify the muscles that help create the movement at each joint?

63

2A Muscular-skeletal System

Topic Test ☑

The image shows a shot-put competitor.

a) **Name** the two **muscles** that cause **movement at the elbow**. **2 marks**
b) **Identify** two **functions the skeleton carries out** during the shot-put throw. **2 marks**

When reading the question, look at what the key words and phrases are asking you to do:

- **Command word:** This is based on the assessment objective (AO). The assessment objective for this question is AO1: you need to demonstrate your knowledge and understanding.
- **Topic:** This is the key area of study the question is about.
- **Qualifying words or phrases:** This is the specific area you need to focus on in your answer.

Doing this will help you to build your answer so that you can access the AO for each question.

Step 1 Demonstrate your knowledge (AO1)

You need to **demonstrate your knowledge and understanding** of skeletal muscle groups. Think of the two muscles that flex and extend the arm.

_____

_____

Step 2 Demonstrate your knowledge (AO1)

You need to **demonstrate your knowledge and understanding** of the functions of the skeleton. The skeleton has four functions: movement, structure, support and production of red blood cells. Which two functions do you think will help the athlete perform the shot-put?

_____

_____

Chapter 2 Exercise Physiology

THE BIG QUESTION

RECAP

A Now that you have developed a knowledge and understanding of the muscular-skeletal system, it's time to have a go at part 1 of the Big Question.

1. A javelin thrower needs to generate speed and power to throw the javelin in a competition.

    a) Identify the bones that articulate at the elbow joint as the thrower prepares to release the javelin. (2 marks)

    b) Identify and explain which muscle fibre type is most likely to be used in the run-up. (2 marks)

    Muscle fibre type: _____

    Reason:

What are the major bones in the arm? (There are three, two in the lower arm and one in the upper arm.)

Think about the fitness components: speed and power. What muscle fibre would be linked to these two components of fitness? Why?

65

2B Cardio-respiratory and Vascular System

In this topic we will work towards answering this part of the Big Question:

2. a) Complete the diagram of the heart by writing the letters from the diagram in the table next to the correct chamber. (2 marks)

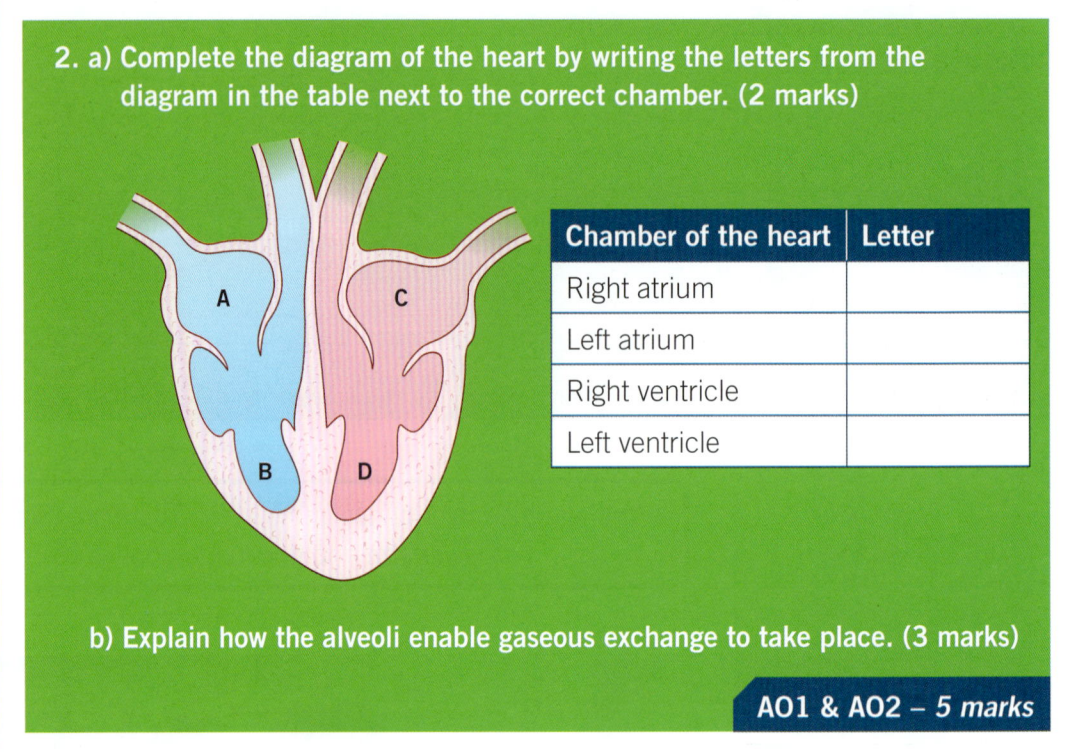

Chamber of the heart	Letter
Right atrium	
Left atrium	
Right ventricle	
Left ventricle	

b) Explain how the alveoli enable gaseous exchange to take place. (3 marks)

AO1 & AO2 – 5 marks

The cardio-respiratory system works to transport oxygen and nutrients to working muscles as well as removing waste products such as carbon dioxide and **lactic acid**.

'Cardio' refers to the heart and **respiration** is the exchange of oxygen for carbon dioxide by breathing. So the cardio-respiratory system includes the heart and the organs that help us to **inhale** and **exhale** air. The **vascular system** is the system of blood vessels in the body.

The Heart

The diagram shows the structure of the heart.

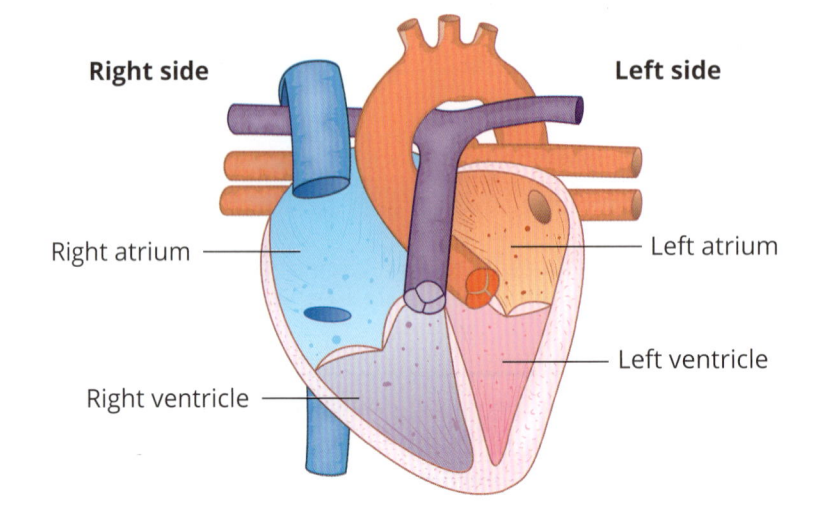

Top Tip

Remember when you see a diagram of the heart it is as if the person's back is against the page; when you look at it the diagram face on, the left side is on the right.

Chapter 2 Exercise Physiology

The heart has four chambers, two at the top and two at the bottom.

The two top chambers are the **left atrium** and the **right atrium**. The two **atria** (plural of atrium) both receive blood from elsewhere in the body.

> Left atrium: Receives **oxygenated blood** from the lungs.
> Right atrium: Receives **deoxygenated blood** from the body.

The two bottom chambers are the **left ventricle** and the **right ventricle**. Each ventricle receives blood from the atrium above it – so the left atrium supplies blood to the left ventricle.

> Left ventricle: Receives oxygenated blood which it then pumps around the body.
> Right ventricle: Receives deoxygenated blood which it pumps to the lungs.

The left side of the heart has thicker muscular walls to pump oxygenated blood all around the body. The right side of the heart receives deoxygenated blood from the body and then pumps it to the lungs to become deoxygenated.

The diagram shows the pathway of blood around the heart and body.

AO2
You will need to identify the chambers of the heart.

AO2
You will need to know the pathways of blood and how deoxygenated blood becomes oxygenated.

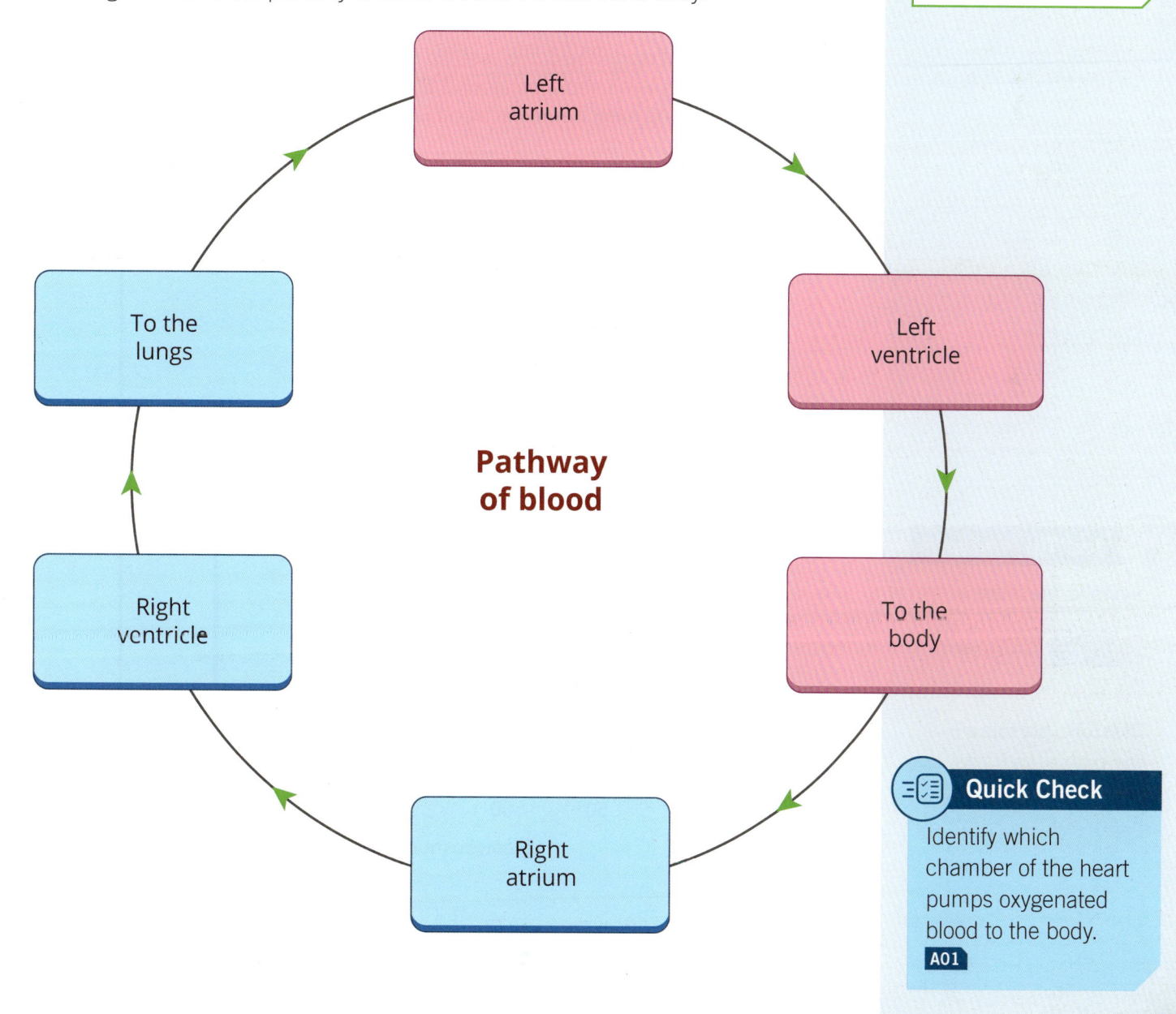

Pathway of blood

Left atrium → Left ventricle → To the body → Right atrium → Right ventricle → To the lungs → Left atrium

Quick Check
Identify which chamber of the heart pumps oxygenated blood to the body.
AO1

67

2B Cardio-respiratory and Vascular System

Cardiac Values

Heart rate (HR) is the number of heartbeats per minute. The average human heart rate at rest is about 70 beats per minute (bpm). Exercise will increase bpm, and different **durations** and **intensities** of exercise will have different effects.

Stroke volume is the amount of blood ejected per beat. This is measured in millilitres (ml). Stroke volume can increase during exercise. Average stroke volume is around 70 ml.

Cardiac output (Q) is the amount of blood that leaves the heart in one minute. It is calculated as heart rate × stroke volume (for example, 70 bpm × 70 ml = 4900 ml per minute). If heart rate and stroke volume increase during exercise, cardiac output therefore also rises.

Blood Pressure

Blood pressure is described using two numbers. The first number is **systolic pressure**, which is the highest blood pressure that is reached as blood is being ejected from the heart. The second, lower number is **diastolic pressure**, which is the blood pressure in the arteries between heartbeats.

In a typical healthy person at rest, the systolic pressure should be around 120 mm Hg, and the diastolic pressure should be around 80 mm Hg. This reading is recorded as 120/80 mm Hg. During exercise, more blood is pumped out of the heart so blood pressure increases.

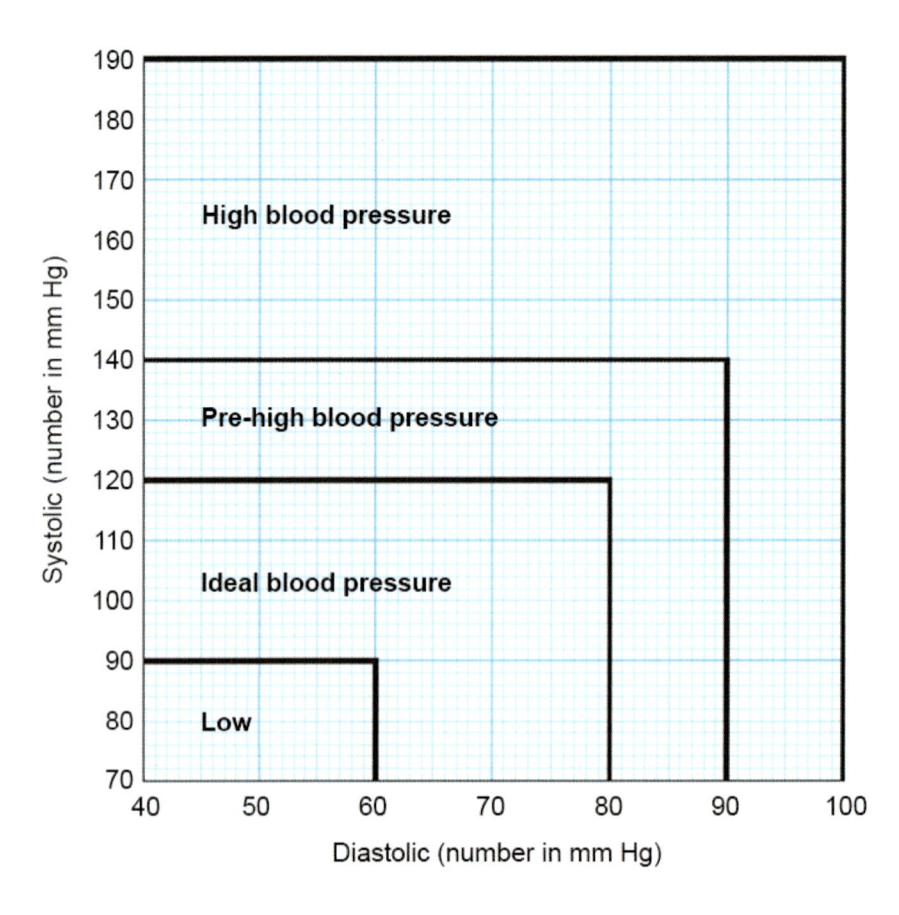

> **Top Tip**
>
> **Systolic pressure** = the contraction (heart emptying) phase of the heartbeat.
>
> **Diastolic pressure** = the relaxation (heart filling) phase of the heartbeat.

Chapter 2 Exercise Physiology

Respiratory System

The respiratory system is made up of complex structures, which rely on changes in pressure for **inspiration** and **expiration** to take place.

Inspiration	Expiration
Diaphragm and intercostals contract	Diaphragm and intercostals relax
Lung size increases and air pressure reduces	Lung size decreases and air pressure increases
Air is pulled into the lungs	Air is forced out of the lungs

Inspiration and expiration are part of the process in which we bring oxygen into the body (inspiration) and remove carbon dioxide from the body (expiration). The exchange of oxygen and carbon dioxide (gaseous exchange) takes place in the alveoli (air sacs) found inside the lungs.

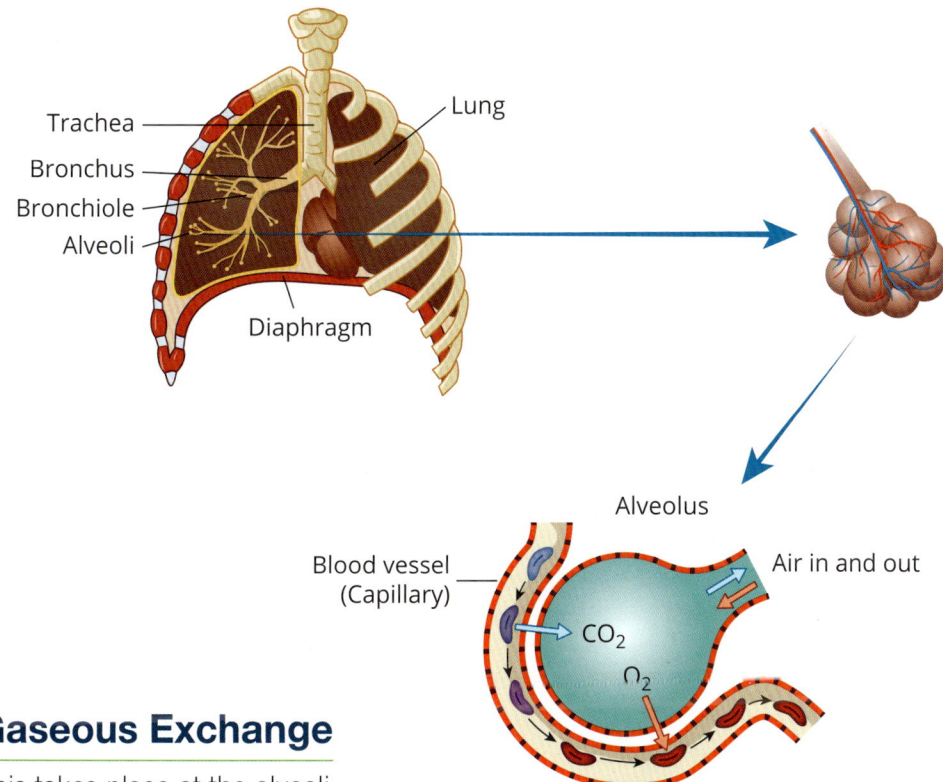

Top Tip
The diffusion of gas is the exchange from an area of high concentration to an area of low concentration.

Quick Check
Identify where gaseous exchange take place. **A01**

What gases are exchanged? **A01**

A02
You will need an understanding of gaseous exchange in the alveoli.

Gaseous Exchange

This takes place at the alveoli.
The thin, moist walls of the alveoli allow **diffusion** to take place. **Capillaries** are closely wrapped around the alveoli to reduce the distance of diffusion and increase efficiency. Oxygen enters the blood stream through the thin walls of the capillaries and attaches to haemoglobin in the **red blood cells**. This haemoglobin is oxidised to become oxyhaemoglobin and it then travels to the heart to be pumped around the body. (You need to know about diffusion and haemoglobin if you are studying for the WJEC exam, but not if you are studying for Eduqas.)

As oxygen moves from the alveoli into the blood stream, carbon dioxide moves from the red blood cells into the alveoli to be exhaled.

69

2B Cardio-respiratory and Vascular System

Respiratory Values

You need to know about these respiratory values:

Tidal volume is the amount of air that is breathed in or out during a breath.

Vital capacity is the maximum amount of air that someone can breathe out after breathing in as far as they can.

Breathing frequency is the number of breaths per minute.

Minute ventilation is the volume of air breathed in or out per minute. Minute ventilation = breathing frequency × tidal volume.

Tidal volume and vital capacity are shown in the spirometry trace.

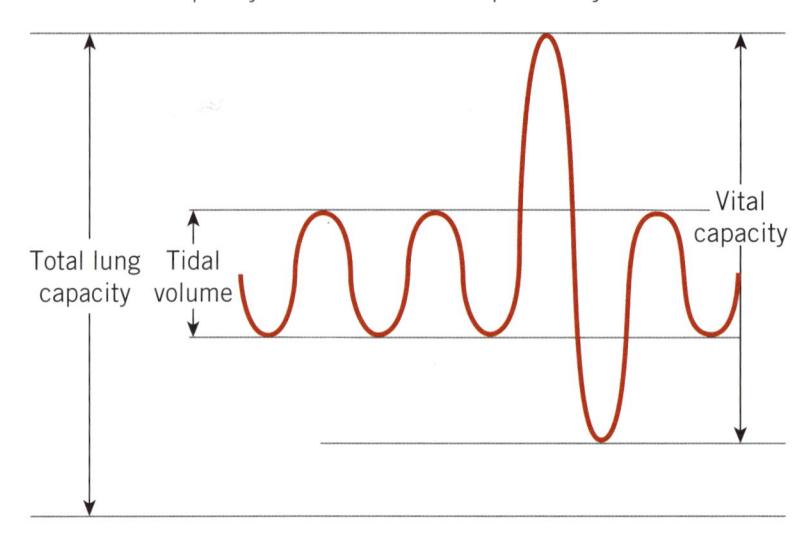

> **Top Tip**
>
> Explore your breathing frequency by counting the number of breaths you take per minute.

> **Quick Check**
>
> Explain why there will be an increase in tidal volume during exercise. **AO2**

During exercise:
- **tidal volume** will increase
- **breathing frequency** will increase
- **minute ventilation** will increase.

The intensity and duration of exercise will influence these values.

> **Knowledge Check**
>
> Answer the following questions using your knowledge about this topic.
>
> 1. Which **one** of the following best describes stroke volume (SV)? **AO1**
>   - ☐ The amount of blood ejected per beat
>   - ☐ The amount of blood that leaves the heart in one minute
>   - ☐ The number of beats per minute
>
> 2. Complete the following sentences using the words in the box below.
>
> | air | tidal volume | vital capacity | maximum |
>
> The amount of _____ that is breathed in or out during a breath is referred to as _____ _____. The _____ amount of air that someone can breathe out after taking a deep breath is called the _____ _____.

Vascular System

Blood vessels transport blood to and from the heart. There are three different types of blood vessels with different characteristics and functions.

Characteristics of Blood Vessels

Arteries
- Carry blood away from the heart
- Blood is carried at high pressure
- Thick muscular walls
- They carry mainly oxygenated blood
- They have no valves

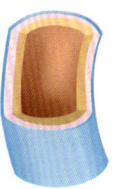

Veins
- Carry blood towards the heart
- Blood is carried at low pressure
- Thin muscular walls
- They carry mainly deoxygenated blood
- They have valves

Capillaries
- Thin walls only one cell thick
- Allow for diffusion of gas (gaseous exchange)
- They have no valves

Functions of Blood Vessels

1. Transportation of nutrients, oxygen and waste products

The oxygen we breathe in is transported to the working muscles, and waste products such as carbon dioxide and lactic acid are removed from the body. In addition, the blood transports nutrients to the body's cells.

2. Thermoregulation

The body regulates body temperature through thermoregulation. Temperature is regulated by thermoreceptors in the body, which inform the brain's thermoregulatory centre.

In hot conditions, the body allows more blood to flow close to the surface of the skin, causing a red appearance. This is achieved by widening blood vessels near the skin's surface to allow more blood through, a process called **vasodilation**. This allows more heat loss from the blood through the skin.

If the body is cold, it reduces blood flow near the surface of the skin, which helps keep the body warm. Blood vessels close to the skin become narrower and let less blood through. This is called **vasoconstriction**.

Top Tip

You might find this a useful way of remembering the difference between arteries and veins:

Arteries start with **a** and they carry blood **a**way from the heart.

V**e**ins contain the word **in** and they carry blood towards (or **in**to) the heart.

Quick Check

Which type of blood vessel carries blood away from the heart?
AO1

2B Cardio-respiratory and Vascular System

Practical investigation

Now that you have an understanding of the cardio-respiratory and vascular systems, complete this practical investigation to show how good your understanding of the circulatory system is. It is important to know that the body has two circulatory systems:

> **pulmonary circulatory system**: transfers blood between the heart and the lungs

> **systemic circulatory system**: transfers blood between the heart and the body.

This investigation will help you to understand the two systems.

Equipment

You will need the following:

> a photocopy of the blank circulatory systems worksheet in Appendix 2.2
> a pen or pencil
> two coloured pens (red and blue)
> a glue stick.

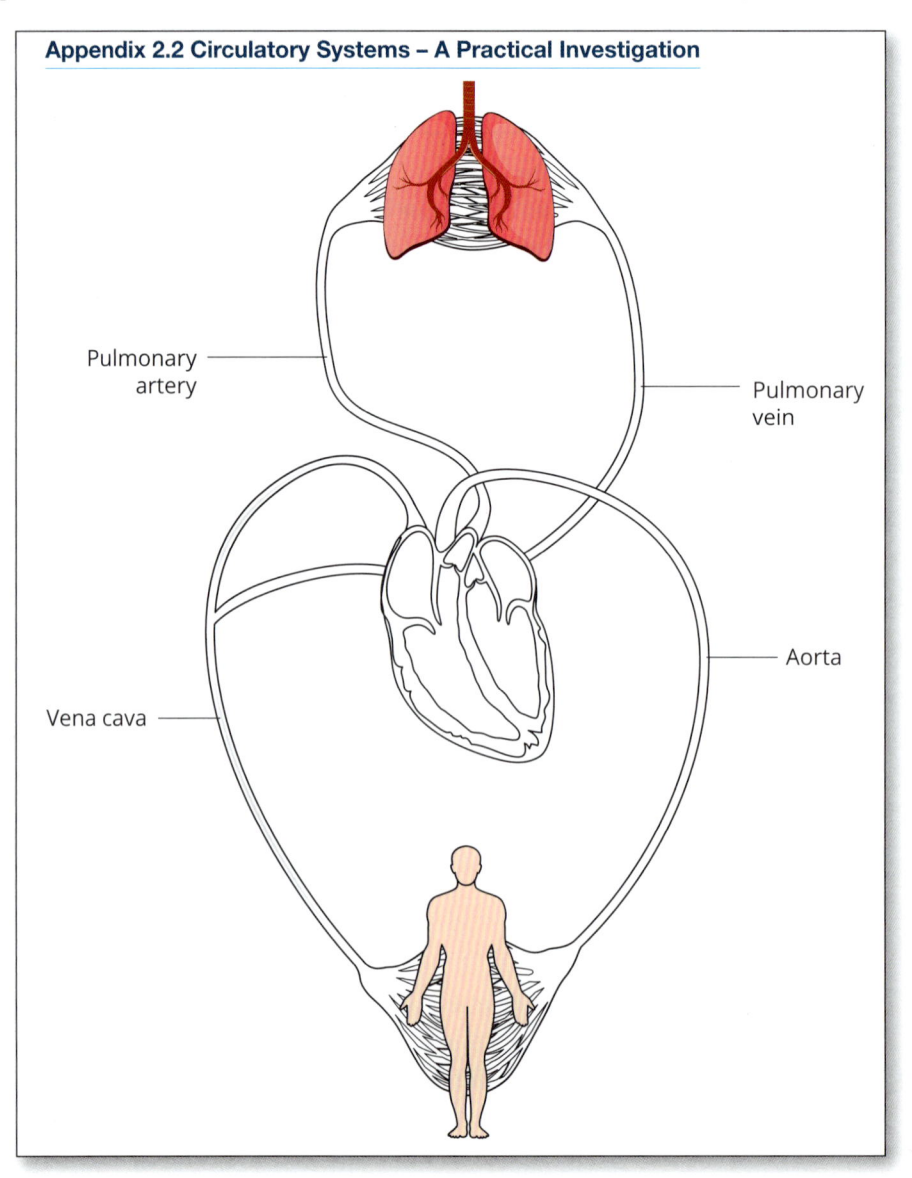

Appendix 2.2 Circulatory Systems – A Practical Investigation

Pulmonary artery

Pulmonary vein

Aorta

Vena cava

Method

Use your copy of the circulatory systems worksheet from Appendix 2.2 to complete the following tasks.

1. The body contains two circulatory systems. The pulmonary circulatory system transports blood to and from the lungs, and the systemic circulatory system transports blood to the tissues of the body. Label each system on your worksheet.

2. Using your coloured pens:

   a) Identify the part of the system carrying oxygenated blood from the lungs to the working muscles in the body and colour this **red**.

   b) Identify the part of the system carrying deoxygenated blood from the body to the lungs to be oxygenated and colour this **blue**.

3. Draw arrows (→) to show the path of blood through both systems.

4. Use the following terms relating to the circulatory systems and label your diagram:

   lungs; body; right atrium; left atrium; right ventricle; left ventricle.

5. Stick your completed worksheet in your exercise book using the glue stick.

Extension Activity

Complete this task using your worksheet and the words in the box (you may need to use some words more than once). You may wish to complete the sentences in your book around your model if you have space.

1. Oxygenated blood in the left _____ travels into the left _____ .

2. Oxygenated blood is then pumped out of the heart and transported around the _____ through the _____ .

3. When the oxygen is used up around the body, the _____ blood travels to the right _____ and then enters the right _____ .

4. The deoxygenated blood travels to the _____ , where gaseous exchange occurs, the blood becomes _____ and carbon dioxide is exhaled.

5. The oxygenated blood travels to the left _____ and then the process begins again.

oxygenated	deoxygenated
blood vessels	lungs
atrium	ventricle
body	

2B Cardio-respiratory and Vascular System

Topic Test

Blood vessels transport blood to and from the heart.
Draw a line from each **blood vessel** to the description that best describes the **characteristic of that blood vessel.** 2 marks

Artery		Carries blood towards the heart
Vein		Carries blood away from the heart
Capillary		Thin walls only one cell thick

When reading the question, look at what the key words and phrases are asking you to do:

- **Command word:** This is based on the assessment objective (AO). The assessment objective for this question is AO1: you need to demonstrate your knowledge and understanding.
- **Topic:** This is the key area of study the question is about.
- **Qualifying words or phrases:** This is the specific area you need to focus on in your answer.

Doing this will help you to build your answer so that you can access the AO for each question.

Demonstrate your knowledge (AO1)

Using what you have learned you need to **demonstrate your knowledge and understanding** of the vascular system. Revisit the characteristics of blood vessels in Section 2B to consolidate your knowledge and understanding before completing this question.

Artery		Carries blood towards the heart
Vein		Carries blood away from the heart
Capillary		Thin walls only one cell thick

Can you recall what the different blood vessels in the body are? Check back on page 71 if you need a reminder.

Chapter 2 Exercise Physiology

THE BIG QUESTION

RECAP

B You are starting to build the knowledge and understanding you need to answer the Big Question. You have already answered part 1 at the end of the last topic. Now it's time to answer part 2 and apply your knowledge and understanding of the cardiovascular system.

2. a) Complete the diagram of the heart by writing the letters from the diagram in the table next to the correct chamber. (2 marks)

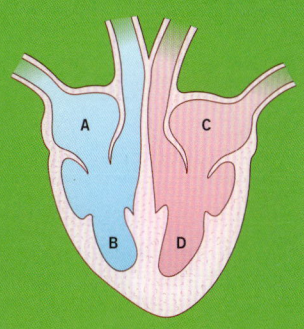

Chamber of the heart	Letter
Right atrium	
Left atrium	
Right ventricle	
Left ventricle	

b) Explain how the alveoli enable gaseous exchange to take place. (3 marks)

Think about how the positioning of the heart is interpreted in the diagram. Which is the left side?

75

2C Aerobic and Anaerobic Exercise

In this topic we will work towards answering this part of the Big Question:

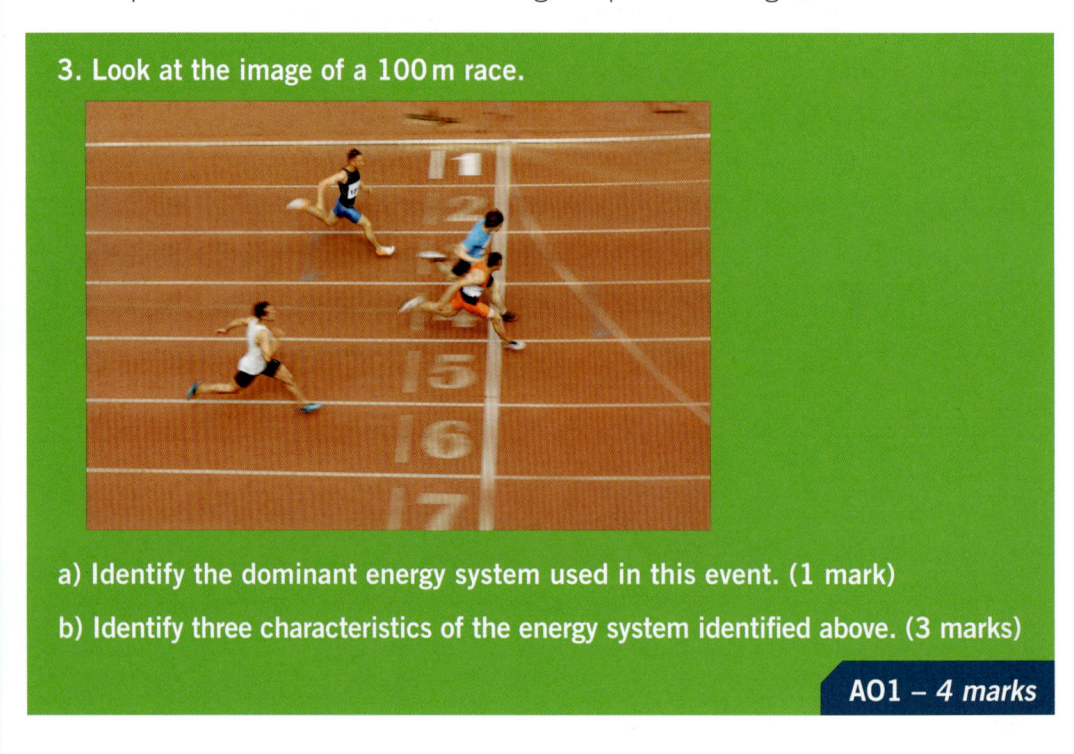

> 3. Look at the image of a 100 m race.
>
> a) Identify the dominant energy system used in this event. (1 mark)
>
> b) Identify three characteristics of the energy system identified above. (3 marks)
>
> AO1 – 4 marks

Aerobic Exercise

Aerobic exercise is when the body has enough oxygen to meet the energy demands of the activity. So when exercising at a low to moderate intensity we use the **aerobic energy system**.

▲ Jogging at a moderate pace is an example of aerobic exercise.

Top Tip

The **lactic acid system** is also known as anaerobic **glycolysis**.

Anaerobic Exercise

Anaerobic exercise is when the body produces energy without the use of oxygen. To maintain exercise at high intensity for a short duration you would use the **anaerobic energy system**. The body has two types of anaerobic energy systems:

› The **creatine phosphate (CP) system** uses a chemical that is stored in the body's cells called creatine phosphate. It provides cells with energy faster than the other energy systems, so it is used for explosive movements. However, it can only provide energy for up to about ten seconds before the body has to replenish it. This energy system is also called the **ATP-CP system**.

› The **lactic acid system** is used to sustain high-intensity exercise for longer than ten seconds. Glycogen is broken down into glucose in the cells. But without the presence of oxygen this process produces lactic acid as a waste product, causing fatigue and discomfort. This system can provide energy for up to about 90 seconds.

After using the two anaerobic systems, the body needs extra oxygen to break down the lactic acid in the muscles and replenish its stores of creatine phosphate. The need to 'repay' the body with extra oxygen by breathing heavily after anaerobic exercise is called **oxygen debt**.

> **Top Tip**
>
> Aerobic = Using oxygen to produce energy.
>
> Anaerobic = Using carbohydrates without oxygen to produce energy.

◀ Sprinting over a short distance is high intensity and uses the anaerobic energy system.

Factors Affecting Aerobic and Anaerobic Exercise

Which energy system the body uses during exercise will depend on:

› the intensity of the exercise
› the duration of the exercise
› the amount of nutrients available for fuel.

2C Aerobic and Anaerobic Exercise

> **AO2**
> You will need to be able to apply your knowledge of the key characteristics of each energy system.

> **Top Tip**
> Sometimes you will see creatine phosphate referred to as ATP-CP; they are both the same.

> **Quick Check**
> What three factors will determine whether an activity is aerobic or anaerobic? **AO1**

Sometimes an activity will vary between different intensities and durations. Therefore the performer may switch between aerobic and anaerobic exercise. There will come a point when the performer may not have enough oxygen supply to meet the demands of the exercise and lactic acid will start to build up. This is known as the **anaerobic threshold** – the point when there is not enough oxygen to sustain the intensity of the exercise.

Characteristics of the three energy systems:

Characteristics	Creatine phosphate (ATP-CP system)	Anaerobic glycolysis (lactic acid system)	Aerobic energy system
Oxygen required?	No	No	Yes
Speed of energy supply	Very fast	Fast	Slow
Fuel source	Creatine phosphate stored in the muscles	Carbohydrates (glycogen)	Carbohydrates and fat. Protein in extreme circumstances
Amount of ATP production	Limited	Limited	Unlimited
By-products (waste products)	None	Lactic acid	Water and carbon dioxide
Intensity	Explosive	High	Low to moderate
Duration	0–10 seconds	Up to 90 seconds	Indefinite
Cause of fatigue	Limited supply of creatine phosphate (ATP-CP)	Lactic acid	None
Activity	Power-based activities, e.g. shot put, 100m sprint	Sprint endurance, e.g. 400m	Long distance, e.g. marathon running

The Role of Nutrition and Exercise

The energy systems we use require fuel for exercise:

> Aerobic exercise working at a low intensity will use fat and carbohydrates (glycogen) as fuel.

> Anaerobic exercise, which is high intensity, will use creatine phosphate and carbohydrates (glycogen).

As well as carbohydrates and fats, water is an important nutrient and should be an essential part of a performer's preparation before, during and after exercise. Water not only helps to keep the body hydrated but also plays a role in breaking down carbohydrates. Staying hydrated helps to keep the **viscosity** of blood low. This will allow blood to move quickly and smoothly through blood vessels.

Chapter 2 Exercise Physiology

Hydration is important during exercise as it maintains the body's functions as well as decision-making. Dehydration can affect judgement, increase heart rate and increase body temperature. Overhydration can also be dangerous, resulting in high levels of water retention in the body, which can lead to water entering the cells rather than remaining in the blood stream.

◀ It's important to stay hydrated during exercise as it affects your judgement, your heart rate and your body temperature.

When taking part in aerobic exercise at a low intensity for long periods of time, energy is required from starchy carbohydrate sources (such as rice, bread, potatoes and bananas) as well as fats (like those from dairy products such as butter, cheese and milk). The aerobic system produces the majority of our energy when exercising at a low intensity for long periods of time. Glucose from carbohydrates and fat supplies the energy.

Top Tip
Glucose + oxygen → energy + water + carbon dioxide

When performing anaerobic exercise (which requires explosive movements) energy is needed from creatine phosphate and carbohydrate, which is stored as glycogen in the skeletal muscles and the liver and can be used as an immediate source of energy. The anaerobic system produces energy very quickly by breaking down glucose into lactic acid. Glucose is derived from carbohydrates.

Top Tip
Glucose → energy + lactic acid

2C Aerobic and Anaerobic Exercise

Practical Investigation

All three energy systems contribute together at the start of exercise. But depending on the intensity and duration of the activity, one energy system will dominate.

Use the energy continuum worksheet to develop your understanding of energy systems.

Equipment

You will need the following:

› a photocopy of the worksheet in Appendix 2.3

› a pen or pencil

› three highlighters/ coloured pens (green, blue, red).

Method

Energy systems interact to provide energy for varying lengths of time.

Complete a thorough warm-up before completing the following tasks to develop your understanding of energy systems. As you complete each task, record how you felt in the table on the worksheet:

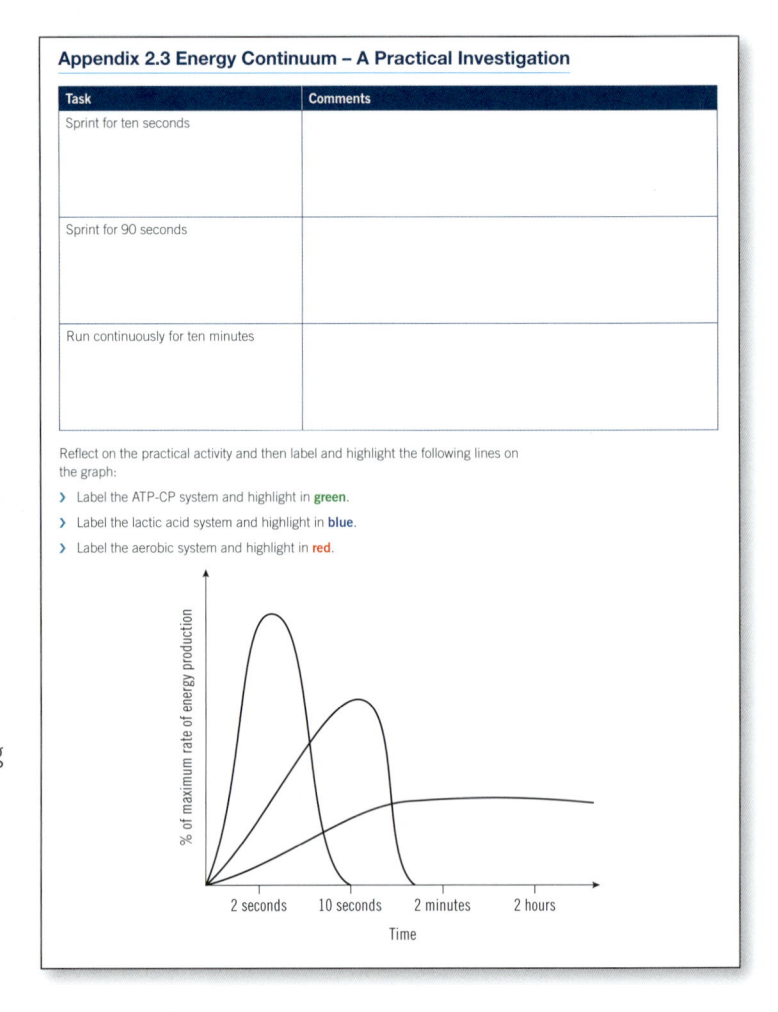

Appendix 2.3 Energy Continuum – A Practical Investigation

Task	Comments
Sprint for ten seconds	
Sprint for 90 seconds	
Run continuously for ten minutes	

Reflect on the practical activity and then label and highlight the following lines on the graph:

› Label the ATP-CP system and highlight in green.
› Label the lactic acid system and highlight in blue.
› Label the aerobic system and highlight in red.

› Explore the ATP-CP system by running as fast as you can for ten seconds. Record how you felt in the table.

› Rest for five minutes (full recovery).

› Run as fast as you can continuously for 90 seconds. Record how you felt in the table.

› Rest for five minutes (full recovery).

› Run continuously for ten minutes at a manageable pace. Record how you felt in the table.

Chapter 2 Exercise Physiology

Investigation

Reflect on the practical activity and then label and highlight the following lines on the graph on the worksheet:

› Label the ATP-CP system and highlight in **green**.

› Label the lactic acid system and highlight in **blue**.

› Label the aerobic system and highlight in **red**.

Extension Activity

Complete the gap-fill task using the words in the box.

The **ATP-CP** system lasts for up to _____. It is used for _____ -intensity exercise. It is used for activities like _____, _____ and _____.

The **lactic acid** system is used for _____ -intensity exercise, which lasts up to about _____. The fuel used for this system is _____ which are stored in the muscle as _____. The lactic acid system is used for speed endurance events like _____ and _____ athletic track events.

The **aerobic** system requires _____. It is used for _____ to _____ -intensity exercise, for example _____ and _____ running. The fuel needed for this system comes from _____, _____ and, in extreme circumstances, _____.

carbohydrates	marathon
high	fats
proteins	shot put
90 seconds	ten seconds
carbohydrates	200 m
high	glycogen
400 m	short sprints
10,000 m	oxygen
low	medium
discus	

81

2C Aerobic and Anaerobic Exercise

Topic Test

The main component of fitness needed by a 100 m sprinter is speed.

a) **Identify** the main *energy system* used *during a 100 m race*. **1 mark**

b) **Outline** one reason for your answer. **1 mark**

When reading the question, look at what the key words and phrases are asking you to do:

- **Command word:** This is based on the assessment objective (AO). The assessment objective for this question is AO1: you need to demonstrate your knowledge and understanding.
- **Topic:** This is the key area of study the question is about.
- **Qualifying words or phrases:** This is the specific area you need to focus on in your answer.

Doing this will help you to build your answer so that you can access the AO for each question.

Step 1 Demonstrate your knowledge (AO1)

You need to **demonstrate your knowledge and understanding** of energy systems by identifying which is used during a 100 m race.

The main energy system used in a 100 m is _____

Step 2 Demonstrate your knowledge (AO1)

You need to outline the reason for your answer.

_____
_____
_____
_____

Use the terms in the tick list of terminology to help you plan your answer to meet AO1. Look at how many marks are available to help you decide how much detail to include:

- ☐ High intensity
- ☐ Aerobic
- ☐ ATP-CP
- ☐ No oxygen
- ☐ Short duration
- ☐ Anaerobic
- ☐ Lactic acid

Chapter 2 Exercise Physiology

THE BIG QUESTION

RECAP

C You are building the knowledge and understanding you need to answer the Big Question. You have already answered parts 1 and 2. Now it's time to answer part 3 and apply your knowledge and understanding of aerobic and anaerobic exercise.

3. Look at the image of a 100 m race.
   a) Identify the dominant energy system used in this event. (1 mark)
   b) Identify three characteristics of the energy system identified above. (3 marks)

> Think about the factors that determine the energy systems used in an activity. Apply these to a 100 m race.

> Think about the characteristics of the energy system. The following key words may help you: oxygen, fuel, intensity, duration, fatigue, waste product.

83

2D Short- and Long-term Effects of Exercise

This is the question we're going to be working towards answering at the end of this section.

> 4. Explain the long-term adaptations to the cardiovascular system after following an eight-week training programme. (3 marks)
>
> AO2 – 3 marks

Short-term Effects of Exercise

As we begin to exercise, our muscles and the cardio-respiratory system all work harder to meet the demands of the intensity and duration of the exercise we are doing.

Short-term effects are the ones that happen immediately when we begin to exercise. The body responds to exercise in order to meet the demands of its intensity and duration. This affects which energy system we use.

Muscular system

Whatever type of exercise we do, our muscles will contract and so require an increased supply of oxygen. As we begin to exercise they:

- increase muscle contractions
- produce more carbon dioxide
- produce lactic acid when oxygen is not available
- fatigue
- increase in temperature.

Cardiovascular system

This system will respond to exercise by increasing the flow of blood by:

- increasing heart rate
- increasing stroke volume
- increasing cardiac output
- vasodilation in working muscles
- vasoconstriction in the digestive system
- releasing heat through blood vessels near the skin.

Respiratory system

The respiratory system responds to exercise by:

- increasing respiratory rate and the number of breaths per minute
- increasing tidal volume
- increasing the volume of air inhaled and exhaled per minute
- increasing the rate of gaseous exchange.

Temperature control (thermoregulation)

When we exercise, our bodies produce heat; we control this increase in temperature by:

- moving blood to the surface of the skin through vasodilation to release heat
- producing sweat, which evaporates on the skin to reduce body temperature.

Quick Check

Identify three short-term effects of exercise on the body. AO1

1. _____
2. _____
3. _____

Chapter 2 Exercise Physiology

Long-term Effects of Exercise

A regular pattern of exercise will make your body become more efficient and stronger. Your body will adapt to change after a period of regular training. The changes to your body will depend partly on the intensity and duration of your training sessions.

1. Muscular-skeletal system
2. Cardiovascular system
3. Respiratory system
4. Health and fitness
5. Energy systems

> **Top Tip**
> Long-term adaptations are generally increases in size, efficiency and volume.

1. Muscular-skeletal system

The muscular-skeletal system will become stronger. The following long-term adaptations will enable it to work harder for longer as well as reducing the risk of injury:

- improving muscle endurance and strength
- increasing the size of muscle (**hypertrophy**)
- increasing the elasticity of muscles
- increasing the density and strength of bones through weight-bearing exercises, which reduces the risk of osteoporosis
- reducing the risk of injury by improving stability at joints.

> **Top Tip**
> 'Muscular-skeletal' means relating to the muscles and skeleton. It includes the bones, joints, tendons and muscles.

85

2D Short- and Long-term Effects of Exercise

> **Top Tip**
> Cardiovascular = heart and vascular system

2. Cardiovascular system

Over time this system will become stronger, enabling it to efficiently circulate blood around the body. This happens by:

- increasing the size of the heart (**cardiac hypertrophy**), which will then be able to pump more blood around the body
- increasing resting stroke volume (the amount of blood pumped out of the heart during one contraction is increased)
- increasing cardiac output (the amount of blood pumped out of the left ventricle in one minute is increased)
- increasing the number of red blood cells, so there is more haemoglobin to carry more oxygen around the body
- reducing resting heart rate
- increasing number of capillaries
- arteries becoming more elastic
- reducing blood pressure.

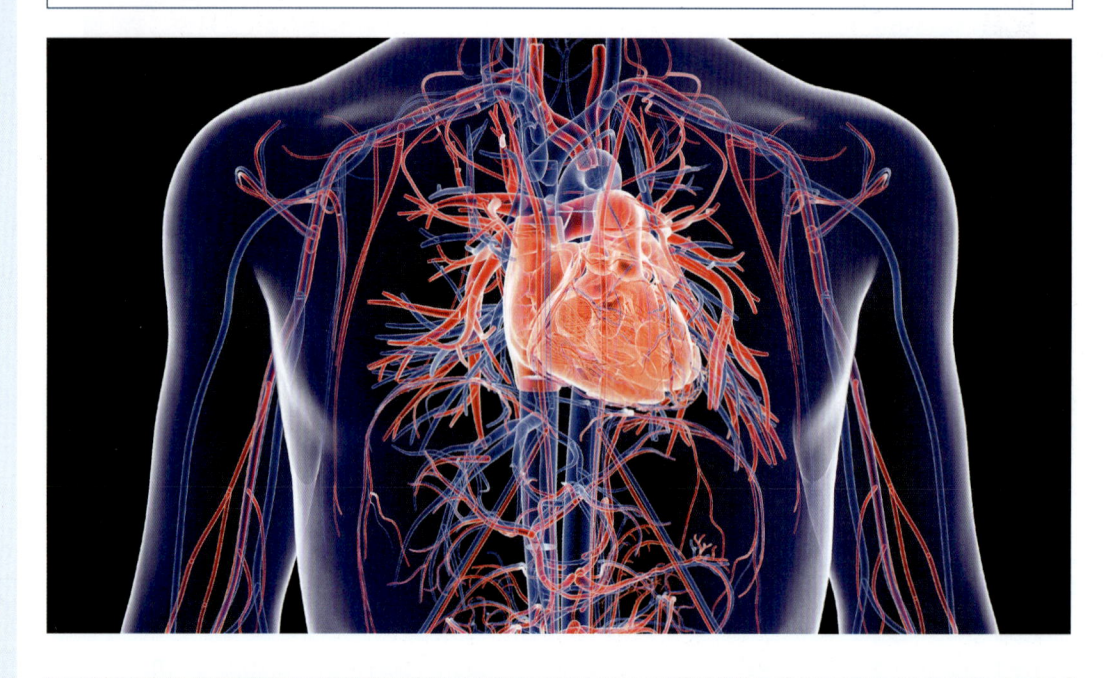

▶ The cardiovascular system circulates blood around the body.

> **Top Tip**
> Respiratory = lungs

3. Respiratory system

This system will adapt and become stronger, enabling it to deliver more oxygen to the working muscles by:

- increasing lung volume as the diaphragm and intercostal muscles become stronger
- increasing tidal volume
- increasing the efficiency of gaseous exchange by forming more capillaries around the alveoli
- increasing VO2 max (the maximum amount of oxygen inhaled and used during exercise)
- decreasing breathing frequency as a result of greater efficiency
- increasing vital capacity.

4. Health and fitness

The body will adapt to long-term training and will:

- allow you to train harder and for longer
- improve your overall health
- improve your overall performance
- improve recovery time
- reduce the risk of injury
- improve flexibility
- improve self-esteem and self-image.

Quick Check

Identify three long-term health and fitness benefits of regular exercise. **A01**

1. _____
2. _____
3. _____

◀ Long-term training will reduce your risk of injury.

5. Energy systems

Increase in capillarisation of blood vessels in the muscles and lungs to:

- transport oxygen to working muscles
- remove waste products (carbon dioxide and lactic acid) from working muscles.

Knowledge Check

Match each long-term adaptation to their specific system. **A01**

Long-term adaptation	System
Increase in muscle hypertrophy	Cardiovascular system
Increased cardiac output	Muscular system
Increased efficiency of gaseous exchange	Respiratory system

87

2D Short- and Long-term Effects of Exercise

Topic Test

Explain one **short-term** effect of **exercise on the body.** `2 marks`

When reading the question, look at what the key words and phrases are asking you to do:

- **Command word:** This is based on the assessment objective (AO). The assessment objective for this question is AO2: you need to apply your knowledge and understanding.
- **Topic:** This is the key area of study the question is about.
- **Qualifying words or phrases:** This is the specific area you need to focus on in your answer.

Doing this will help you to build your answer so that you can access the AO for each question.

Step 1 Demonstrate your knowledge (AO1)

You need to **demonstrate your knowledge and understanding** of the short-term effects of exercise on the body by identifying one of them. Remember, short-term effects are immediate. So how does your body respond to exercise while it is happening?

_____

Use the terms in the tick list of terminology to help you plan your answer to meet AO1. Look at how many marks are available to help you decide how much detail to include:

- ☐ Sweating
- ☐ Temperature
- ☐ Breathing rate
- ☐ Heart rate
- ☐ Muscle contractions

Step 2 Apply your knowledge and understanding (AO2)

You need to **apply your knowledge and understanding** of the short-term effects of exercise on the body in order to **explain** the effect you have chosen.

_____
_____
_____
_____
_____

Use the terms in the tick list of terminology to help you plan your answer to meet AO2. Look at how many marks are available to help you decide how much detail to include:

- ☐ Increase in temperature
- ☐ Increase in carbon dioxide
- ☐ Increase in oxygen
- ☐ Increase in muscle contractions

Chapter 2 Exercise Physiology

THE BIG QUESTION

RECAP

D Now it's time to answer part 4 and apply your knowledge and understanding of short- and long-term effects of exercise.

4. Explain the long-term adaptations to the cardiovascular system after following an eight-week training programme. (3 marks)

What makes up the cardiovascular system?

Generally long-term adaptations are increases in size, volume and efficiency.

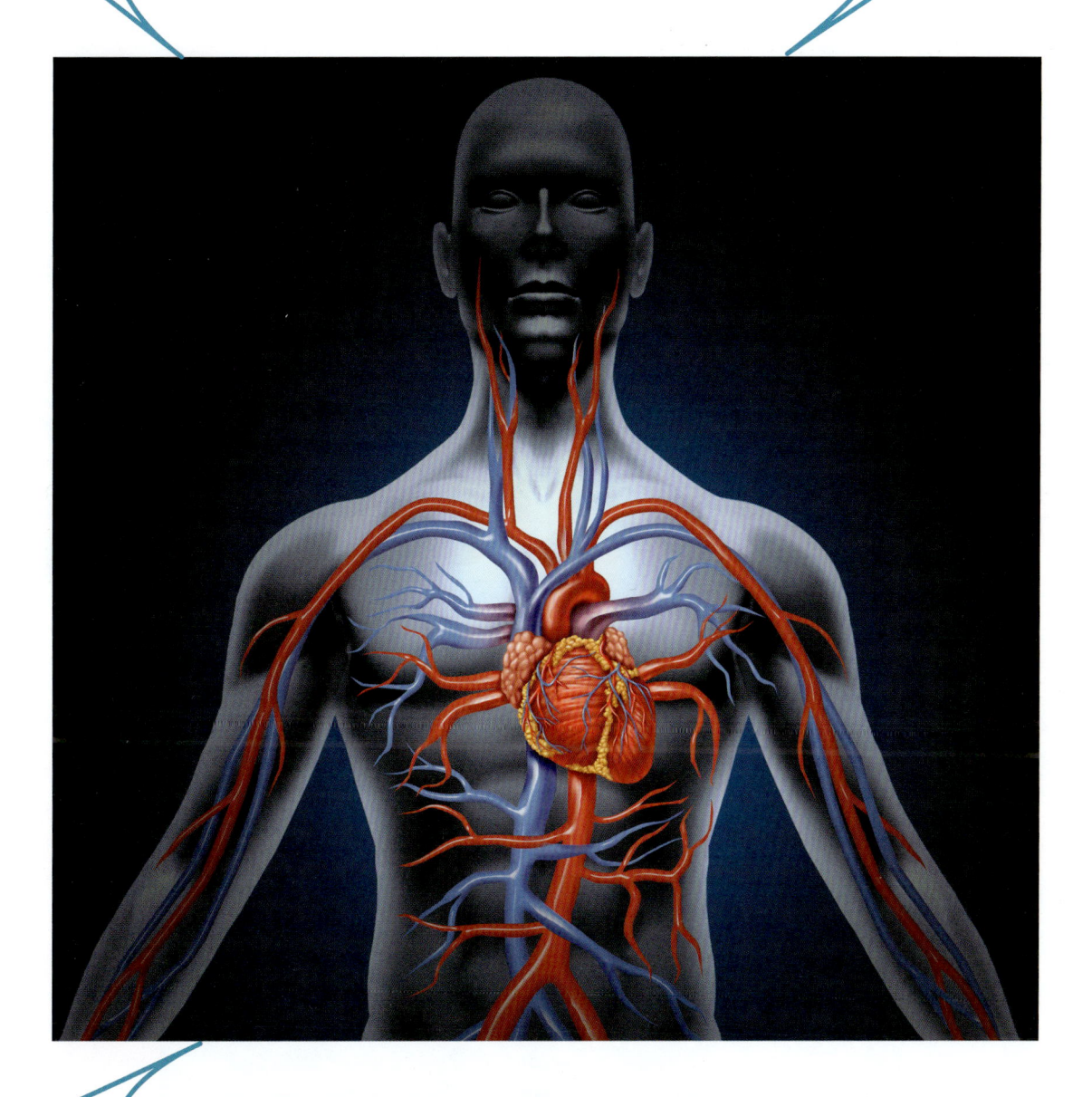

Think about your own eight-week training plan. Can you relate your adaptations during the plan to the question?

89

CHAPTER 3

Movement Analysis

Movement analysis helps coaches and athletes understand the different types of movements within specific sports. Part of your exam asks you to analyse specific movements that take place in sport. To do so you need to fully understand movement analysis and be confident in the terminology used.

THE BIG QUESTION

Imagine gymnasts preparing for a major competition. They will require a range of movements to complete a fluent routine. As you complete this chapter, you will develop the knowledge, understanding and skills you need to analyse the movements of the gymnasts and answer the Big Question. By the end of each topic in this chapter you should be able to answer one of the question parts outlined below.

These are the topics you'll need to answer the Big Question:

A **Muscle contraction:** When performing a handstand in a routine, what contractions will take place in the arms?

B **Lever systems:** If a gymnast performs a split leap and pushes off the floor with one foot, what class of lever do they use and how much mechanical advantage does it benefit from?

C **Planes and axes of movement:** As the gymnast runs to gain speed in preparation for a somersault, what plane would they be moving through? When performing a cartwheel, what axis would the gymnast rotate around?

D **Sports technology:** How can the gymnast and their coach use technology to help improve the gymnast's performance?

As you work through this chapter, we will cover all the skills and knowledge you'll need to be able to answer the Big Question. If you can do that, you will have brilliant AO1 and AO2 skills ready to use in your GCSE.

In this chapter you will learn about:

> the major muscle groups and their antagonistic muscle actions
> isotonic and isometric muscle contractions with application to sporting examples
> the classification of each lever system, identifying the mechanical advantage or disadvantage of each lever system
> the different planes and axes of movement, as well as how they relate to joint and muscle movements in different sporting activities
> the role of technology in the analysis of movement and how it can be used by coaches to improve sporting performance
> the role of technology in officiating.

In this chapter you will be using the following key terms. You can look up the meaning of these terms in the Glossary (page 184 onwards).

Key Terms

Agonist (prime mover)	Antagonist	Axis (plural axes)	Effort
Effort arm	Fulcrum	Lever arm	Load
Load arm	Mechanical advantage	Mechanical disadvantage	Motivation
Notational analysis	Perpendicular	Plane	Qualitative data
Quantitative data	Technology	TMO	VAR

3A Muscle Contraction

In this topic we will work towards answering this part of the Big Question:

> 1. Athletes preparing for major competitions require a range of movements to compete fluently.
>
> a) A gymnast performs a handstand during a routine. Explain which muscle contraction takes place to hold a balance. (4 marks)
>
> **AO2 – 4 marks**

Analysing muscular contractions helps an athlete and coach to develop training programmes meeting the specific needs of their sport or activity. It allows identification of movement patterns, contractions and the development of specific actions and muscles.

Muscle Contractions

You need to know about **muscle contractions** so that you can understand how the muscles of the body work to produce movement. **Skeletal muscles** are responsible for producing movement through different muscle contractions which pull on the skeletal system to cause movement at a joint. It is important to understand the different types of muscle contractions and how muscles work together to produce different movements.

Before we can explore the different muscle contractions, it is a good opportunity to recap on the major skeletal muscles covered on page 59:

Deltoids
Abduction of the arm at the shoulder joint

Pectorals
Involved in the abduction of the arms

Biceps
Flexion of the arm at the elbow joint

Abdominals
Flexion of the trunk

Quadriceps
Extension of the leg at the knee joint

Trapezius
Rotation of the shoulder

Triceps
Extension of the arm at the elbow joint

Latissimus dorsi
Adduction of arm movement at the shoulder

Hamstrings
Flexion of the leg at the knee joint

Gastrocnemius
Extension at the ankle

In order to produce movement our muscles must shorten or lengthen. Muscle contractions can be divided into two types: **isotonic** and **isometric**.

> **Top Tip**
>
> Muscles only contract. Skeletal muscles contract, pulling on tendons that are attached to bone, causing movement at a joint.

Chapter 3 Movement Analysis

Isotonic Contraction

An isotonic contraction produces movement. The muscles involved in the contraction produce tension which controls the speed and types of contraction. There are two types of isotonic contraction:

- concentric contraction
- eccentric contraction.

The image shows a biceps curl. To lift the weight, the biceps muscle will need to contract. This means the muscle becomes shorter under tension, causing flexion at the elbow joint. This is known as a **concentric contraction**.

Concentric contraction

Concentric contraction of biceps

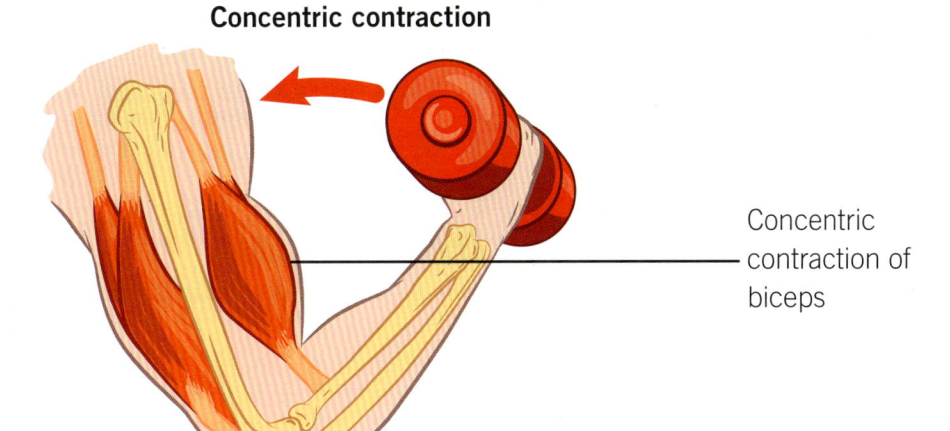

When lowering the weight, the biceps muscle will need to lengthen under tension so that the weight is lowered under control causing extension at the elbow. This is known as an **eccentric contraction**.

Eccentric contraction

Eccentric contraction of biceps

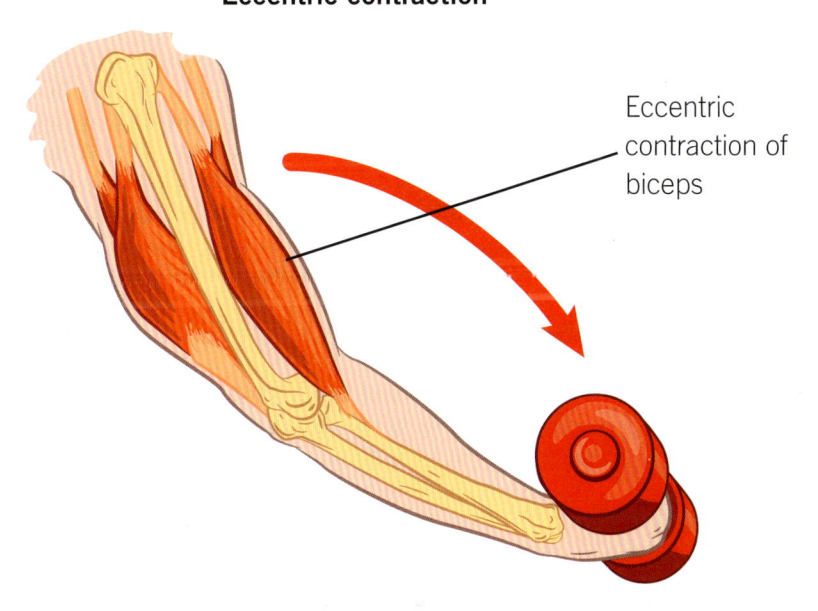

This page talks about **types of contractions**, so is only concentrating on one muscle; in this instance the biceps. When the biceps lifts the weight it gets smaller and when it lowers the weight it gets longer.

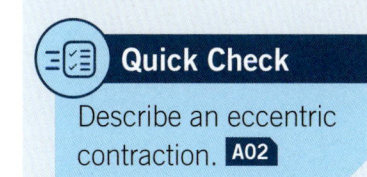

Quick Check

Describe an eccentric contraction. A02

3A Muscle Contraction

> **Top Tip**
>
> Here is one way to remember the two main types of contraction.
>
> Is**oto**nic contraction = movement.
> Two 'o's in isotonic = two movements (concentric and eccentric).
>
> Is**o**metric contraction = static. One 'o' in isometric looks like a zero = no movement.

Isometric Contraction

In an isometric contraction the muscle is under tension but there is no movement. When holding the plank position during a workout, the abdominal muscles are under tension, keeping the body in a static position. There is no movement.

▲ An example of an isometric contraction is a plank exercise.

The image above shows a plank position being held. There is no movement (it is static) so the muscle remains under tension with no lengthening or shortening.

Muscle contraction	Details
Isotonic	The muscle contracts under tension producing movement through the shortening or lengthening of the muscle
Isometric	The muscle contracts under tension but there is no movement
Concentric contraction	A type of isotonic contraction where the muscle contracts and gets shorter
Eccentric contraction	A type of isotonic contraction where the muscle contracts, but is lengthening under a load

Antagonistic Muscle Actions

Muscles work in pairs to produce movement at a joint. In order to produce movement, one muscle will need to contract (shorten), pulling on a bone, and another muscle will need to relax. To produce the opposite movement, the roles of the muscles will change. This is known as an **antagonistic muscle action**.

Chapter 3 Movement Analysis

The quadriceps and the hamstrings work in pairs to flex and extend the leg at the knee. Look at the images.

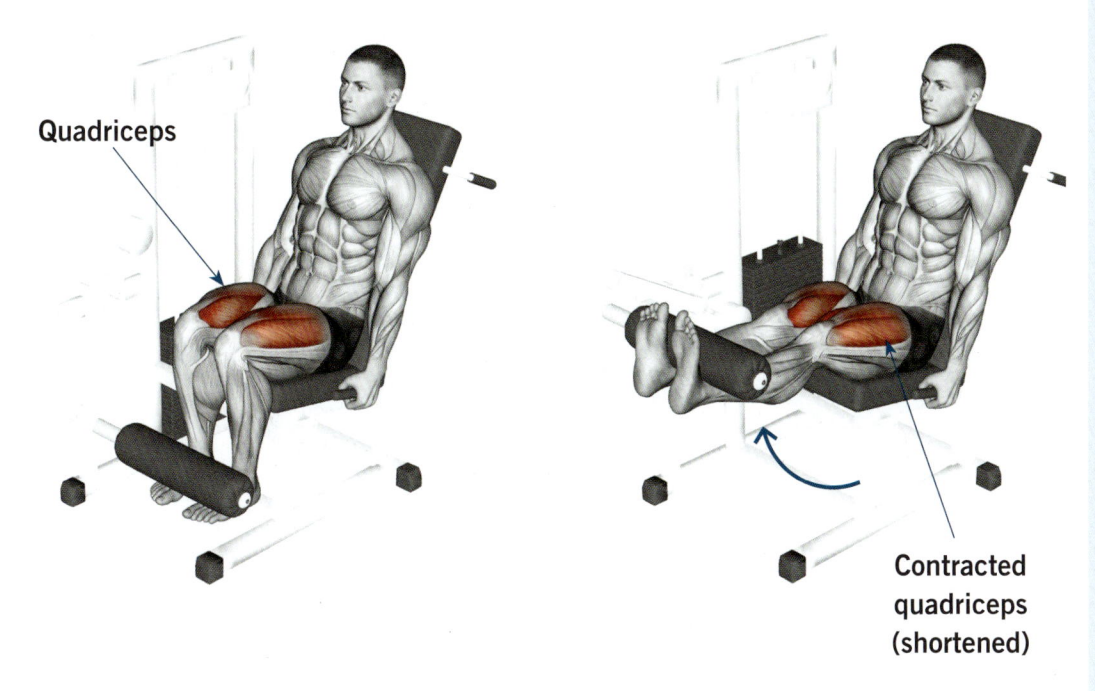

Quadriceps

Contracted quadriceps (shortened)

During a leg extension the quadriceps muscles are used to extend the leg at the knee joint. The quadriceps muscles contract (shorten), controlling the movement, so the quadriceps are the **agonist** or **prime mover**.

The hamstring muscles relax (lengthen) to allow the movement to take place. They are the **antagonist**.

A hamstring curl is the reverse of the previous action. In a hamstring curl, the hamstrings contract to produce flexion at the knee. In this exercise the hamstrings now become the agonist or prime mover as they are controlling the movement.

The quadriceps relax (lengthen) to allow this movement to take place. They are the antagonist.

Hamstrings

Contracted hamstrings (shortened)

> **Top Tip**
> Skeletal muscles contract to produce movement at a joint.
> Skeletal muscles work in antagonistic pairs, e.g. biceps and triceps.

> **Top Tip**
> The agonist controls the movement, so it is also known as the prime mover.

> **Quick Check**
> Identify two types of movement that can be produced by an isotonic contraction. **A01**
> During the lifting phase of a biceps curl identify which muscle is the agonist (prime mover). **A01**

> **A02**
> You will need to apply your knowledge of specific terms such as 'flexion' and 'extension'.

95

3A Muscle Contraction

Practical investigation

Equipment

You will need the following:

> a photocopy of the cut-out images in Appendix 3.1
> scissors
> glue
> split pin.

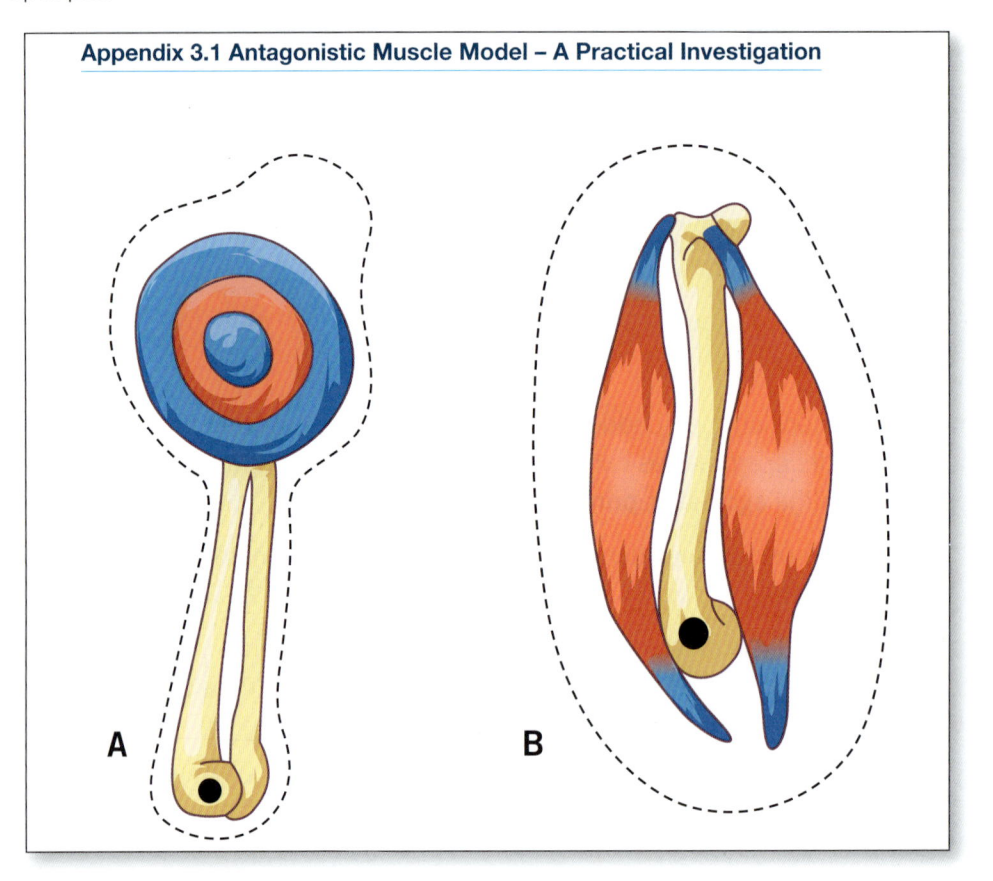

Appendix 3.1 Antagonistic Muscle Model – A Practical Investigation

A   B

Method

1. Using scissors, carefully cut around the dotted lines of images A and B, showing the humerus and the radius and ulna.

2. Carefully pierce the paper where the black dots are. The holes will then be used to place the split pin.

3. Push the split pin through hole A of the radius and ulna and then through hole B at the bottom of the humerus. This will create the elbow joint.

4. Now that your model is together, identify an area on a blank page of your book where you will stick your model. **Make sure you position your model so you have space around the outside to annotate it to complete the investigation**. On the back of the humerus **only**, paste some glue on the top half of the image and stick this section only to your page. Make sure you leave room so that the radius and ulna can move freely.

Investigation

Using your model, annotate your page to identify the following:

1. biceps
2. triceps
3. humerus
4. radius
5. ulna
6. tendon.

Extension Activity

Explore your model and complete this task. You may wish to complete the sentences in your book around your model if you have space.

1. An arm lifting a weight using this movement creates a _____ muscle contraction.

2. The _____ muscle contracts (shortens) to control this movement and is known as the _____ or _____ mover.

3. In this movement the _____ muscle works with the biceps. It relaxes (lengthens) and is the _____.

4. When the arm lowers the weight, it creates an _____ muscle contraction where the biceps muscle is still under tension but lengthens during the lowering of the weight.

5. The biceps muscle is attached to the radius by a _____ which pulls on the bone to produce movement at the _____ joint.

Use the following words to fill the gaps:

biceps	elbow
triceps	eccentric
tendon	agonist
concentric	antagonist
prime	

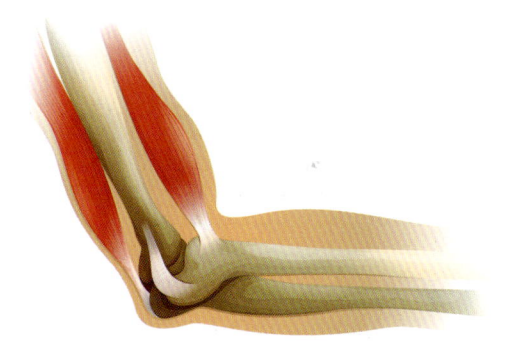

3A Muscle Contraction

Topic Test

A gymnast preparing for a major competition requires a range of movements to complete a fluent floor routine.

a) Identify the movement at the knee, labelled A, in the image below. **1 mark**
Tick (✓) one box only.

	Tick (✓)
Flexion	
Extension	
Abduction	
Adduction	

b) **Explain** the antagonistic muscle actions of the quadriceps and hamstrings when causing this movement at the knee. **3 marks**

When reading the question, look at what the key words and phrases are asking you to do:

- **Command word:** This is based on the assessment objective (AO). The assessment objective for part a) is AO1 and the assessment objective for part b) is AO2: you need to demonstrate and apply your knowledge and understanding.
- **Topic:** This is the key area of study the question is about.
- **Qualifying words or phrases:** This is the specific area you need to focus on in your answer.

Doing this will help you to build your answer so that you can access the AO for each question.

Step 1 Demonstrate your knowledge (AO1)

You need to **demonstrate your knowledge and understanding** by **identifying** the movement at the knee. What is happening to the joint with the leg in that position?

Step 2 Apply your knowledge and understanding (AO2)

You need to **apply your knowledge and understanding** of antagonistic muscle actions in order to **explain** the movement.

Use the terms in the tick list of terminology. Look at how many marks are available to help you decide how much detail to include.

Isotonic	
Shortens	
Concentric	
Eccentric	
Lengthens	
Flexion	
Extension	
Quadriceps	
Hamstrings	
Knee	

Chapter 3 Movement Analysis

THE BIG QUESTION

RECAP

A Now that you have developed a knowledge and understanding of muscle contraction and completed the Topic Test, have a go at part a) of the Big Question.

1. **Athletes preparing for major competitions require a range of movements to compete fluently.**

   a) A gymnast performs a handstand during a routine. Explain which muscle contraction takes place to hold a balance. (4 marks)

The image shows a gymnast holding a handstand on the parallel bars.

We know that a handstand is a balance – not a movement. So what is the role of the muscles?

Think about the muscles used in the upper arm and shoulder.

What type of muscle contraction is taking place in the arms and shoulder?

99

3B Lever Systems

In this topic we will work towards answering part b) of the Big Question.

> 1 Athletes preparing for major competitions require a range of movements to compete fluently.
>
> b) In order to perform a split leap, a gymnast pushes off the floor with one foot.
>
> (i) Identify the class of lever shown in the image. (1 mark)
>
> (ii) Explain the mechanical advantage of the class of lever shown in the image. (2 marks)
>
> **AO1 & AO2 – 3 marks**

Imagine you are coaching the gymnast in the question. You will need an understanding of the mechanics of levers and how they produce movement. You will also need an understanding of the relationships between the muscular and skeletal systems, and how they allow the body to apply a **force** to create movement. For this information to be helpful to both the coach and the athlete, specific terminology is used to analyse the movements taking place.

Components of a Lever

Levers are normally used to make physical work easier, for example to move a heavy load or to move something quickly. When we exercise, most of our movements will involve the use of levers; for example, when we run, lift weights, kick or throw a ball, all of these actions use levers.

A lever system within the body uses a **lever arm** (a bone) to move an object. For example, when we run, we are the object being moved, but when kicking a ball, the object being moved is the ball.

All lever systems are made up of **four components** called the lever arm, **fulcrum**, **load** and **effort**. These terms describe the relationships between the part of the body producing the movement and the load which the body part is trying to move.

Look at the table and familiarise yourself with each component name, image and how it links to the body or mass being moved.

Chapter 3 Movement Analysis

Component	Description
Lever arm	In the body, a lever arm is a bone that helps to produce a movement
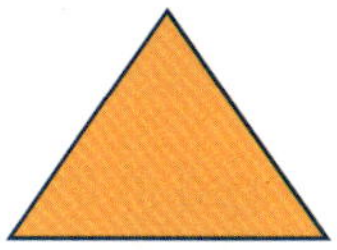 Fulcrum	The fulcrum is a pivot. This is a joint of the body from which the lever produces movement
 Load	The load is the resistance (weight/mass) that the athlete is trying to move. This can be body weight or an external weight like a dumb-bell
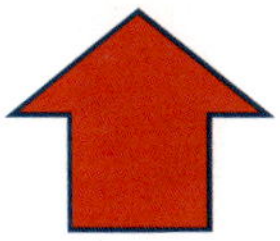 Effort	The effort is the force created by a muscle which is connected to the bone that is trying to move the load

Classification of Levers

Levers are classified based on the relationships between the components. Levers can be classified as first class, second class or third class. Each class of lever has its own advantages and disadvantages.

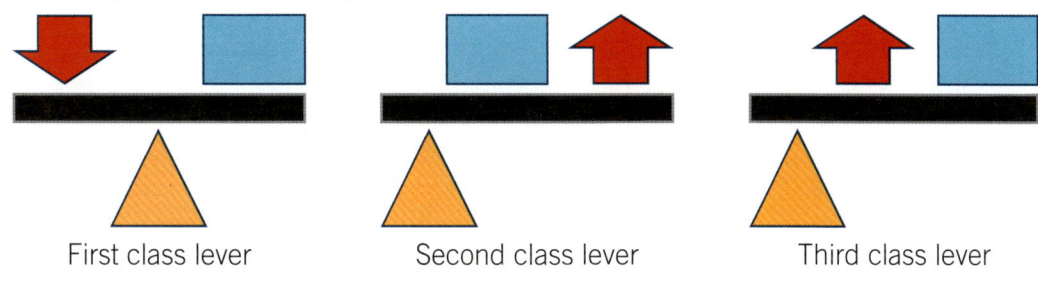

First class lever   Second class lever   Third class lever

You can use **FLE123** to help you remember the classes of lever. Forget about the lever arm for now and concentrate on the fulcrum, load and effort (FLE). Whatever component is in the middle will determine the class of lever.

In the illustration below we can see that the **effort** is between the **fulcrum** and the **load**. When we look at the FLE123 grid, we can see that the **effort** sits above **3**, therefore the example is a **third class lever**.

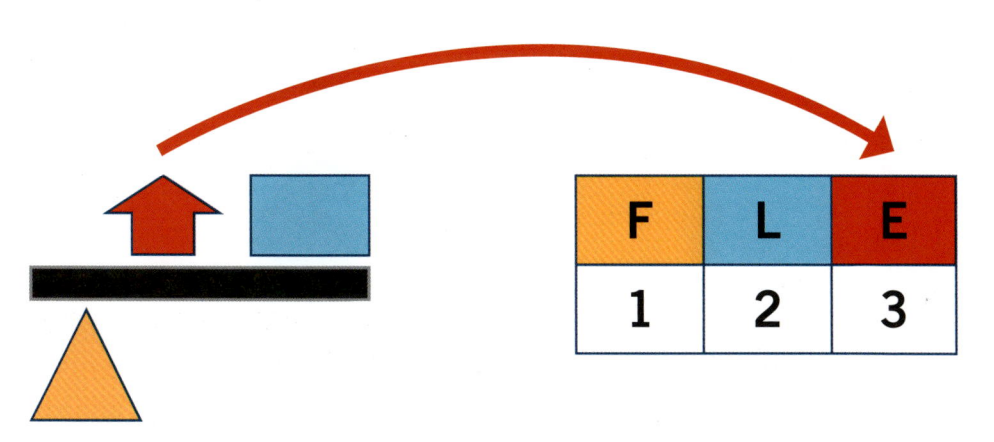

F	L	E
1	2	3

Top Tip
Remember FLE123 to identify the class of a lever. Whichever component is in the middle of the diagram determines the class of lever.

F	L	E
1	2	3

Quick Check
Can you identify the following levers using FLE123? **A01**

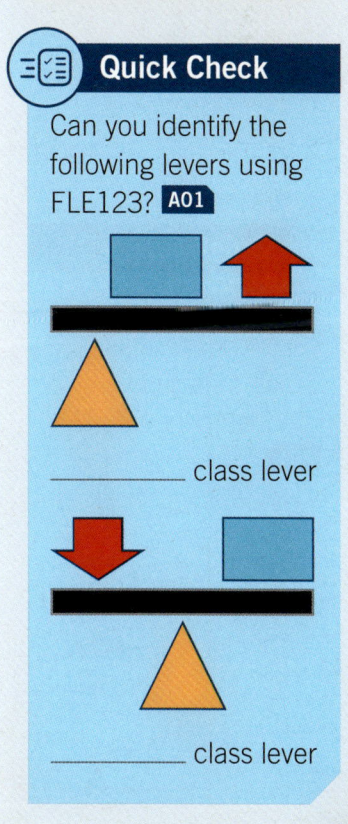

_____ class lever

_____ class lever

101

3B Lever Systems

Levers in the Body

Each classification of lever can be found in the body. The images below will help you to identify the relationships between the muscle and skeletal systems that help the body produce movement.

First Class Lever

The image shows first class levers in action. The components are arranged in the order E**F**L. The **effort** is the muscle used to produce the movement, the **fulcrum** is the neck joint where the movement takes place and the **load** is the weight of the cranium that is being moved.

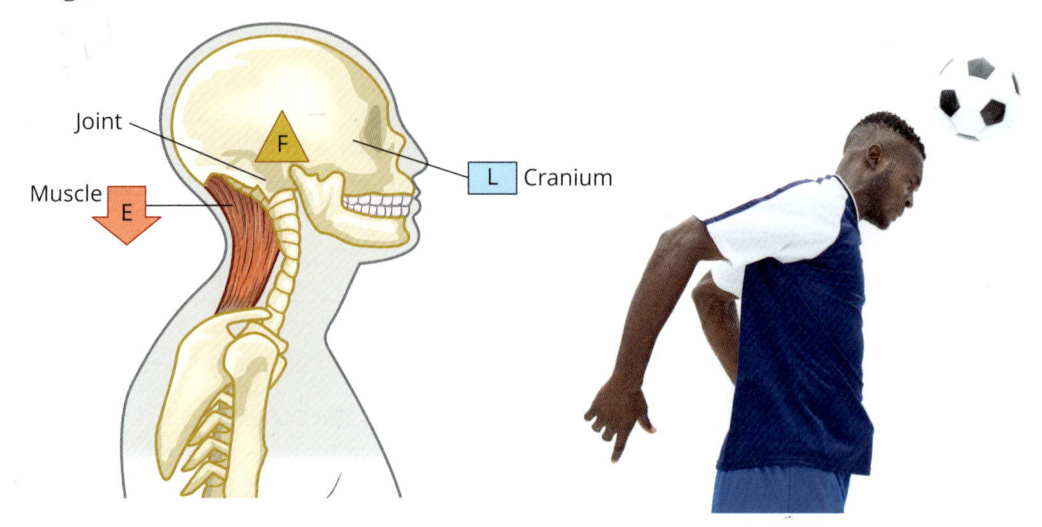

There are not many examples of first class levers in the body. Nodding of the head is an example so sports that require head movement, e.g. heading a ball or watching the flight of an object, are examples of a first class lever in sport.

Second Class Lever

For a second class lever the components are arranged in the order of E**L**F. The image shows an example of a second class lever. The **effort** is the muscle (calf/gastrocnemius) used to produce the movement, the **load** is the weight of the body that is being moved and the **fulcrum** is the ball of the foot where the movement takes place.

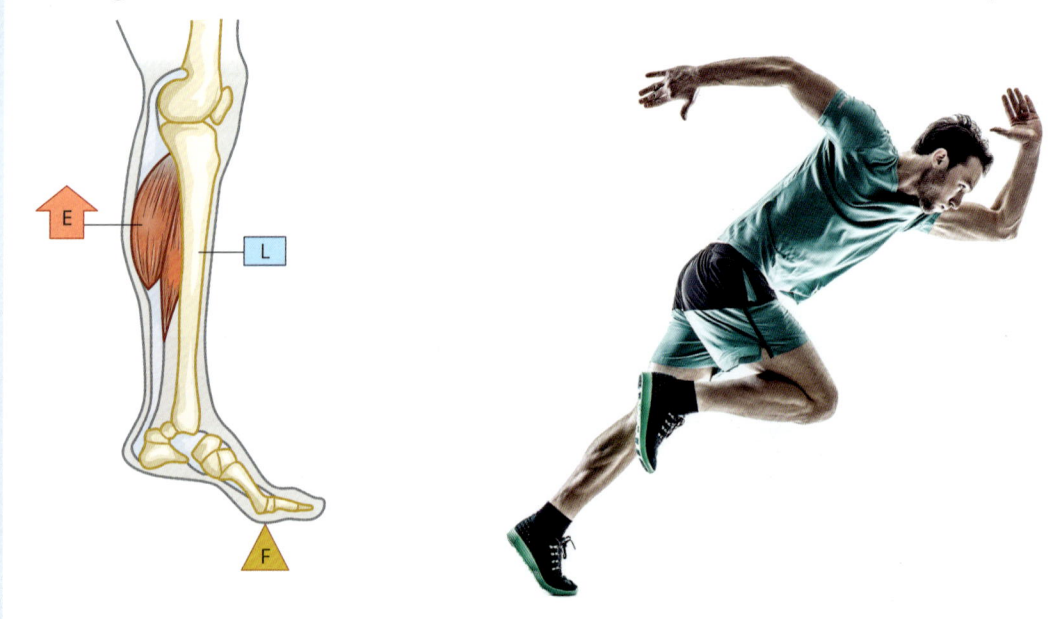

> **Quick Check**
> Which part of the human body acts as the fulcrum in all lever systems? **AO1**

> **Quick Check**
> In the image of a second class lever, which muscle is producing the effort? **AO1**

Again, there are not many examples of second class levers in the body. However, there are many sporting examples where body weight is lifted up on the ball of the foot, e.g. running or preparing to jump.

Third Class Lever

The third class lever in the image below shows the components arranged in the order F**E**L. The **fulcrum** is the elbow joint where the movement takes place, the **effort** is the muscle (biceps) used to produce the movement and the **load** is the weight of the object being held in the hand and moved.

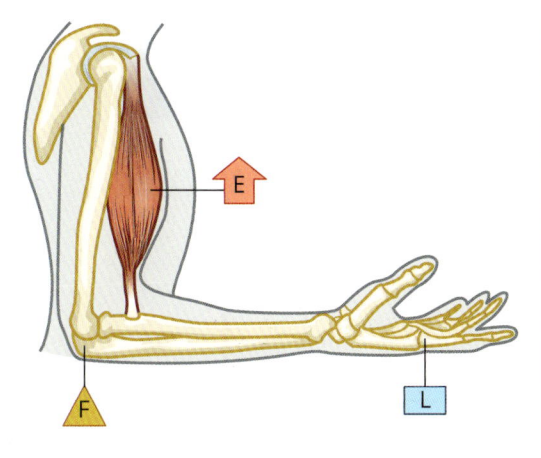

> **Quick Check**
> During flexion of the elbow, which muscle contracts and produces the effort? **AO1**

The third class lever is the most common type of lever in the body. This lever is involved in many movements and there are many examples of their use in sport, e.g. the elbow when performing biceps curls, and the use of the arm in racket sport or striking activities. Third class levers can also be found in the knee (when kicking a ball), the hip (when running) and the shoulder (when moving the arm out and upwards).

> **Quick Check**
> Other than the elbow, where in the body might you find another third class lever? **AO1**

Knowledge Check

Identify the type of lever seen at point A and point B in the image below. **AO1**

A = _____

B = _____

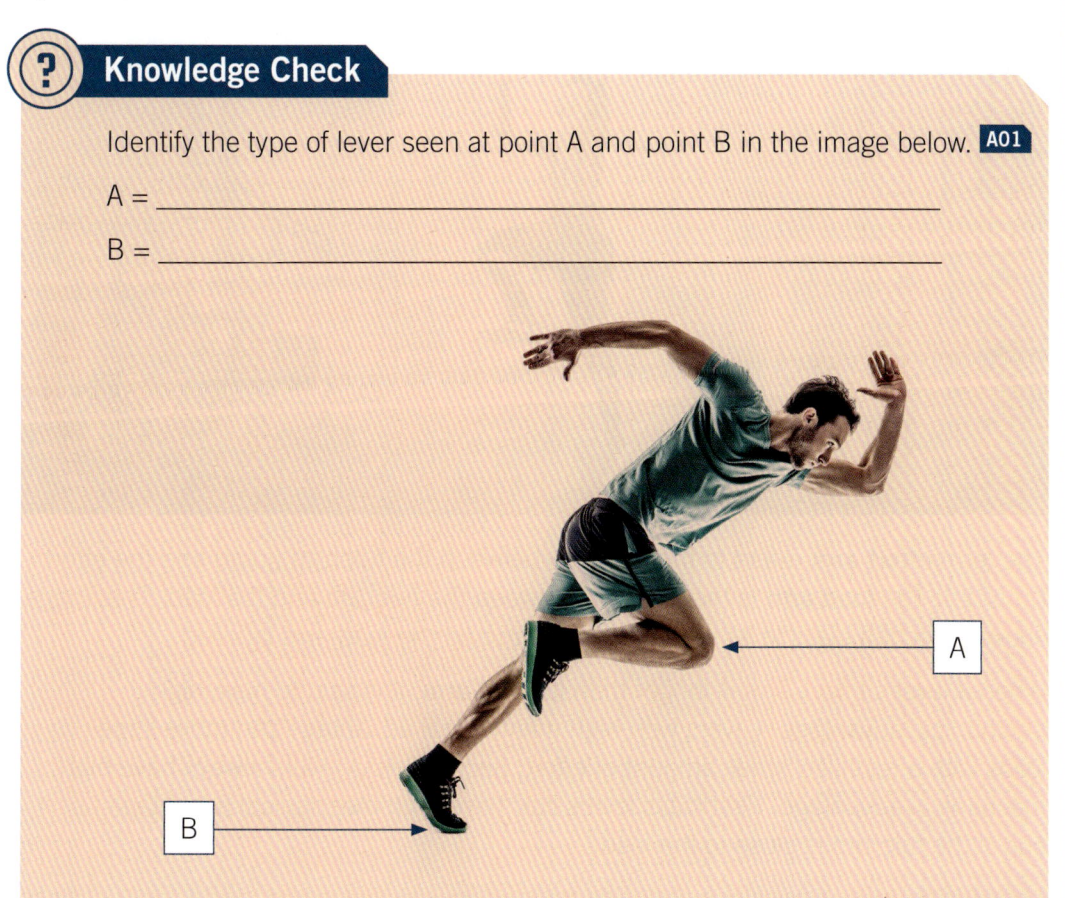

3B Lever Systems

Mechanical Advantage of Levers

Mechanical Advantage

The main functions of levers are to move heavy loads and to move loads at speed. Some levers operate with a **mechanical advantage**. This means that the lever can move a large load with relatively little effort.

In general terms levers have more mechanical advantage where the fulcrum is closer to the load. These levers tend to move slowly but are good at lifting a heavier load.

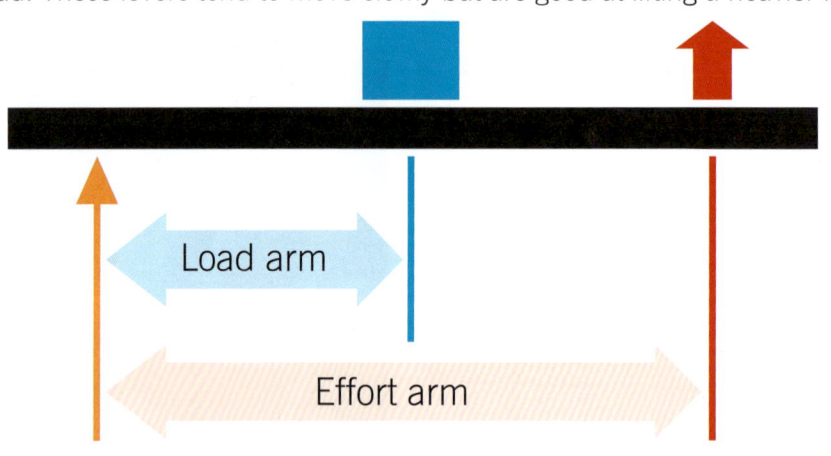

> **Top Tip**
> A lever is said to have a mechanical advantage when it can move a heavy load efficiently.

A second class lever has a mechanical advantage. You can easily lift your body weight (load) by contracting your calf muscle (effort) to raise your body up onto tiptoes to perform a layup in basketball.

▶ A second class lever at the ankle is used when a basketball player jumps.

The term **effort arm** refers to the distance between the fulcrum (joint) and the effort (muscle). The **load arm** is the distance between the fulcrum and the load. The image shows a second class lever with the effort arm and the load arm labelled.

When a lever's **effort arm** is longer than its **load arm**, it is said to have high mechanical advantage. Levers with high mechanical advantage can move large loads with a relatively small amount of effort. Second class levers always have high mechanical advantage. First class levers can have high mechanical advantage but only if the fulcrum is close to the load.

Mechanical Disadvantage

A **mechanical disadvantage** occurs if the **effort arm** is shorter than the **load arm**. This means that more effort will be required to overcome the load.

Third class levers are not advantageous for applying large amounts of force so they are the least efficient. However, they are good for accelerating objects quickly. They amplify the speed of the movement.

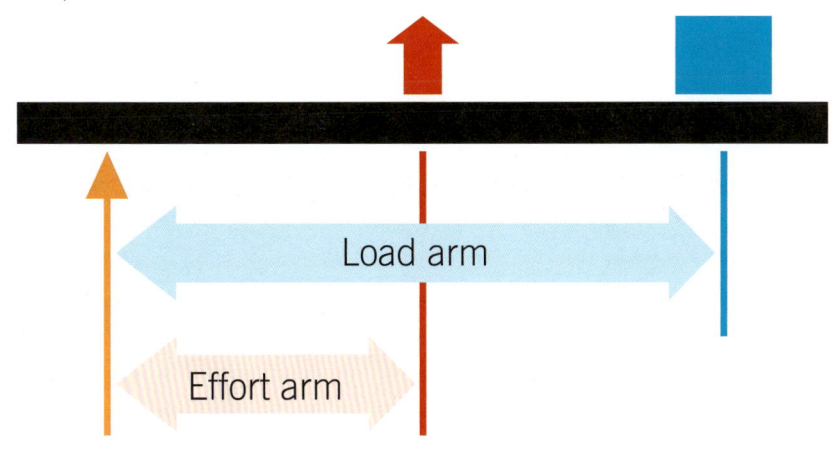

So, to summarise:

Mechanical advantage = a shorter **load arm** and a longer **effort arm**, allowing a heavier load to be lifted.

Mechanical disadvantage = a shorter **effort arm** and a longer **load arm**, allowing for faster movements over a larger range.

The general rules of mechanical advantages and disadvantages can be seen in the following table:

Class of lever	Diagram	Mechanical advantage/disadvantage	Movement example
First class lever		Can have a mechanical advantage (if the effort arm is longer than the load arm) or a mechanical disadvantage (if the load arm is longer)	Nodding the head
Second class lever		Always has a mechanical advantage, because the effort arm is longer than the load arm	Rising onto the ball of the foot
Third class lever		Always has a mechanical disadvantage, because the load arm is longer than the effort arm	Flexing the elbow or knee

Quick Check

Which of the following equations best describes a mechanical advantage? A01

1. Effort arm + load arm
2. Effort arm ÷ load arm
3. Effort arm × load arm

A02

You will need to apply your knowledge of the components of a lever and how they link to the skeletal and muscular systems. Make sure you know the terminology.

Quick Check

Match each class of levers to the correct components list. A01

> First class lever
> Second class lever
> Third class lever

fulcrum – load – effort

load – fulcrum – effort

load – effort – fulcrum

3B Lever Systems

Practical Investigation

Equipment

You will need the following:

> a range of sporting equipment linked to your chosen exercise/sporting activity
> a camera to capture the images of your chosen activities
> a pencil and paper to sketch the class of lever shown and record your results.

▲ Sporting equipment needed for the practical investigation.

Method

1. Take part in either an exercise or a sporting activity that uses each of the lever systems.

2. Using a camera, capture an image which shows an example of the lever system you are trying to demonstrate. (If you have no access to a camera then describe your chosen activity.)

3. Record your results.

Investigation

Analyse the movements involved in each of your chosen activities and complete a table like the one below:

Class of lever	Mechanical advantage or disadvantage	Exercise or sporting activity	Image or description of activity	Sketch of the lever involved

Results

Complete your table by:

> identifying whether the type of lever has mechanical advantage or disadvantage

> identifying your activity

> taking a picture or describing your activity

> sketching the lever involved in the activity, including the fulcrum, load and effort.

Class of lever	Mechanical advantage or disadvantage	Exercise or sporting activity	Image or description of activity	Sketch of the lever involved
First class	Mechanical advantage if the load is closer to the fulcrum than the effort	Heading a ball in football		

3B Lever Systems

Topic Test

Look at the image of a pole-vaulter who is running to gather speed as she approaches the bar.

a) **Identify** the classification of lever shown at point **A** and point **B** in the image. **2 marks**

Point	Classification of lever
A – neck	1st
B – knee	3rd

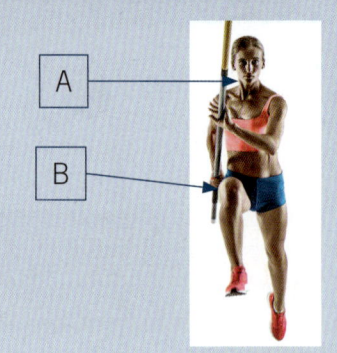

b) **Assess** the differences between the two classifications of lever. **4 marks**

When reading the question, look at what the key words and phrases are asking you to do:

- **Command word:** This is based on the assessment objective (AO). The assessment objective for part a) is AO1 and the assessment objective for part b) is AO3: you need to demonstrate your knowledge and understanding and perform some analysis or evaluation.
- **Topic:** This is the key area of study the question is about.
- **Qualifying words or phrases:** This is the specific area you need to focus on in your answer.

Doing this will help you to build your answer so that you can access the AO for each question.

Step 1 Demonstrate your knowledge (AO1)

To answer part a) you need to **demonstrate your knowledge and understanding** of levers. Note down the components of a lever then use them to determine the class.

Use FLE123 to help you answer:

F	L	E
1	2	3

_____

_____

Step 2 Analyse and evaluate (AO3)

You need to **analyse and evaluate** the properties of levers in order to **assess** the classifications of lever.

Think about the lever components. Which differences between the levers helped you work out their classifications? Will each lever have a mechanical advantage? How will they affect movement?

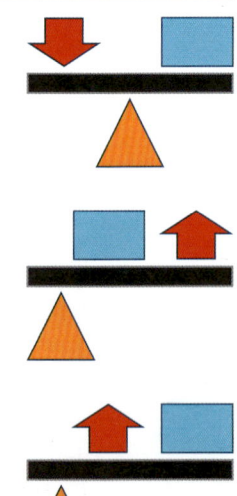

_____

_____

_____

_____

Chapter 3 Movement Analysis

THE BIG QUESTION

RECAP

B You are starting to build the knowledge and understanding you need to answer the Big Question. You have already answered part a) at the end of the last topic. So now it's time to answer part b) and apply your knowledge and understanding of lever systems.

> 1. Athletes preparing for major competitions require a range of movements to compete fluently.
>
>   b) In order to perform a split leap, a gymnast pushes off the floor with one foot.
>
>   (i) Identify the class of lever shown in the image. (1 mark) *2nd class*
>
>   (ii) Explain the mechanical advantage of the class of lever shown in the image. (2 marks)

Top Tip

Annotate the question using the colours we've used in this book: topic, command word, qualifying words.

What component is in the middle?

Does the lever give a mechanical advantage or disadvantage?

How easy is it to lift your body weight up on to your tiptoes?

The fulcrum is the ball of the foot. Where are the load and the effort?

3C Planes and Axes of Movement

In this topic we will work towards answering part c) of the Big Question.

> 1. Athletes preparing for major competitions require a range of movements to compete fluently.
>
> c) A gymnast performs a routine that includes a somersault and a cartwheel.
>
>   (i) The gymnast runs forwards to gain speed in preparation for the somersault. Identify the plane of movement she moves through. (1 mark)
>
>   (ii) Identify the axis of movement that the gymnast's body rotates around while she performs a cartwheel. (1 mark)
>
> AO1 – 2 marks

Top Tip

You move through a plane and rotate around an axis.

When you know about **planes** and **axes** you can better understand different movements in different sports. And you can also link those movements to the joints and muscles that work to create them.

To analyse the movement that takes place in sport we need an understanding of planes and axes of movement as well as the terminology linked to planes and axes. A knowledge of planes and axes will allow you to understand:

› movements in sport

› how to link movements to joints within the body

› how muscles help create the specific movements.

Anatomical Position

Whether you are a sports performer or a coach, an understanding of movement is important when analysing performance. All movements will occur through a specific plane and all rotations will occur around a specific axis.

Although you don't need to know the term 'anatomical position' for your exam, it may help you to visualise the different planes. It is also important to note that movement analysis is closely linked with the skeletal and muscle systems covered in Chapter 2.

Before we discuss the body plane it is a good idea to understand the anatomical position of the body. This can help you visualise the movements that happen in both planes and axes when we cover them later in this topic.

The anatomical position of the body (as shown in the following image) refers to the body's position when:

1. your head and eyes are facing straight ahead
2. your arms are to the side with your palms facing forwards
3. you are standing up straight
4. your feet are together.

1. Head and eyes facing straight ahead

2. Arms to the side with palms facing forwards

3. Standing up straight

4. Feet together

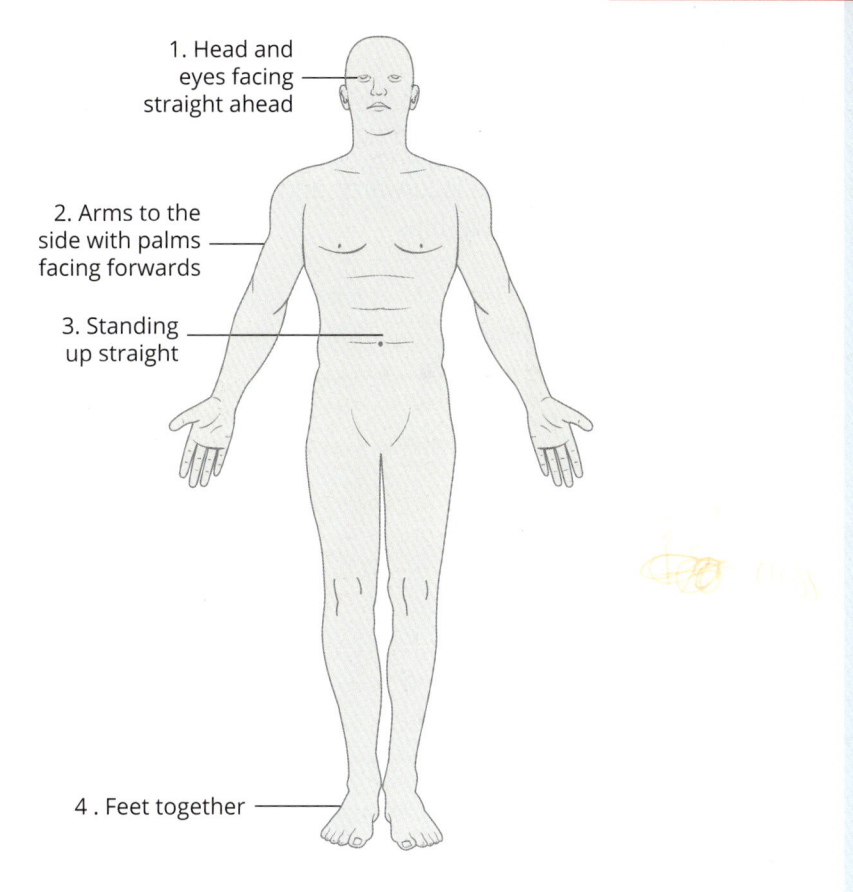

Planes of Movement

The body can move through **three** different planes. The body's movement can be either within or along each plane. When we say plane, we're referring to an imaginary surface which divides the body.

Before we look at the planes in detail, read the table to recap on types of movement first covered on page 62.

Movement	Example
Flexion	This is where a joint closes. An example would be flexion at the elbow when performing a biceps curl
Extension	This is where a joint will open. An example would be when a tennis player throws the ball into the air during a serve
Abduction	This is movement towards the midline of the body. An example would be when performing star jumps, the arms return to the side of the body
Adduction	This is movement away from the midline of the body. In a star jump it would be when the arms are lifted out to the side
Rotation	This is when there is a twisting movement at a joint. An example would be when a golfer rotates the hips to perform a drive to the fairway.
Circumduction	This is where the joint moves in a circle. The shoulder joint of a bowler in cricket would perform circumduction when bowling the ball.

A03

You will need to know the types of movement and the specific terminology.

Quick Check

Other than the elbow, name another joint where flexion and extension can occur.
A01

3C Planes and Axes of Movement

Sagittal Plane

The sagittal plane runs through the midline of the body from the head down to the feet. It divides the body into left and right sides.

Movement through this plane is forwards and backwards and can involve flexion and extension at the shoulders and hips.

Running – forwards through the sagittal plane. There is also flexion and extension at the knee and elbow joints, which are also movements through the sagittal plane

Squats – flexion and extension at the knee through the sagittal plane

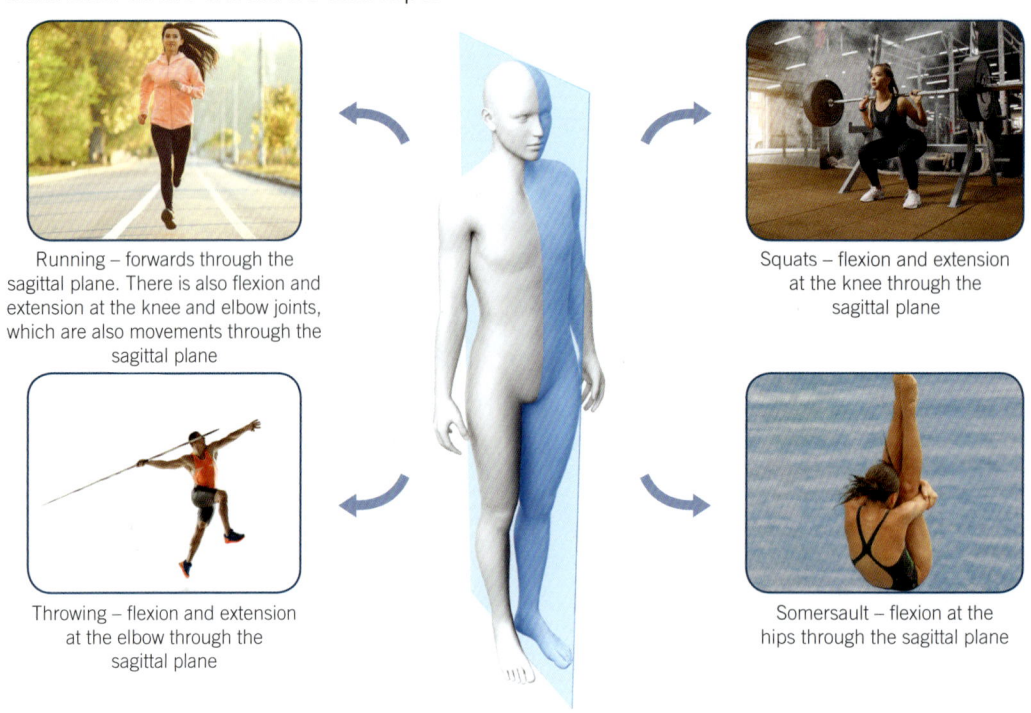

Throwing – flexion and extension at the elbow through the sagittal plane

Somersault – flexion at the hips through the sagittal plane

Frontal Plane

This plane runs through the midline of the body from the left side to the right side and it divides the body into front and back.

Movement through this plane includes side to side movements along with abduction and adduction at the arms and legs.

AO2

You will need to know the types of movement through each plane.

Lateral raises – during the lifting phase the movement at the shoulder joint is abduction and during the lowering phase it is adduction

Star jumps – abduction at the shoulder and hips to create the star shape and then adduction when bringing the limbs in to the body

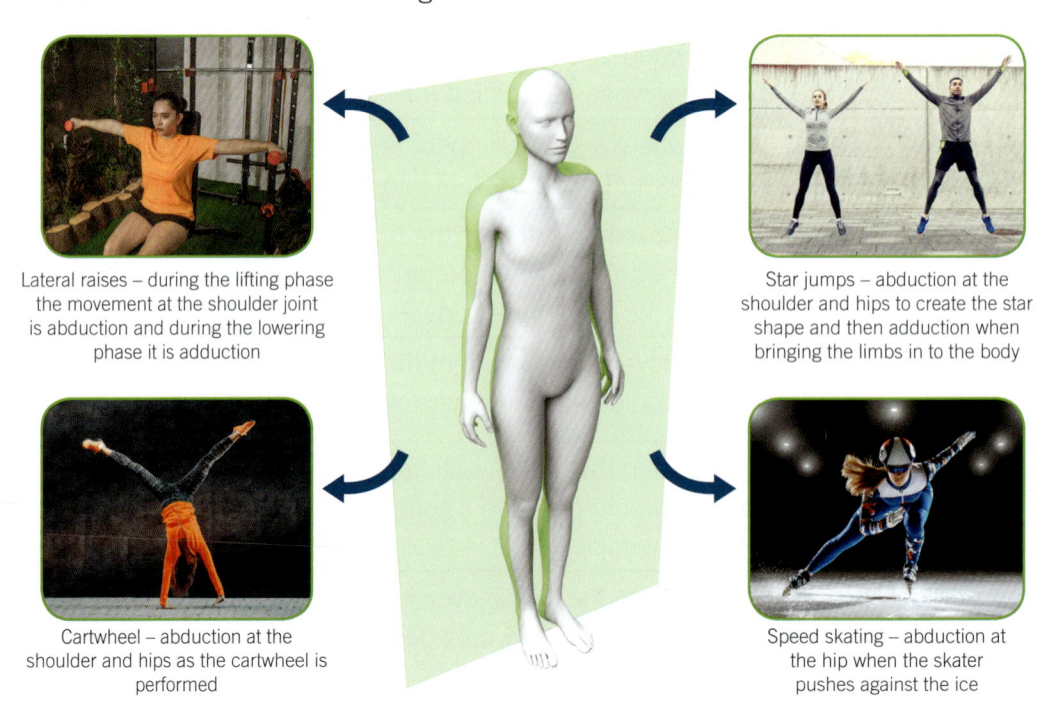

Cartwheel – abduction at the shoulder and hips as the cartwheel is performed

Speed skating – abduction at the hip when the skater pushes against the ice

Transverse Plane

This planes divides the body into top and bottom halves.

Movement through this plane includes turning movements like rotation at the hips and shoulders.

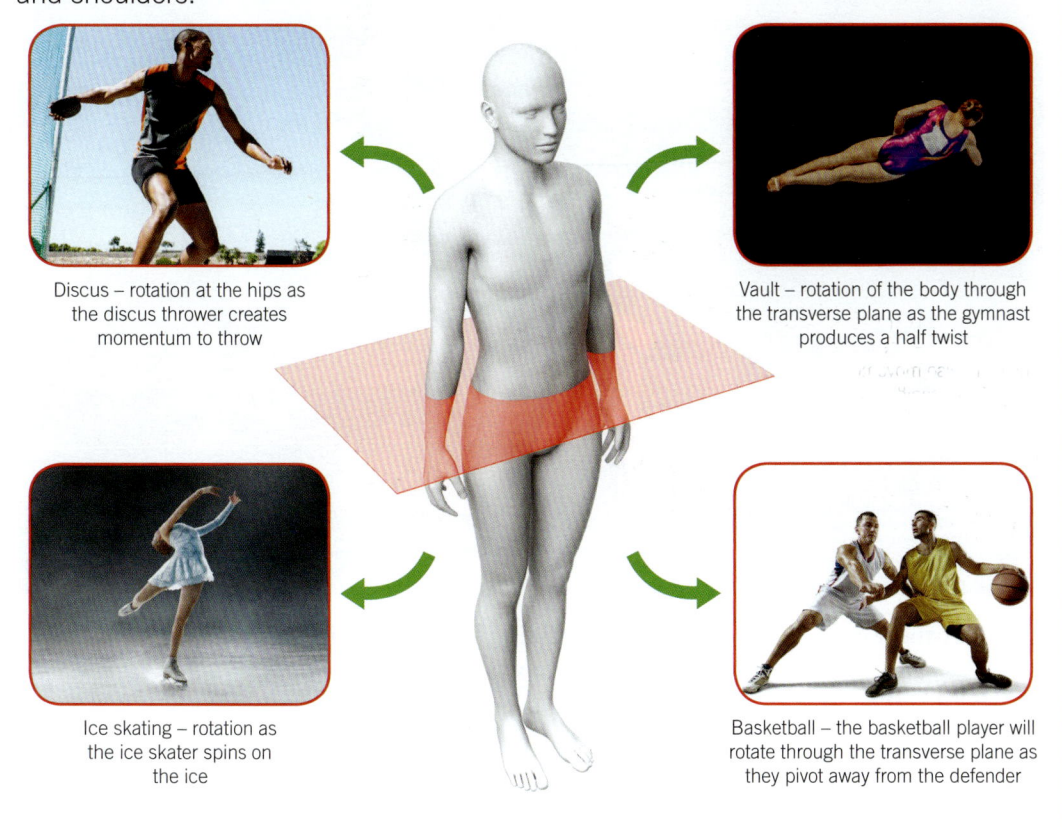

Discus – rotation at the hips as the discus thrower creates momentum to throw

Vault – rotation of the body through the transverse plane as the gymnast produces a half twist

Ice skating – rotation as the ice skater spins on the ice

Basketball – the basketball player will rotate through the transverse plane as they pivot away from the defender

Axes of Movement

An axis is an imaginary rod running through the body. The imaginary rod intersects the body's centre of gravity where rotational movements occur. This means that the body can rotate around **three** different axes.

The three axes of rotation are the:

1. **sagittal axis**
2. **frontal axis**
3. **vertical axis**.

Axes of movement are sometimes called different terms depending on what you read and where you read it. For your exam you will need to know the sagittal, frontal and vertical axes. You will also need to know their application in sporting movements.

A02

You will need to know the types of movement through each plane.

Top Tip

To remember how the body is divided, use the first letter for each plane:

sagittal = sides (divides the body into left and right sides)

frontal = front and back (divides the body into front and back)

transverse = top and bottom (divides the body into top and bottom)

Quick Check

Identify the three planes of movement.
A01

3C Planes and Axes of Movement

Sagittal Axis

The sagittal axis runs from front to back through the body's centre of gravity.

An example of rotation around this axis is a cartwheel in gymnastics.

▲ A cartwheel is an example of rotation around the sagittal axis.

Frontal Axis

The frontal axis runs from side to side through the centre of gravity just like a player in table football.

An example of rotation around this axis is a back somersault in diving.

▲ A back somersault in diving is an example of rotation around the frontal axis.

AO2

You will need to know the types of rotation at each axis.

Top Tip

Use the following combinations to help you work out which plane goes with which axis:

SF = **S**agittal plane / **F**rontal axis

FS = **F**rontal plane / **S**agittal axis

TV = **T**ransverse plane / **V**ertical axis

Chapter 3 Movement Analysis

Vertical Axis

The vertical axis runs from head to feet through the centre of gravity.

An example of rotation around this axis is a pirouette in skating.

▲ A pirouette is an example of rotation around the vertical axis.

To remember how the body is divided, use the first letter for each plane:

Sagittal axis = Spear

(think of 's' = speared through the belly)

Frontal axis = Football

(think of table football)

Vertical axis = Very long

(runs through the length of the body top to bottom)

> **Quick Check**
>
> Identify the three axes of rotation. **A01**

> **Quick Check**
>
> Match the planes with the appropriate axes: **A01**
>
> sagittal plane =
>
> _____ axis
>
> transverse plane =
>
> _____ axis
>
> frontal plane =
>
> _____ axis

> **? Knowledge Check**
>
> Here are some words to help you. You might need to use them more than once.
>
> | vertical   through   sagittal   around   frontal   transverse |
>
> Movement happens _____ a plane and _____ an axis. The names of the three planes are _____, _____ and _____. There are also three axes which are _____, _____ and _____. **A01**

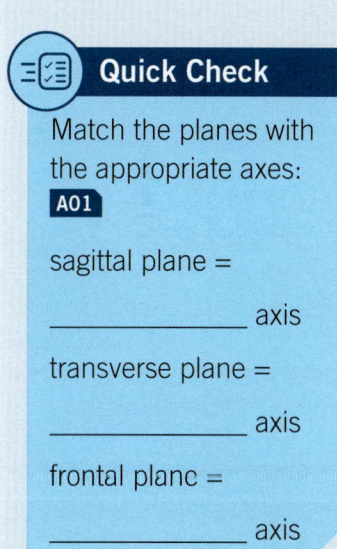

115

3C Planes and Axes of Movement

Practical Investigation

Equipment

You will need the following:

› three jelly babies
› three cocktail sticks
› three small pieces of card/paper.

Method

Take three jelly babies and three cocktail sticks.

1. Position the first jelly baby in the upright position (anatomical position). Take the cocktail stick and push it through the middle of the jelly baby to represent the frontal axis (from left side to the right side).

   a) When you twist the cocktail stick, what plane does the jelly baby move through? (Think of a highboard diver performing a somersault into the pool.)

   b) If you rotate the jelly baby around the frontal axis, what sort of movement might the body be doing?

2. With your second jelly baby, take another cocktail stick and pierce it through the belly button (front to back) so it represents the sagittal axis.

   a) What plane does the jelly baby move through when you twist the cocktail stick?

   b) If you rotate the jelly baby around the sagittal axis, what sort of movement might the body be doing? (Think of a gymnast doing a floor routine.)

3. Take your third jelly baby and pierce it with the cocktail stick through the head to the feet so it represents the vertical axis.

   a) What plane does the jelly baby move through when you twist the cocktail stick?

   b) If you rotate the jelly baby around the vertical axis, what sort of movement might the body be doing? (Think of a trampolinist.)

Now you will need to remove your cocktail sticks and put them to one side whilst you do the next few steps in the investigation.

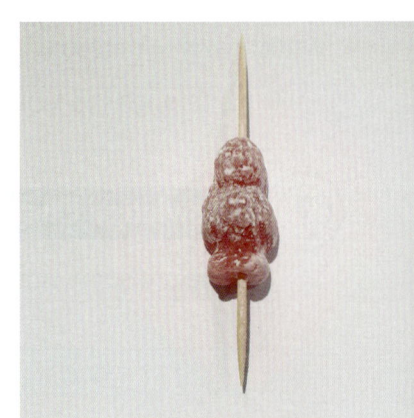

4. Take your three pieces of card/paper and label them with the three planes (sagittal plane, frontal plane and horizontal or transverse plane). Follow instructions a, b and c below and then place the card/paper between the two pieces to show the plane of movement. Then pierce the card/paper and jelly baby with your cocktail stick.

   a) Cut jelly baby 1 (frontal axis) to split it down the sagittal plane (divide it into left and right).

   b) Cut jelly baby 2 (sagittal axis) to split it down the frontal plane (divide it into front and back).

   c) Cut jelly baby 3 (vertical axis) to split it down the transverse plane (divide it into top and bottom).

> **Top Tip**
>
> When you complete step 4 of the investigation, each plane is **perpendicular** to the associated axis.

Investigation and results

Using your models investigate the rotation around the different axes to identify:

› the plane of movement that the body moves through when rotating around each axis

› types of movement that are most associated with the axis and plane of movement, e.g. flexion, extension, abduction, etc.

› examples of these actions in sporting activities.

Complete the chart below based on what you discover from your models.

Plane	Axis	Movement	Sporting example
	Frontal		
	Sagittal		
	Vertical		

117

3C Planes and Axes of Movement

Topic Test

Using **planes and axes of movement** *explain* how a gymnast would **perform a forward roll**. Use appropriate terminology in your explanation. `4 marks`

When reading the question, look at what the key words and phrases are asking you to do:

- **Topic:** This is the key area of study the question is about.
- **Command word:** This is based on the assessment objective (AO). The assessment objective for this question is AO2: you need to apply your knowledge and understanding.
- **Qualifying words or phrases:** This is the specific area you need to focus on in your answer.

Doing this will help you to build your answer so that you can access the AO for each question.

Step 1 Demonstrate your knowledge (AO1)

You need to **demonstrate your knowledge and understanding** of theories, definitions, and concepts of planes and axes of movement.

_____
_____
_____

Use the terms in the tick list of terminology to help you plan your answer to meet AO1. Look at how many marks are available to help you decide how much detail to include.

- ☐ Sagittal plane
- ☐ Transverse plane
- ☐ Sagittal axis
- ☐ Frontal plane
- ☐ Frontal axis
- ☐ Vertical axis

Step 2 Apply your knowledge and understanding (AO2)

You need to **apply your knowledge and understanding** to a gymnast performing a forward roll by **explaining** relevant concepts.

_____
_____
_____
_____
_____

Use the terms in the tick list of terminology. Look at how many marks are available to help you decide how much detail to include.

- ☐ Forwards
- ☐ Flexion
- ☐ Circumduction
- ☐ Elbow
- ☐ Backwards
- ☐ Abduction
- ☐ Rotation
- ☐ Knee
- ☐ Extension
- ☐ Adduction
- ☐ Hips

Chapter 3 Movement Analysis

THE BIG QUESTION

RECAP

C You are starting to build the knowledge and understanding you need to answer the Big Question. You have already answered parts a) and b), so now it's time to answer part c) and apply your knowledge and understanding.

1. Athletes preparing for major competitions require a range of movements to compete fluently.

   c) A gymnast performs a routine that includes a somersault and a cartwheel.

   (i) The gymnast runs forwards to gain speed in preparation for the somersault. Identify the plane of movement she moves through. (1 mark)

   Tick (✓) one box only.

	Tick (✓)
Sagittal plane	✓
Frontal plane	
Transverse plane	

   (ii) Identify the axis of movement that the gymnast's body rotates around while she performs a cartwheel. (1 mark)

   Tick (✓) one box only.

	Tick (✓)
Sagittal axis	✓
Frontal axis	
Vertical axis	

Where would you place an imaginary rod to allow the movement of a cartwheel?

Remember the top tip for axes – S, F and V.

3D Sports Technology

In this topic we will work towards answering part d) of the Big Question:

> 1. Athletes preparing for major competitions require a range of movements to compete fluently.
>
>   d) Explain, using appropriate examples, how a gymnast and a coach may use technology to help improve the gymnast's performance.
>
>   *AO2 – 4 marks*

We live in a world where **technology** in our everyday lives is forever advancing and this is no different with technology in sport. Technology will affect every aspect of sport at every level from grassroots through to elite level. We will explore performance, coaching, officiating and even watching sport.

Technology and Performance

The advancement of technology can play a part in preparation and recovery as well as analysis to develop, support or improve performance. We often associate the use of technology with elite performers and their ability to access high-tech training facilities. But this is not always the case because technology is now available for performers at all levels.

Technology can be used by athletes in many ways:

- to monitor or analyse their own performance or the performance of others
- to aid their performance by using the right equipment
- to help them recover from performance
- before, during or after competitions.

> **Monitoring performance** GPS and heart rate monitors are just some examples of technologies which allow athletes to monitor their bodies' responses to exercise and analyse performance, as well as being a useful tool to provide the athlete with **motivation**.

> **Analysis of performance** Athletes can analyse performance using a range of software. Performance is recorded using a video camera and software can then be used to analyse the movement depending on what the athlete and the coach specifically focus on.

> **Equipment for performance** Specialist equipment and clothing can be used to improve and develop performance, such as swimsuits designed to reduce drag and specialist tennis rackets. Innovative technology also provides disabled athletes with more opportunities for participation in sports, e.g. running blades, racing wheelchairs and sit skies.

> **Recovery from performance** Athletes use technology to aid and speed up the recovery process. Compression clothing and massage therapy devices are just some of the uses of sports technology.

AO3

You will need to know how technology can benefit performers, coaches, officials and spectators as well as understanding the positives and negatives of using technology.

Positives and negatives for the use of technology as a performer:

Positives	Negatives
› Health, wellbeing and fitness can be monitored	› Can be costly
› Develop better performance through analysis	› Requires knowledge of using software
› Speed up recovery times	› Could develop a win-at-all-cost attitude leading to deviance
› Specific and accurate feedback to develop technique and understanding	› Could encourage forcing the body to do more, leading to injury
› Better equipment for performance and protection	

AO3

It's important to have an understanding of the positives and negatives in order to answer questions with the command word discuss.

Data Analysis

A GPS running device connected to a heart rate monitor was used to collect data for a runner competing in a half marathon. The line on the graph indicated the runner's heart rate during the half marathon.

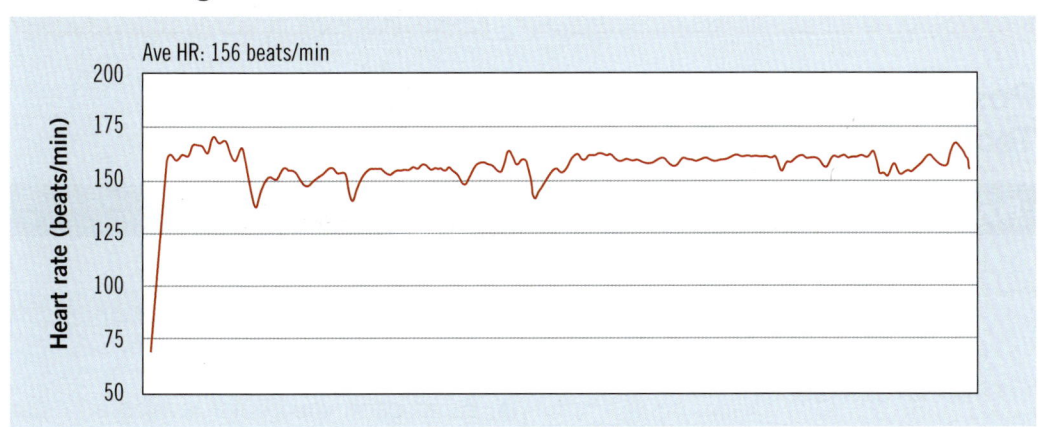

Ave HR: 156 beats/min

(Graph showing heart rate in beats/min on y-axis from 50 to 200, staying around 150–170 throughout the race.)

1. What was the highest recorded heart rate during the race?
2. Suggest why the runner's heart rate dropped below 150 beats/min during the race.

Technology in Coaching

Technology has benefits for coaches as well as athletes. Some of the technology used by the performer will also be used by the coach but the information gained from the technology will be used in slightly different ways. Coaches use a variety of methods to **analyse movement and performance**. They use the information to support their coaching by analysing team strategies and tactics for both their own team or athletes and the opposition's.

Quick Check

How can technology be used to develop the performance of a skill? **AO2**

3D Sports Technology

Monitoring performance

Coaches use a range of technology such as GPS and heart rate monitors to track the progress of their athletes. The technology provides the coach with **quantitative data** to **feed back** to the athlete or team as well as enabling the coach to make tactical decisions.

Analysis of performance

A coach uses a range of software, apps and devices to analyse their athlete's performance. The **qualitative data** received from this technology allows the coach to plan specific coaching sessions to develop the athlete's or team's performance.

Equipment for coaching

A coach uses specialist equipment to support athletes to develop techniques. For example, in gymnastics a coach might use a harness to develop the movement of a somersault.

Positives and Negatives for the Use of Technology for a Coach

> **AO2**
> It's important to provide an account of the topic, along with reasoning and explanations, in order to answer a question with the command word explain.

Positives	Negatives
› Health, wellbeing and fitness can be monitored to support athletes	› Can be costly
› Clear identification of performance through analysis	› Could be time-consuming when training to use the software
› Allows for specific focus in training sessions based on analysis	› As a coach you could develop a win-at-all-costs attitude leading to deviance
› Support technique development through specific and accurate feedback	› May come to rely on the technology which will prevent natural feedback between coach and athlete
› Better equipment for the delivery of coaching sessions	
› Helps with selection	

Data Analysis

During training and competition, coaches use technology to analyse performance. Video analysis can help with improving a technique or analysing specific movements through slow motion, camera sequencing or comparing clips. In training it could be used to analyse techniques. During competition, it may be used to analyse the performance of the athlete or the opponent to identify strengths and weaknesses. Afterwards, the coach and the athlete may review the performance together to identify strengths and weaknesses. These techniques provide qualitative data.

To help with analysing tactics they might use **notational analysis** which uses data collected to monitor trends in performance, for example shots on goal or number of unforced errors. This can supply the coach with quantitative data.

Technology for the Officials

Sports technology now plays a major role in supporting officials to make accurate and informed decisions, reducing the likelihood of human error. As the pressure of sport increases, so does the pressure on officials to make correct decisions which in the past have sometimes been influenced by the reaction of players and spectators. The introduction of sports technology has minimised these influences and often adds to the excitement, which engages the spectator in the process.

> **Quick Check**
>
> How can social media be used to access information on teams and individual athletes? **AO3**

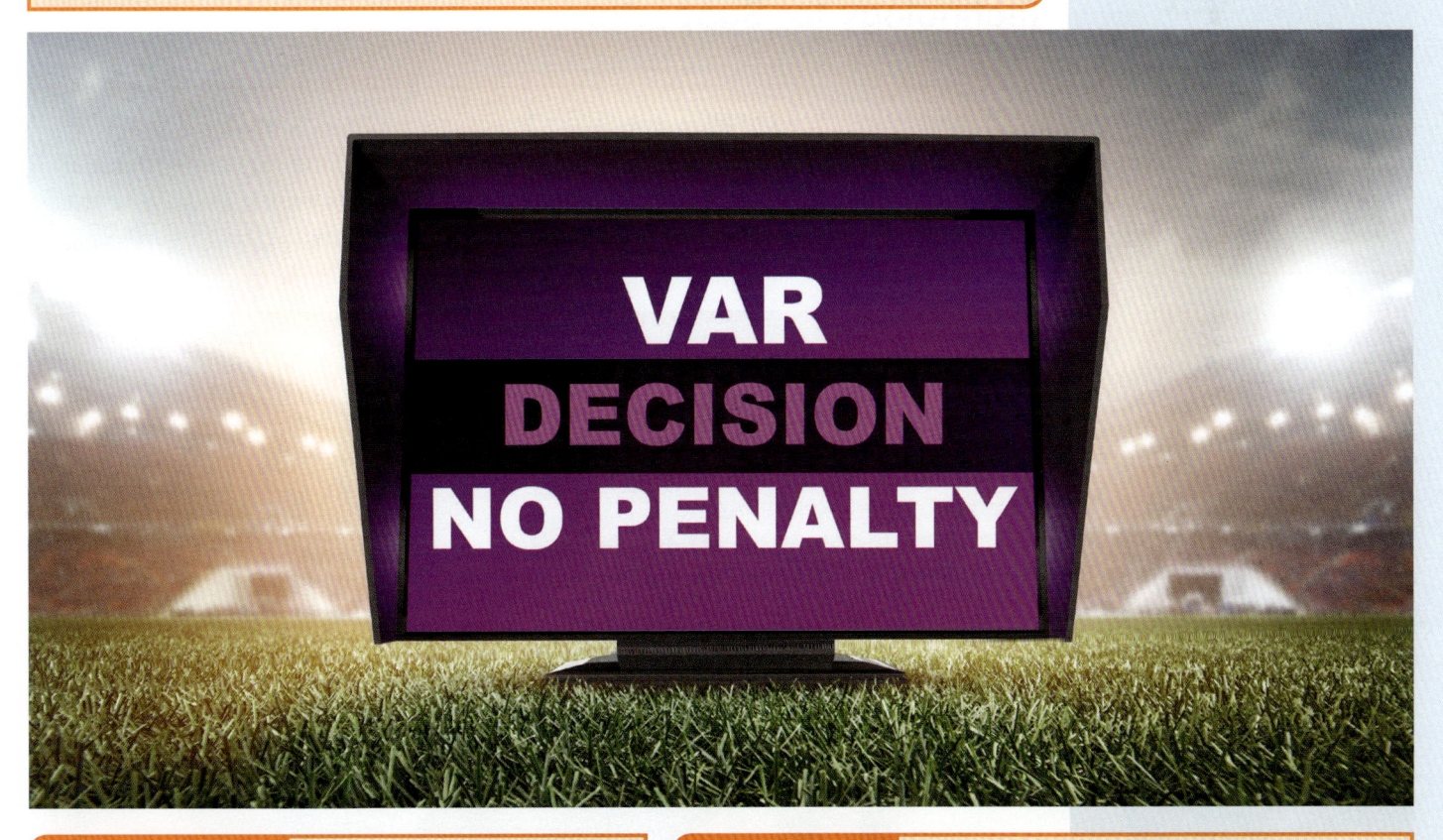

Making a decision Officials use technology to make accurate and informed decisions. Some of the examples we see today are: **VAR**, **TMO**, **Hawk-Eye**, and many more.

Scoring/measuring Sports technology provides accurate measurements when it comes to measuring and scoring. In athletics, for example, time and distance are measured more accurately, reducing human error.

Communicating Another advancement of sports technology is the ability for officials to be in constant contact throughout games. Microphone communication via headsets allows officials to communicate to reduce foul play as well as coming to informed decisions.

123

3D Sports Technology

Positives and Negatives for the Use of Technology for the Officials

Positives	Negatives
> Reduces pressure to make a decision	> Technology can be wrong
> Improved communication to share information	> Reduces the accountability of the officials and goes against the tradition of the game
> Decisions become more reliable and accurate	> Not available at all levels of competition
> Confidence is increased so the officials can trust the process	> Disrupts the flow of the game as decisions can take time
> Prevents controversy and the ability for players to manipulate the officials' decisions	> May reduce the confidence of an official if the technology proves the official is wrong
> Helps with selection	

> **AO3**
> It's important to have an understanding of the positives and negatives to answer a question with the command word **discuss**.

> **Quick Check**
> Technology is used to support officials in making decisions. What impact has this had on sport? **AO3**

Technology for Supporters

Coverage of sport Sports technology has advanced to allow spectators to engage more with sport. Coverage of sport has become so commercialised that the spectators' experience is vitally important. One way in which it has been enhanced is through a range of camera angles, requiring different types of technology such as player cam, ref cam and spider cam, as well as cameras that can give a range of views around stadiums.

Performance data Spectators now have access to performance data. Analysis which was previously only generated for coaches is now readily available to supporters, providing detailed analysis of teams' and individual athletes' performances.

Social media Digital media allows spectators access to more detailed information about teams and athletes. Spectators have a closer connection to high-profile athletes through a range of social media platforms.

Positives and Negatives for the Use of Technology for Supporters

Positives	Negatives
› Improved coverage and greater range of camera angles provide a better experience	› Replays and highlights may take the focus away from the actual play
› Increased information through statistical data on teams' and athletes' performances	› Adverts and breaks due to commercialisation and sponsorship may take attention from the actual play
› Digital media allows access to events and updates wherever you are through apps	› Grassroots sports not supported, only focus on elite
› Social media allows for a closer connection with teams and athletes	› Some events may become less accessible due to pay per view
› Encourages participation through the promotion of positive role models	

◀ A greater range of camera angles provide a better viewing experience.

Practical Investigation

Conduct a research project exploring the use of sports technology for a sport of your choice.

Method

Explore how technology can have an impact on a performer, a coach, a spectator and an official. To complete the task use the following steps:

1. Choose a sport to conduct your research on.

2. Take a piece of paper and divide it into four sections. Label each section with the following headings:

    a) Performer

    b) Coach

    c) Spectator

    d) Official

3. For each heading consider the following points:

    › the role of analysing movement

    › improving sports performance or the experience of spectators

    › the advantages and disadvantages of using technology.

4. Record your findings in each section on your piece of paper. Your work should be laid out as follows:

My chosen sport is _____

Performer	Coach
Spectator	Official

Chapter 3 Movement Analysis

Stretch and Challenge

During your research project, complete the following tasks.

1. Identify sports technology used in your chosen sport. **A01**

2. Explain how this technology is used in your chosen sport. **A02**

3. Analyse the advantages and disadvantages of its use in your chosen sport. **A03**

Advantages of technology	Disadvantages of technology

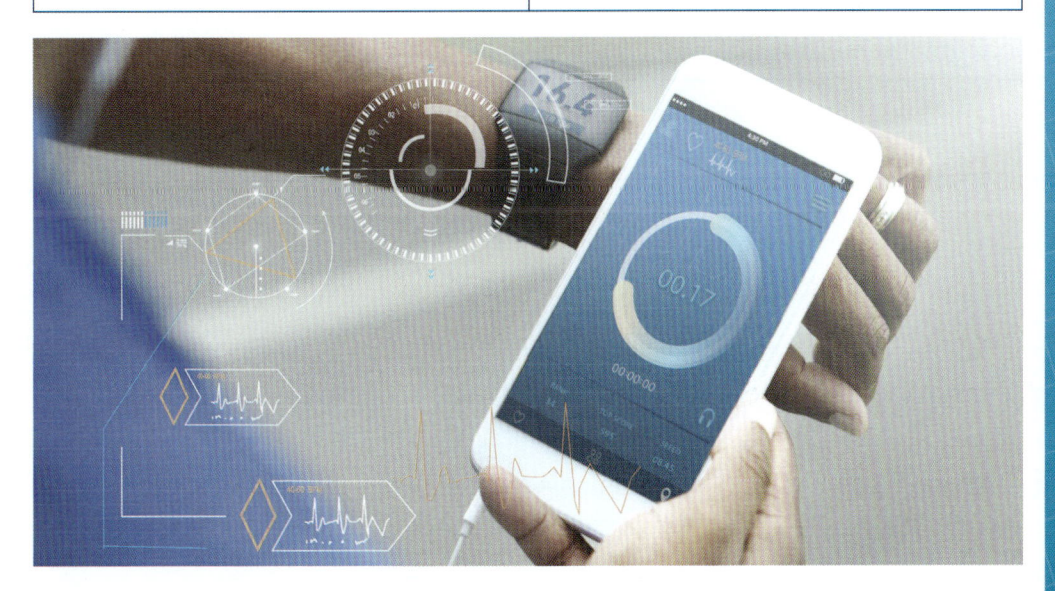

▲ What are the advantages and disadvantages of using technology in sport?

127

3D Sports Technology

Topic Test

Using appropriate examples, explain how technology could be used as a motivational tool for non-elite athletes. `4 marks`

When reading the question, look at what the key words and phrases are asking you to do:

- **Command word:** This is based on the assessment objective (AO). The assessment objective for this question is AO2: you need to apply your knowledge and understanding.
- **Topic:** This is the key area of study the question is about.
- **Qualifying words or phrases:** This is the specific area you need to focus on in your answer.

Doing this will help you to build your answer so that you can access the AO for each question.

Step 1 Demonstrate your knowledge (AO1)

You need to **demonstrate your knowledge and understanding** of technology used in sport.

_____
_____
_____

Use the terms in the tick list of terminology. Look at how many marks are available to help you decide how much detail to include.

- ☐ GPS
- ☐ Phones
- ☐ Apps
- ☐ Heart rate monitors

Step 2 Apply your knowledge and understanding (AO2)

You need to **apply your knowledge and understanding** in order to **explain** how technology can help motivation in non-elite athletes.

_____
_____
_____
_____
_____

Use the terms in the tick list of terminology. Look at how many marks are available to help you decide how much detail to include.

- ☐ Monitor progress
- ☐ Adherence
- ☐ Compare to others
- ☐ Motivation
- ☐ Engage with activity
- ☐ Develop confidence
- ☐ Engage with the activity

Chapter 3 Movement Analysis

THE BIG QUESTION

RECAP

D You have built a knowledge and understanding of muscle contractions, levers, planes and axes of movement, and sports technology. You have already answered parts a), b) and c), so now it's time to answer part d).

1. Athletes preparing for major competitions require a range of movements to compete fluently.

   d) Explain, using appropriate examples, how a gymnast and a coach may use technology to help improve the gymnast's performance. (4 marks)

Think about different camera views.

What are the benefits of recording a performance compared to watching it only once in real time?

How can the recording be used?
› Identify strengths and weaknesses
› Compare the performance to other performances
› Share information with the athlete

How would the performer benefit from watching their performance?

How can the playback options of a recording, e.g. slow motion, freeze frame, etc., help?

Technology plays a major part in analysing performance. By using performance analysis, coaches and athletes can identify where improvements can be made. Knowledge and an understanding of movement analysis (parts a) to d) of the Big Question) will allow for sporting improvements to be made.

129

CHAPTER 4

Psychology of Sport and Physical Activity

Many successful performers use psychology in sport to improve performance; for example, setting goals to improve health, wellbeing and performance helps them to increase focus and maintain motivation. Information processing allows performers to understand the process of decision-making and the value of feedback. Coaches need an understanding of classifications of skill, methods of guidance and practices to develop their performers. All performers need motivation to adhere to their chosen goals. Understanding the types of motivation is useful for both the performer and the coach in order for them to achieve success. Once this has been understood, it is up to the performer to prepare; mental preparation is a tool which can be used to improve performance.

THE BIG QUESTION

Psychology in sport can have a big impact on sporting performance. For performers, coaches and trainers an understanding of a range of methods helps with focus and motivation to achieve the desired outcome.

These are the topics you'll need to answer the Big Question:

A **Goal-setting:** How can goal-setting help you plan your personal fitness programme?

B **Information processing:** Why is feedback important when learning a new skill?

C **Guidance and practice:** How do how coaches use guidance for performers in different stages of learning?

D **Mental preparation and motivation:** What mental preparation techniques might a cyclist use before a race?

E **Classification of skill:** What are the characteristics of a skilful performance?

As you work through this chapter, we will identify all the skills and knowledge you'll need to be able to answer the Big Question. If you can do that, you will have brilliant AO1 and AO2 skills ready to use in your GCSE.

In this chapter you will learn about:

› how goal-setting can influence performance as well as health and wellbeing
› the information processing model, and how it can be used to process information during sport and physical activity
› the different stages of learning and the relationship between guidance, learning and practice
› different strategies used for mental preparation and how this can help with motivation
› the characteristics of a skilled performer
› the skills continua.

In this chapter you will be using the following key terms. You can look up the meaning of these terms in the Glossary (page 184 onwards).

Key Terms

Adherence	Anxiety	Arousal	Associative stage of learning (intermediate)
Autonomous stage of learning (expert)	Basic skill	Closed skill	
	Externally paced skill	Feedback	Cognitive stage of learning (beginner)
Complex skill	Long-term memory	Manual guidance	
Input	Output	Self-paced skill	Goal-setting
Open skill	Mechanical guidance	Short-term memory	SMART target
Verbal guidance	Visual guidance		

131

4A Goal-setting

This is the question we're going to be working towards answering at the end of this topic.

> 1. Before you start to plan a personal fitness programme, it is important to know what you want to improve.
>
>   Discuss how goal-setting can help you plan a personal fitness programme.
>
>   *AO3 – 6 marks*

Goal-setting can help to focus attention and to maintain motivation. This will in turn help with **adherence** to your activity and training goals over a set time. A goal gives you a sense of purpose and direction. The main strategy to help you set goals is to produce **SMART targets**.

A goal can be a **performance goal**, which will relate to an area of performance, e.g. a 100 m sprinter may aim to improve their sprint start. Or it could be an **outcome goal**, e.g. to win a race or competition. Outcome goals can often be unrealistic; it is recommended that goals be focused on performance.

Setting a goal can also have an impact on:

> the health and wellbeing of a performer as it may motivate them to improve their fitness, resulting in improved physical health and wellbeing by meeting their daily exercise needs

> the performance by encouraging the performer to focus on and adhere to their training programme to help them achieve their goal

> improved effort to commit to training as the performer concentrates on the progress they are making towards their goal

> helping the performer to maintain motivation by seeing the physical progress they are making through their efforts.

▲ A coach and performer discussing goals.

Setting SMART targets gives your goals clarity and a sense of direction as well as making them practical and rational. A SMART target is:

S	**SPECIFIC**	The goal must meet the demands of the individual and the sport.
M	**MEASURABLE**	The goal must be measurable so that progress can be monitored.
A	**AGREED**	Sharing the goal between performer and coach/trainer means it is accepted and all parties have a clear role to play in helping the performer achieve the desired goal.
R	**REALISTIC**	The goal is achievable, which is essential for motivation.
T	**TIME PHASED**	A time must be set to achieve the planned goal by. This must be realistic and gives the goal a defined end-point to help the performer and coach monitor progress.

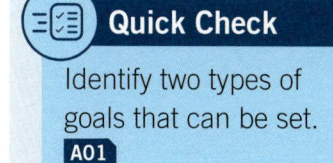

If too many SMART targets are used or if they are unrealistic, this will have a negative effect on motivation. Making sport too goal-driven can take away the fun and enjoyment.

> **Top Tip**
> All goals should follow the SMART principle.

> **Quick Check**
> Identify two types of goals that can be set.
> **AO1**

▲ Make sure SMART targets are measurable.

133

4A Goal-setting

Practical Investigation

Setting SMART targets is a strategy used to create achievable goals. Complete the table in Appendix 4.1 to show your understanding of SMART targets.

Equipment

You will need the following:

> a photocopy of the SMART targets worksheet (see Appendix 4.1)
> writing equipment

Appendix 4.1 SMART targets – A Practical Investigation

	Goal	
S	Specific	
M	Measurable	
A	Agreed	
R	Realistic	
T	Time phased	

Method

To complete the table:

> Identify a SMART target linked to a particular activity and add this to the 'Goal' row in the table. You may want to link this goal to one of the chosen activities for your PE GCSE. An example of a SMART target is 'To improve my personal best of 52.06 seconds in the 400m by June'.

> Explain how you will use each component of SMART to achieve your goal.
> - Specific: How is the goal specific to your sport/activity?
> - Measurable: How will you measure your progress? Could you use fitness testing? If so, what test will you use?
> - Agreed: Who will you agree your goal with and why?
> - Realistic: Is this goal achievable and why?
> - Time phased: What time duration will you set to achieve this goal, is it realistic and why?

S	**SPECIFIC**	**Explanation:** The goal must be clear and it must focus on what you want to improve. **Application examples:** > To improve my successful pass rate in netball. > To improve my cardiovascular fitness so that I can last the full duration of a match in football without getting tired.
M	**MEASURABLE**	**Explanation:** You must have something to measure your goal against if it is to be successful. **Application examples:** > I want to improve my pass rate to 90% successful passes in a game of netball. > I want to improve my multi-stage fitness test (MSFT) score by six shuttles to achieve 'excellent' against national norms.
A	**AGREED**	**Explanation:** The goal must be agreed with a coach/teacher. **Application examples:** > I have discussed the goal with my coach and we will focus on developing this area in both training and matches. > I have discussed the goal with my teacher and we both agree the target is achievable and realistic in the time we have.
R	**REALISTIC**	**Explanation:** The goal must take into account a variety of factors including time, facilities and individual fitness and skill levels. When these have been considered, it must be realistic for the individual. **Application examples:** > My pass rate is currently 85% so my coach and I agree that a 5% increase is realistic. > My frequency of training has increased since returning from injury and I have included more aerobic work. My teacher and I believe this is an achievable target.
T	**TIME PHASED**	**Explanation:** The goal must have a time frame to complete so that you can monitor and see the effects of training. **Application examples:** > By the end of the season, I am going to achieve a 90% pass rate. I will monitor my progress at different points. > In eight weeks I am going to increase my MSFT score by six shuttles. I will monitor my progress after four weeks of training and adjust my goal accordingly.

4A Goal-setting

Topic Test

Athletes must set themselves **effective goals** in order to achieve their potential. **Outline the difference between outcome goals and performance goals.** `2 marks`

When reading the question, look at what the key words and phrases are asking you to do:

- **Command word:** This is based on the assessment objective (AO). The assessment objective for this question is AO1: you need to demonstrate your knowledge and understanding.
- **Topic:** This is the key area of study the question is about.
- **Qualifying words or phrases:** This is the specific area you need to focus on in your answer.

Doing this will help you to build your answer so that you can access the AO for each question.

Demonstrate your knowledge (AO1)

You need to **demonstrate your knowledge and understanding** of the two types of goals by **outlining** the difference between them.

_____
_____
_____
_____

Use the two images to help you with your answer.

Team talk when the team are behind by four points.

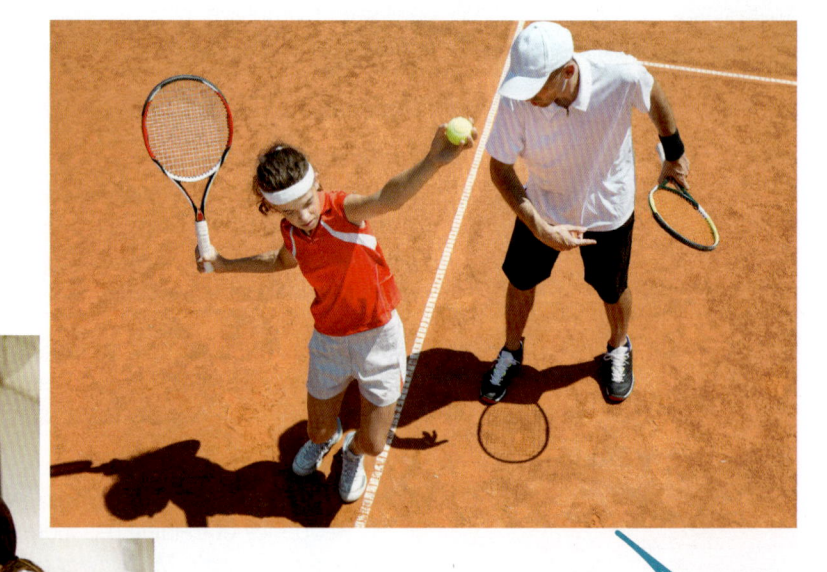

The coach is helping the athlete develop an aspect of their performance.

136

Chapter 4 Psychology of Sport and Physical...

THE BIG QUESTION

RECAP

A Now that you have developed a knowledge and understanding of goal-setting, it's time to have a go at part 1 of the Big Question.

1. Before you start to plan a personal fitness programme, it is important to know what you want to improve.

   Discuss how goal-setting can help you plan a personal fitness programme. (6 marks)

How can it motivate you?

Think about SMART targets.

How will you show success through planning and monitoring progress?

How can you link it to adherence?

137

4B Information Processing

This is the question we're going to be working towards answering at the end of this topic.

> 2. Feedback is an important component of information processing during sport.
>
> Using examples from sport, explain why feedback is important when learning a new skill.
>
> **AO2 – 4 marks**

A performer is required to take in information and make decisions to produce the desired outcome in their chosen sport or activity. The information processing model shows the clear stages that are involved to make these decisions.

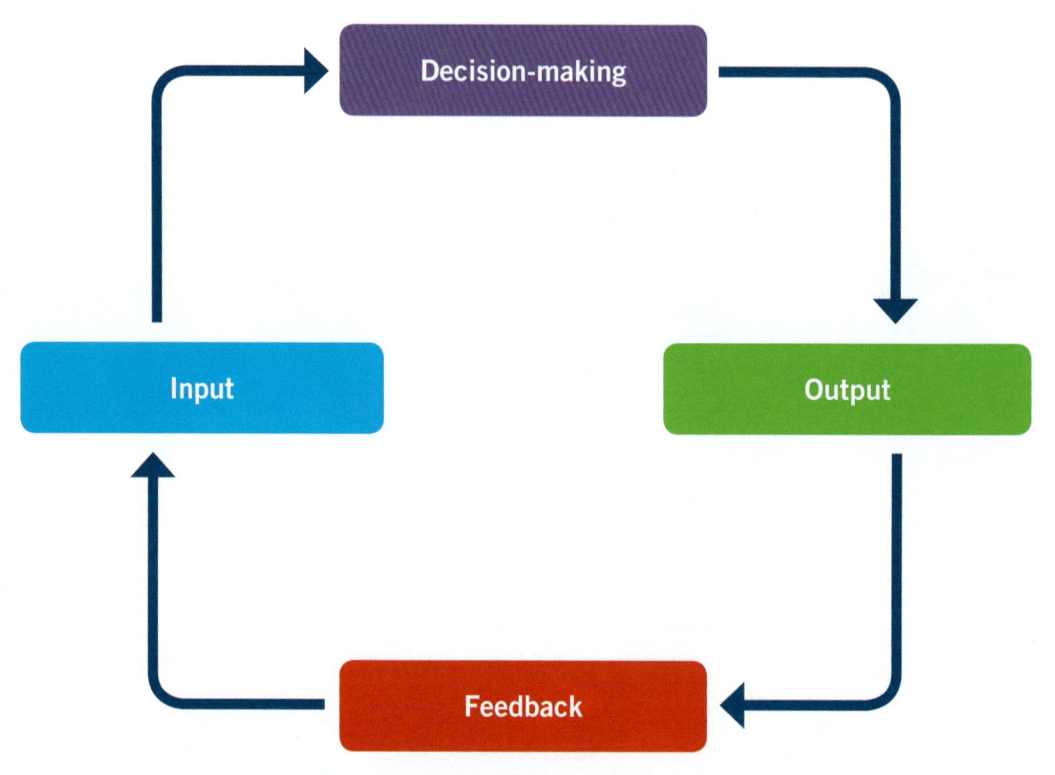

```
        Decision-making
         ↗          ↘
      Input         Output
         ↖          ↙
         Feedback
```

Input: **Input** is information taken in through our senses (sight, hearing, touch, etc). The performer selects the information they feel is important. The more experienced the performer is, the more information they can take in and process while filtering out the non-important information. This is known as **selective attention**.

Intermediate and expert performers (in the **associative** and **autonomous stages of learning**) are able to do this very effectively. Beginners (in the **cognitive stage of learning**) have difficulty processing large amounts of information from their senses and therefore cannot filter the required information. They will therefore make many mistakes.

Decision-making: This is where the performer selects the appropriate response. The performer uses information from their **short-term memory** (STM) and **long-term memory** (LTM) to make decisions.

Output: **Output** is the performer's action in response to the situation.

Top Tip

Look at Topic 4C to find out more about the three stages of learning.

Quick Check

Which of the following key terms is connected to 'input'? **AO1**

› Short-term memory
› Selective attention
› Long-term memory

Feedback: This is when the performer is provided with information on the success of the output. **Feedback** is vital to the learning process as it will affect how you perform the skills in the future. The performer can receive feedback in two ways:

- **Intrinsic feedback** comes from inside the performer – it is what the performance or the skill has felt like.

- **Extrinsic feedback** comes from external sources, such as coaches or spectators.

To be effective, feedback should be accurate, concise, immediate and truthful.

Feedback can provide two different types of knowledge:

- **Knowledge of performance:** This is knowledge about the technical quality of the performance, such as whether a movement was executed correctly.

- **Knowledge of results:** This is knowledge of the outcome or result of the performance, such as the score awarded to a gymnast or whether the team won a match.

> **Quick Check**
> Identify two types of feedback. **A01**

> **Top Tip**
> Beginners tend to need positive feedback, extrinsic feedback and knowledge of results.
>
> Elite performers tend to need knowledge of performance and can provide themselves with intrinsic feedback.

> **Quick Check**
> Feedback that comes from yourself is called what? **A01**

139

4B Information Processing

Practical Investigation

Method

Make a copy of the information processing model in Appendix 4.2 and fill it in using examples relating to a sport of your choice. If you can, think of recent examples from your own experience.

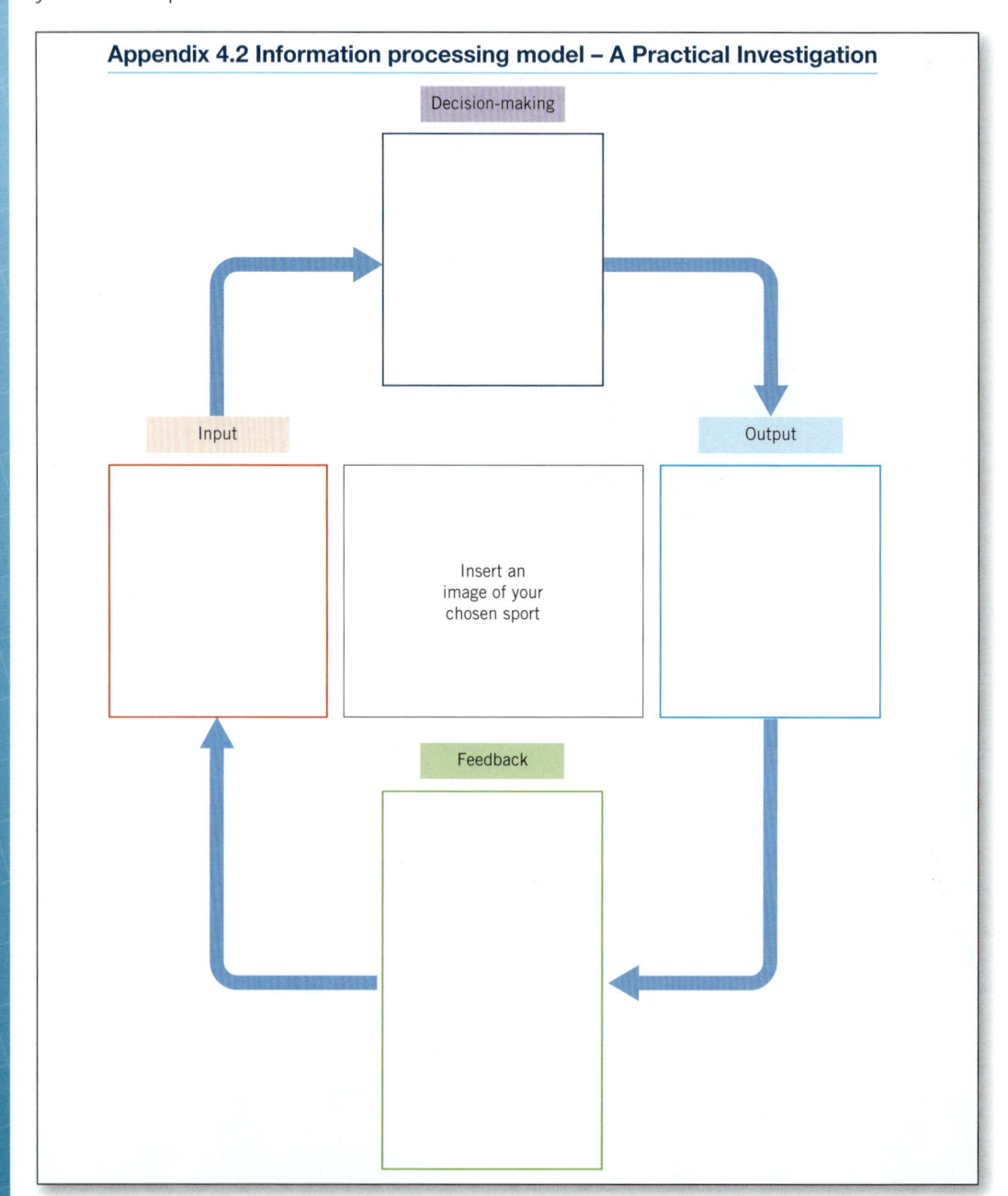

Appendix 4.2 Information processing model – A Practical Investigation

Decision-making

Input

Output

Insert an image of your chosen sport

Feedback

Explain the:

> input: what information did your senses take in?

> decision-making: from the information, what decision did you make?

> output: what did you do?

> feedback: what was the feedback? Think about both intrinsic and extrinsic feedback, and consider your knowledge of the results and knowledge of your performance.

Chapter 4 Psychology of Sport and Physical...

Extension Activity

Complete the following table focusing on:

› input: selective attention

› decision-making: long- and short-term memory

› output

› feedback: intrinsic and extrinsic feedback.

Information processing		Example
Input	**Selective attention** This is where you focus on the important information (stimuli). Describe the important information you will focus on.	
Decision-making	**Long-term memory** This is the information you have stored from rehearsal/practice for future reference. Describe what you already know.	
	Short-term memory This only lasts a few seconds. It is a working memory you use whilst completing a skill (e.g., what direction the ball is coming from or where an opponent is).	
Output	The action you have decided on. Describe your response.	
Feedback	**Intrinsic feedback** This is internal feedback on your own response. How did the outcome make you feel?	
	Extrinsic feedback This is external feedback on your response. How do you know the success of the outcome?	

▲ Using short-term memory in cricket to react to the bowler.

4B Information Processing

Topic Test

Using examples describe the input stage of the information processing model. 2 marks

When reading the question, look at what the key words and phrases are asking you to do:

- **Command word:** This is based on the assessment objective (AO). The assessment objective for this question is AO1: you need to demonstrate your knowledge and understanding.
- **Topic:** This is the key area of study the question is about.
- **Qualifying words or phrases:** This is the specific area you need to focus on in your answer.

Doing this will help you to build your answer so that you can access the AO for each question.

Step 1 Demonstrate your knowledge (AO1)

You need to **demonstrate your knowledge and understanding** of the information processing model by **describing** the input stage. Think about how you receive information during physical activities.

_____
_____
_____
_____

Step 2 Demonstrate your knowledge (AO1)

Can you demonstrate your understanding of selective attention?

_____
_____
_____
_____

How fast is the player running? How far away is he?

Selective attention is where you focus on the important information (stimuli).

Chapter 4 Psychology of Sport and Physical...

THE BIG QUESTION

RECAP

B You are starting to build the knowledge and understanding you need to answer the Big Question. You have already answered part 1 at the end of the last topic. So now it's time to answer part 2 and apply your knowledge and understanding of information processing.

> 2. Feedback is an important component of information processing during sport.
>
> Using examples from sport, explain why feedback is important when learning a new skill. (4 marks)

How will the feedback given make you feel?

How is the performance making you feel?

How will the feedback given help you to improve?

Coach congratulating you on a successful shot (extrinsic).

Feeling of achievement after a successful shot (intrinsic).

143

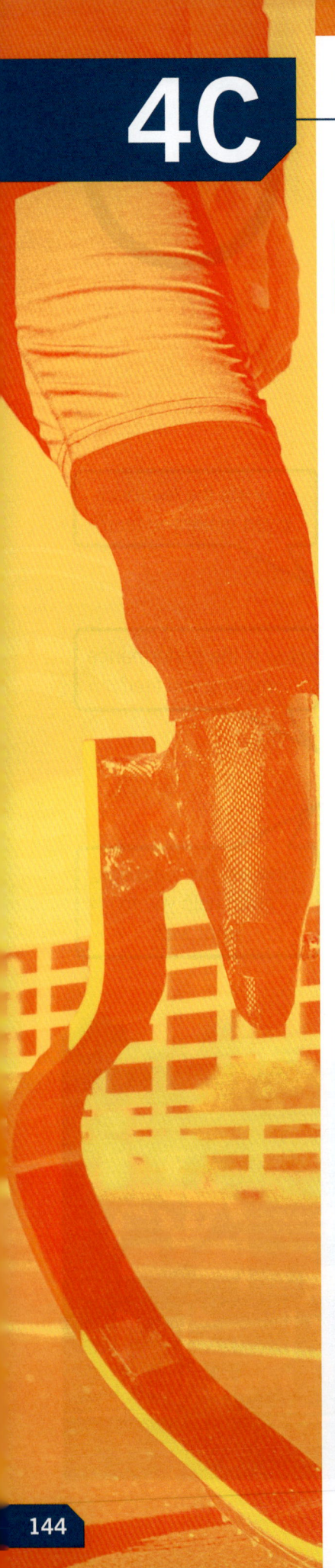

4C Guidance and Practice

This is the question we're going to be working towards answering at the end of this section.

> 3. Compare how coaches use guidance for performers in the cognitive and autonomous stages of learning.
>
> **AO2 – 4 marks**

Stages of Learning

Practice is important for performers to develop new skills as well as existing ones. To help with this, performers need **guidance**.

The types of guidance and practice that are most useful to a performer partly depend on their stage of learning. There are three stages of learning:

1. Cognitive stage (beginner). A performer at this stage is inconsistent in their performance, making many mistakes and lacking fluency.
2. Associative stage (intermediate). A performer at this stage understands the movement, is becoming more consistent and fluent, and is moving towards skills that are more complex.
3. Autonomous stage (expert). A performer at this stage is consistent, effective, fluent and aesthetic in their movements.

Guidance

Performers receive guidance from coaches, trainers, teachers, etc. to support their progress. The types of guidance that can be used are:

> visual   > verbal   > manual   > mechanical

Guidance	Example	Useful for
Visual guidance	Involves demonstrating a performance or showing a video. Visual guidance can be used before, during and after the process of performing a skill to help beginners practise and refine their performance. Visual guidance can include the performer watching recordings of their own performances	This is useful for beginners in the cognitive stage of learning as it shows them how the skill or the performance looks before they try it
Verbal guidance	Given by a coach or teacher, and often includes feedback on what went well and what could be improved	Verbal feedback is useful for all stages of learning but it should be concise and simplified for beginners Those at the autonomous stage interpret verbal guidance better than those at the cognitive stage

Guidance	Example	Useful for
Manual guidance	This is when performers are supported through physical guidance by a coach or teacher	This type of guidance is useful to help performers at all stages of learning experience the correct movement in a safe and supportive environment, which develops confidence
Mechanical guidance	Given by equipment that supports the performer in learning a skill. Mechanical guidance improves confidence and can also help to maintain safety during the acquisition of complex skills and high-risk movements	This is useful for those at the cognitive stage when first learning a movement. It encourages confidence due to the safety element

As shown in the table, performers at different stages of learning tend to benefit from different types of guidance.

Those at the **cognitive stage** require plenty of support; visual guidance through demonstrations tends to work best. They may also require manual and mechanical guidance.

At the **associative stage**, verbal guidance supports performers effectively, as they are gaining an understanding of more complex skills.

Learners at the **autonomous stage** relate to verbal guidance and may use visual guidance to analyse their performance.

Data Analysis

The pie chart shows the type of guidance used by a gymnastics coach over an eight-week period.

Types of guidance used by a gymnastics coach

> **Quick Check**
>
> Match each stage of learning to the best description.
>
> › Cognitive stage
> › Associative stage
> › Autonomous stage
>
> Intermediate
> Expert
> Beginner **AO1**

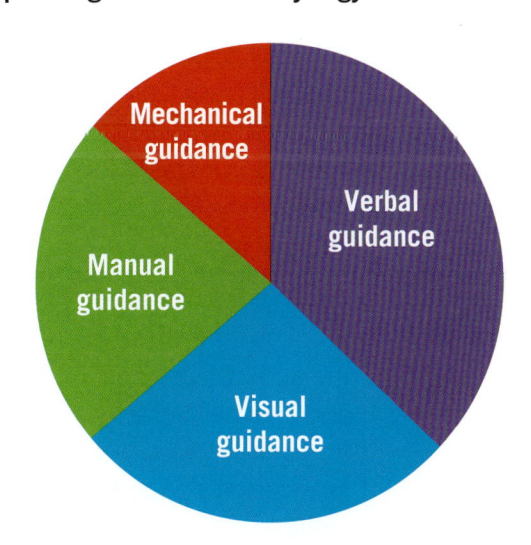

1. Identify the main type of guidance used by the coach.
2. Explain how a coach would use manual guidance with their gymnasts.

4C Guidance and Practice

Practical Investigation

Practice sessions are designed to allow performers to improve their skills. Practice needs to be relevant to the skill and structured in such a way that learning can take place.

There are different types of practice:

> **Whole practice** involves practising a skill as a whole.
> **Part practice** involves breaking a skill up into parts.
> **Fixed practice** involves repeatedly practising a skill.
> **Varied practice** involves changing the practice so the performer is challenged in a variety of situations.

It is important to consider factors such as the environment, the complexity of the skill and the stage of learning when planning which type of practice to use.

Type of practice	Definition	When it is used	Example
Whole practice	This is where the skill is practised as a whole and is not broken down	The performer is near the autonomous stage of learning with the ability to practise the skill as a whole. This is often used for **closed skills**	Practising a tennis serve as a complete technique
Part practice	This is where the skill is broken down into chunks which are practised in isolation	This type of learning is appropriate for learners in the cognitive stage. Can relate to complex skills which can be broken down	Practising just the leg kick in front crawl
Fixed practice	This involves repeatedly practising a skill under constant conditions	The skill is likely to be a relatively closed skill. This type of learning is suitable for those in the cognitive stage of learning	Practising a basketball free throw
Varied practice	This involves practising skills in a situation where the environment is not fixed. The performer is challenged and the skill is applied to different contexts	This type of practice is suitable for those in the associative stage and is usually used for **open skills** as well as **externally paced skills**	A goal kicker towards the post in rugby will need to consider the weather, surface, distance and angle

Top Tip

Fixed practice is used for skills that can be repeated without the impact of other players or the external environment, e.g. a free throw in basketball.

Quick Check

What is part practice?
AO1

Chapter 4 Psychology of Sport and Physical...

▲ Practising a tennis serve.

▲ Practising a leg kick in the swimming pool.

Extension

Using the information in the table, complete the task below for each of the performers:

> **Identify** the type of practice used (think about the level of the performer).

> **Explain** how you would use this type of practice.

A professional golfer	
Type of practice used	Explanation

Learning to kick a ball	
Type of practice used	Explanation

147

4C Guidance and Practice

Topic Test

Identify a *type of practice* that would be suitable for a performer at the **cognitive stage** of learning who is practising a skill for the first time. *Justify* your answer. `3 marks`

When reading the question, look at what the key words and phrases are asking you to do:

- **Command word:** These are based on the assessment objectives (AOs). The assessment objectives for this question are AO1 and AO2: you need to demonstrate your knowledge and understanding and then apply it.
- **Topic:** This is the key area of study the question is about.
- **Qualifying words or phrases:** This is the specific area you need to focus on in your answer.

Doing this will help you to build your answer so that you can access the AO for each question.

Step 1 Demonstrate your knowledge (AO1)

You need to **demonstrate your knowledge and understanding** of the types of practice and stages of learning by **identifying** a suitable type of practice. Is the learner a beginner, an intermediate or an expert?

_____

Step 2 Apply your knowledge and understanding (AO2)

You need to **apply your knowledge and understanding** in order to **justify** the type of practice you have identified.

Use the terms in the tick list of terminology. Look at how many marks are available to help you decide how much detail to include.

☐ Whole   ☐ Part   ☐ Fixed   ☐ Variable

_____
_____
_____
_____
_____

Chapter 4 Psychology of Sport and Physical...

THE BIG QUESTION

RECAP

C You are continuing to build the knowledge and understanding you need to answer the Big Question. You have already answered parts 1 and 2, so now it's time to answer part 3 and apply your knowledge and understanding of guidance and practice.

> 3. Compare how coaches use guidance for performers in the cognitive and autonomous stages of learning. (4 marks)

Explain what type of guidance and why per stage:

- Visual
- Verbal
- Manual
- Mechanical

Coaches will use a range of strategies to help performers learn new skills or develop existing ones. A coach may use specific guidance strategies based on the stage of learning the performer is at.

A tennis coach will use a range of guidance strategies when coaching a performer in a new skill at the early stages of learning.

A coach working with an experienced swimmer will use specific guidance strategies.

149

4D Mental Preparation and Motivation

This is the question we're going to be working towards answering at the end of this section.

> 4. Evaluate two mental preparation techniques a cyclist might use before a race.
>
> AO3 – 5 marks

Mental Preparation

Mental preparation is required for performers to stay focused and manage their emotions to achieve sporting success. Performers may use a range of techniques to develop their confidence and maintain the right mindset to perform at their best – often known as being '**in the zone**'.

Being mentally prepared helps performers by improving:

- **confidence:** having self-belief and trust in their own ability
- **control** over their emotions, dealing well with arousal, anxiety and disappointment
- **concentration:** remaining focused throughout the performance or competition.
- **commitment:** maintaining an enthusiasm for the performance which will maintain motivation and adherence.

A range of mental preparation techniques can be used to help motivate performers and improve their performance, as shown in the table.

Top Tip

Remember the 4 Cs – **c**onfidence, **c**ontrol, **c**oncentration and **c**ommitment.

Technique	Example
Imagery (visualisation)	Imagery (or visualisation) can be used to help reduce arousal and anxiety by visualising success. This can also help increase motivation
	It often involves the performer imagining themselves performing successfully. For example, a goal kicker in rugby might visualise the flight of the ball going between the posts
	It might also involve the performer picturing themselves in a calm environment
	The performer may also use music to help them with this
Mental rehearsal	Mental rehearsal involves a performer picturing themselves executing a skill or performance perfectly to 'practise' it inside their head
	For example, a rock climber might imagine where they will place their hands and feet and how it will feel to complete each move before they attempt a new route
	This could help them build confidence and remember the route better

Rehearsal and visualisation can involve more than one sense. For example, as well as picturing what it will look like to execute a difficult shot, a netball player might imagine how it will physically feel to complete the shot, the smell of the rubber and the sounds made by the other players and the spectators.

Motivation

Motivation is a psychological factor in helping you to achieve goals. There are two types of motivation:

Intrinsic motivation is an inner drive to succeed. The performer is motivated by a sense of pride, fun and enjoyment, for example the love of the game or personal satisfaction.

Extrinsic motivation is performing for external rewards such as prizes, money, trophies and recognition.

Performers' adherence and sporting success are improved by both intrinsic and extrinsic motivation. For example, it would be difficult to train three or four times a week if you did not enjoy what you were doing, but the desire to earn money or win trophies may also increase your motivation.

> **Top Tip**
> Adherence can be affected by motivation.

> **Quick Check**
> Which of the following is a form of intrinsic motivation? **A01**
> ☐ Recognition
> ☐ Prize money
> ☐ Satisfaction of a good performance

◀ Winning a trophy is an example of extrinsic motivation.

> **Knowledge Check**
>
> Describe how a 100m sprinter would use mental preparation before a big race. **A01**
>
> Use the following key terms to help you:
>
> | focused   confidence   emotions   concentration |
> | :---: |
> | in the zone   commitment   control |

151

4D Mental Preparation and Motivation

Topic Test

Explain, using examples, what is meant by the term **extrinsic motivation**. **4 marks**

When reading the question, look at what the key words and phrases are asking you to do:
- **Command word:** This is based on the assessment objective (AO). The assessment objective for this question is AO2: you need to apply your knowledge and understanding.
- **Topic:** This is the key area of study the question is about.
- **Qualifying words or phrases:** This is the specific area you need to focus on in your answer.

Doing this will help you to build your answer so that you can access the AO for each question.

Step 1 Demonstrate your knowledge (AO1)

You need to **demonstrate your knowledge and understanding** of the types of motivation. What does 'extrinsic' mean?

_____
_____
_____

Step 2 Apply your knowledge and understanding (AO2)

You need to **apply your knowledge and understanding** of motivation in order to **explain** extrinsic motivation and rewards. Don't forget to provide examples – what types of rewards would motivate players?

_____
_____
_____
_____
_____
_____

Use the terms in the tick list of terminology to help you plan your answer to meet AO1 and AO2 in Steps 1 and 2. Look at how many marks are available to help you decide how much detail to include:

- ☐ External
- ☐ Rewards
- ☐ Money
- ☐ Recognition
- ☐ Trophy

Chapter 4 Psychology of Sport and Physical...

THE BIG QUESTION

RECAP

D You are continuing to build the knowledge and understanding you need to answer the Big Question. Now it's time to answer part 4 and apply your knowledge and understanding of mental preparation and motivation.

> **4. Evaluate two mental preparation techniques a cyclist might use before a race. (5 marks)**

Before a race, a cyclist will feel a range of emotions. For the cyclist to achieve the goal of winning, they will need to prepare mentally. They may need to apply the 4 Cs:

- Confidence: how can they create self-belief?
- Control: how can they manage the anxiety and stress of the event?
- Concentration: how can they maintain concentration, and take their mind off other competitors?
- Commitment: how can they maintain their motivation to achieve their goal?

153

4E Classification of Skill

> 5. BMX freestylers are regarded as having a high level of skill. Explain two characteristics of a skilful performance using sporting examples.
>
> AO2 – 4 marks

Classifications of Skills

The development of skills in physical activity and sport is essential to performance and moving from the cognitive stage to the autonomous stage of learning.

Skills can be classified along one of three continua depending on their characteristics:

1. open and closed skills
2. basic and complex skills
3. **self-paced** and externally paced skills.

It is often very difficult to pinpoint an exact position for a skill on each continuum, so it is important to provide a reason why you have placed it in that particular position.

Open and Closed Skills

The variable for this continuum is the environment and how much of an impact it will have on performance.

| Open |————————————————————| Closed |

Open skills are affected by many variables, such as other performers/competitors, spectators, weather conditions, the surface. These skills are often externally paced.

Closed skills are not influenced by the surrounding environment and are often self-paced.

Basic and Complex Skills

The variable for this continuum is complexity: how difficult a skill is has an impact on performance.

| Basic |————————————————————| Complex |

Basic skills will require the performer to make very few decisions and tend to be simple and straightforward.

Complex skills are more difficult, requiring the performer to make decisions and interpret information while performing complex movements with fluency and control.

Top Tip

When placing an activity or skill on a continuum it is not about where you place the activity, it is about how you justify where you have placed it.

Self-paced and Externally Paced Continuum

The variable for this continuum is pace. This is based on who controls the speed of the skill being performed.

Self-paced |————————————————————| Externally paced

Self-paced skills are controlled by the performer, for example a javelin throw would be self-paced as the performer is in control.

Externally paced skills are controlled by external factors. The decisions that are made may be influenced by the opposition in a rounders match or a starting pistol in a 100m race.

Characteristics of a Skilled Performance

A skilled performance in sport has many characteristics which contribute to the performer producing a desired outcome. For example, the performance of a golfer teeing off would look very different if performed by an unskilled performer compared to a skilled performer. A skilled performer would show the following characteristics:

Aesthetics
The performance looks good and is pleasing to watch.

Accuracy
The performance is accurate.

Confidence
The performance is positively performed.

Control
The performance shows a high level of control.

Technique
The performance is fluent and uses the appropriate technique.

Efficiency
The performance is made to look easy.

Effectiveness
The performance is effective and achieves the desired outcome.

Consistency
The performance has the desired outcome nearly every time it is performed.

A skilled performer will also be able to adapt their performance to changing situations and still achieve the desired outcome. They make minimal mistakes and seem to be ahead of the game by consistently making the correct decisions.

> **Quick Check**
> On the self-paced and externally paced continuum, where would you place a golfer playing a shot off the tee? Explain your answer. **A02**

> **Top Tip**
> A skilled performer is consistent, confident, effective, controlled and aesthetic.

4E Classification of Skill

Practical investigation

This investigation is designed for you to explore the characteristics of a skilful performer in your chosen activity.

Method

1. Identify a performer in a position or an event in a sport of your choice.
2. Place an image of your selected performer in the middle of a piece of paper, then explore the characteristics they would need to produce a skilful performance.
3. Give an example for each characteristic.

Example for a centre in hockey:

- Effectiveness: selecting the right time to shoot.
- Aesthetics: fluent actions and pleasing to watch.

Use the following hints to help you explore the characteristics of a skilful performance in your chosen sport in more detail:

Your chosen sport

- How effective is the performer in a game/competition?
- Think about the performer's techniques when they perform a skill under pressure.
- Think about their ability to make decisions.

Extension Activity

For each of the characteristics listed in the table, provide an example of how a performer would demonstrate the characteristic within a sport.

Characteristic	Sporting example
Fluency	
Accuracy	
Aesthetics	
Consistency	
Confidence	
Control	
Effectiveness	
Efficiency	
Decision-making	
Technical	
Tactical	

Top Tip

Think about an example that involves the correct skills to link to each characteristic.

▲ What characteristics would a tennis player demonstrate?

4E Classification of Skill

Topic Test ☑

Justify why the **arrow has been placed at this point** on the **open and closed skill continuum**. `3 marks`

Passing the ball in football

Open |————————————————————————| Closed

When reading the question, look at what the key words and phrases are asking you to do:

- **Command word:** This is based on the assessment objective (AO). The assessment objective for this question is AO2: you need to apply your knowledge and understanding.
- **Topic:** This is the key area of study the question is about.
- **Qualifying words or phrases:** This is the specific area you need to focus on in your answer.

Doing this will help you to build your answer so that you can access the AO for each question.

Step 1 Demonstrate your knowledge (AO1)

You need to **demonstrate your knowledge and understanding** of the open and closed skills continuum. What is an open skill?

_____

_____

Step 2 Apply your knowledge and understanding (AO2)

You need to **apply your knowledge and understanding** of open and closed skills in order to **justify** the placement of the arrow. Think about the environment and other people.

_____

_____

_____

Use the terms in the tick list of terminology to help you plan your answer to meet AO1 and AO2 in Steps 1 and 2. Look at how many marks are available to help you decide how much detail to include:

☐ Variable   ☐ Spectators   ☐ Externally paced
☐ Performers   ☐ Self-paced   ☐ Weather conditions

Chapter 4 Psychology of Sport and Physical...

THE BIG QUESTION

RECAP

E Now it's time to answer the final part of the Big Question and apply your knowledge and understanding of classification of skill.

5. BMX freestylers are regarded as having a high level of skill.

Explain two characteristics of a skilful performance using sporting examples. (4 marks)

Remember, in a question the image is only a stimulus. You don't have to talk about BMX freestyle, you can answer the question using any sporting example.

Think about a sport you have knowledge of.

Explain each characteristic.

How does a skilful performer look as they play this sport?

You may decide to identify characteristics from a different sport, e.g., a high jumper in a competition:

Think about how the high jumper approaches the bar.

What does the movement look like when they clear the bar?

Think about the transition from the run-up to the jump.

159

CHAPTER 5

Socio-Cultural Issues in Sport and Physical Activity

Engaging people in physical activity is highly important, not only for improving health and wellbeing but also for managing the pressures that poor health and inactivity place on public services like the NHS. This chapter will explore issues around participation as well as ethical issues and the commercialisation of sport – which can have both a positive and a negative impact on participation.

THE BIG QUESTION

Increasing participation in sport and physical activities can have a big impact on people's health and wellbeing. It is important to understand factors that affect participation, provision and performance as well as the strategies used to develop these areas. Commercialisation can have both a positive and a negative impact on participation as well as contributing to some of the ethical issues in sport.

These are the topics you'll need to answer the Big Question:

1. **Participation and provision in sport and physical activity:** What strategies have been used to increase the involvement of girls in sport?

2. **Commercialisation in sport:** What positive impacts does commercialisation have on sport?

3. **Ethical issues in sport:** Should performance-enhancing drugs be made legal?

In this chapter you will learn about:

› the factors that contribute to and affect participation, provision and performance in sport and exercise

› the influences of school physical education programmes, extra-curricular activities and the wider curriculum

› physical literacy, physical activity, wellbeing and the impact on children's development

› provision for a variety of target groups

› commercialisation of sport, including the role of the media, advertising and the globalisation of sport

› ethical issues, competitiveness, sportsmanship and deviance.

In this chapter you will be using the following key terms. You can look up the meaning of these terms in the Glossary (page 184 onwards).

Key Terms

Anabolic steroids	Brand exposure	Commercialisation	Commodity
Deviance	Disability	Doping	Ethnicity
Globalisation	Media	Mental wellbeing	Participation
Physical wellbeing	Social media	Social wellbeing	Sponsorship
Stereotyping			

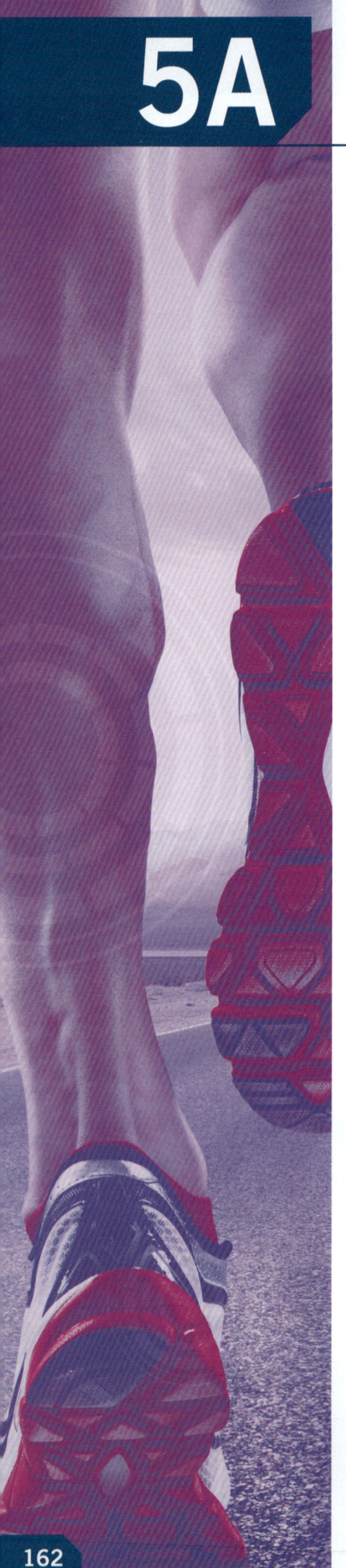

5A Participation and Provision in Sport and Physical Activity

This is the question we're going to be working towards answering at the end of this section.

> 1. Statistics show that boys are more likely to participate in sports than girls. Discuss strategies that have been used to increase the involvement of girls in sport.
>
> **AO3 – 6 marks**

Participation in sport and physical activities can be influenced many factors. People have many different reasons for choosing to participate in different sports and activities, and many factors affect their ability to participate. Some of these factors can be seen in the diagram below.

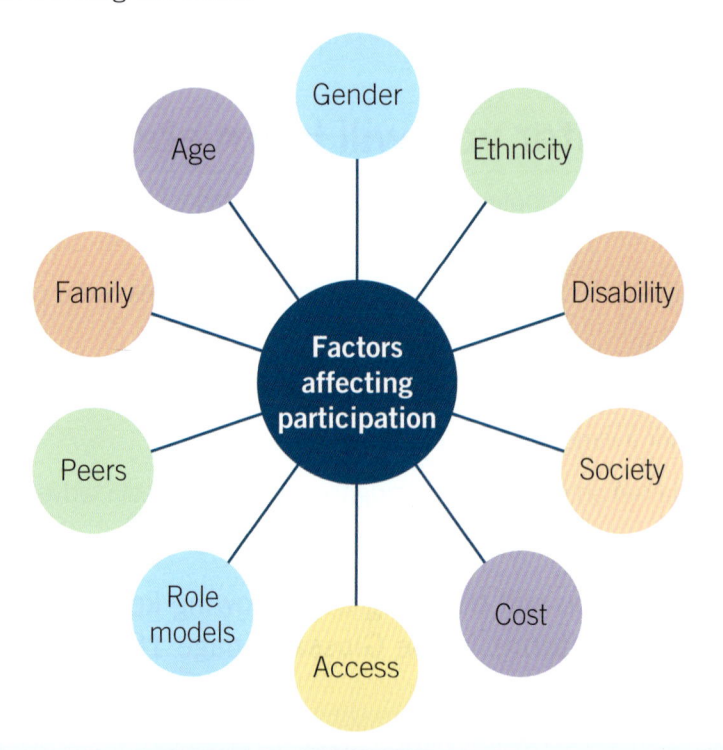

Factor affecting participation	Details
Gender	Some people still hold stereotypical views about which activities males and females 'should' participate in
Ethnicity	Ethnic minority communities may lack role models in leading organisations
Disability	**Stereotyping**, physical barriers and lack of confidence among staff/volunteers may limit opportunities for athletes with disabilities
Society	Government campaigns may try to encourage participation in physical activity so that it is seen as the norm

Factor affecting participation	Details
Cost	Some activities may require a financial commitment (for example, equipment, membership or insurance)
Access	Some activities may only be available in certain parts of the country or may demand travel (for example, some water sports are only available on the coast)
Role models	Positive and negative role models may affect a person's choice of physical activity
Peers	Friends will influence people's decisions to participate in physical activity (or not). This may be either a positive or a negative influence
Family	Family members who participate regularly in sport will often inspire or encourage other family members to stay active
Age	Participation rates can depend on age. For example, participation rates may be high in schools due to easily available opportunities. When people reach working age, participation may decline due to the demands of work and family life

We have some degree of control over some of these factors, as a they have an element of choice. For example, you can choose your friends. Other factors, such as age and ethnicity, are beyond our control.

Age

Age is a factor which changes participation rates over time. During school years participation rates tend to be high due to compulsory PE and opportunities provided by school and community clubs. As children get older, participation rates drop off due to the pressures of exams.

As we move into adulthood, the responsibility of work and family also has an impact on participation levels. Increasing age is often accompanied by an increase in body weight, as well as a decrease in flexibility and strength; this can also affect participation rates.

Top Tip

Participation can be affected by stereotyping, particularly for people of different genders, ethnicities and people with a disability. Stereotypes are sometimes based on tradition or history. This can cause a lack of participation by affecting opportunities, self-confidence and self-esteem.

Quick Check

Explain two factors that affect participation. **AO2**

◀ Participation in sport tends to drop off with age.

5A Participation and Provision in Sport...

Top Tip
It is a good idea to reflect on the reasons why you take part in a sport. This will help you understand questions relating to factors affecting participation in sport.

▶ Stereotypes can influence female participation in sport.

Quick Check
What government campaigns have been launched to help increase female participation levels in sport? **A01**

Gender
As girls reach their teenage years, participation levels decrease. This can be linked to many factors such as body image, limited opportunities, stereotyping and lack of female role models. The government has launched a number of campaigns to tackle these barriers and to support female participation and enjoyment of sport.

Data Analysis
The bar chart shows what percentage of students at a secondary school participated in sport two or more times a week.

From the data, we can see that there is a gradual decrease in both boys' and girls' participation from the ages of 11 to 16.

Participation in Sport Two or More Times per Week

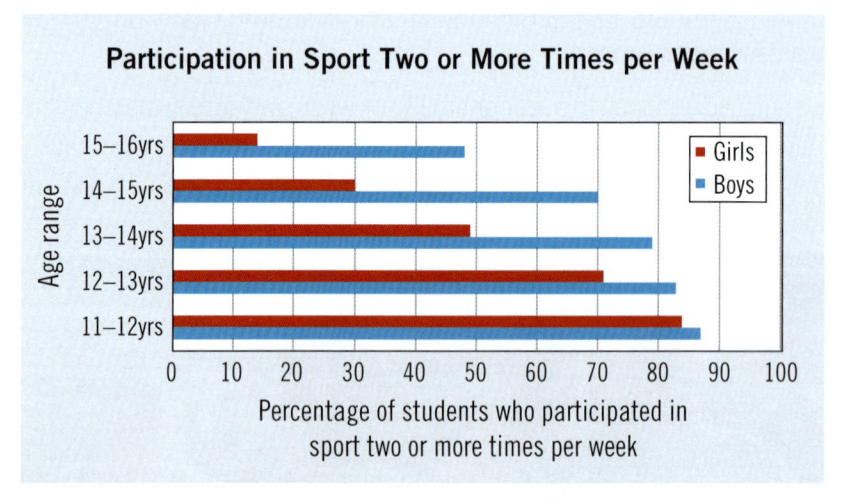

1. Identify **two** reasons why there is a drop in participation for both boys and girls at the age of 15/16.

Ethnicity
Under-representation of ethnic minorities is found in most sports. This can be seen not just at a playing level but also at coaching and managerial levels. Clothing worn to reflect religious beliefs may need to be adapted for sport, and some religious

or ethnic communities are more likely to regard certain sports as outside the norm. Racism in sport is still a problem and needs to be eradicated to improve participation levels.

◀ Ethnic minorities are often under-represented in sport.

Disability

Although participation in sport of people who have a disability has increased in recent years, it is relatively low compared to people without disabilities.

This is due to:

❯ physical barriers: venues may be difficult to access and equipment may need to be adapted to suit the needs of people with disabilities. This can increase costs.

❯ lack of opportunities: people with disabilities may face a lack of available activities, specialist coaches and suitable transport.

❯ psychological barriers: negative attitudes towards athletes with disabilities may have an impact on their confidence to go out and try new activities.

Media coverage and a range of campaigns are attempting to encourage participation by raising the profile of athletes with disabilities and eradicating stereotypical views.

Quick Check

Identify an event that is a flagship for the representation of disability in sport. **AO1**

◀ Over-coming physical and psychological barriers is a major hurdle for people with disabilities.

165

5A Participation and Provision in Sport...

Quick Check

Describe a personal experience that has influenced your participation in sport.
AO1

AO3

You may need to draw on your experience in sport to answer questions in this topic area.

Health Agenda

Health and wellbeing are high on the government's agenda for the following reasons:

> To improve people's health and fitness; this has many advantages, including:
> - improving people's **physical wellbeing**
> - maintaining a fit and healthy workforce (reducing sickness)
> - reducing the pressure placed on the NHS by the health complications that arise from an unfit population.

> To improve **social wellbeing** by providing opportunities for social interaction and friendships.

> To improve **mental wellbeing** by ensuring people spend time doing positive things.

Strategies to Improve Participation in Sport and Physical Activity

To increase participation, organisations sometimes run campaigns to promote their sport. The government and sporting governing bodies also administer campaigns to target specific types of people. Some past campaigns are discussed below.

Female Participation

There have been many nationwide campaigns aimed at encouraging girls and women to take part in sport. An example is the 'This Girl Can' campaign, which aimed to inspire women to get active, no matter how well they did or how they looked. This was set up to overcome judgement, build self-esteem and confidence.

Disabilities in Sport

Increasing participation can mean making it physically possible for people with disabilities to participate. In some cases, people may need access to specially-adapted equipment, may follow different rules, or may encounter barriers when accessing venues. Powerchair football and wheelchair tennis are examples of sports adapted for wheelchair accessibility. Goalball is an example of a sport designed specifically for visually impaired players – it is played with a ball containing bells that can be located by sound. Campaigns and resources for disabled sport are therefore highly important.

▶ A specially-modified wheelchair for playing tennis.

Disability Sport Wales support opportunities for people with disabilities to take part in activities ranging from archery to weightlifting; it is committed to 'transforming lives through the power of sport'.

Activity Alliance launched the 'Together We Will' campaign aimed at increasing the numbers of people with disabilities who take part in regular sport and exercise.

Campaigns like these, along with the Paralympic movement, have helped shift the perception of people with disabilities in sport. An increase in reporting and media coverage, including promotion of the games as well as positive role models, have had a significant impact on participation levels.

Kick It Out

The Professional Footballers' Association (PFA) and the Commission for Racial Equality (CRE) released a campaign in 1993 called 'Kick It Out' which aimed to tackle racist attitudes existing within the game. This campaign has been supported by Sky Sports which encourages fans to report incidents of discrimination.

Provision for Sport and Activity

Provision for sport and activity comes from three different sectors:

The **public sector** is funded locally and nationally from government taxation. The public sector provision includes:

- facilities and equipment made available to everyone at a low cost (or free to some groups, e.g. free swimming during school holidays)
- community facilities like local leisure centres/community centres, which give a sense of belonging
- the ability to use these facilities to implement government initiatives, e.g. walking netball
- links with education and the school curriculum, e.g. duel-use facilities such as swimming pools at local leisure centres that can also be used by schools.

The **private sector** consists of privately owned organisations run for profit. They provide sport and leisure facilities for paying members. The private sector's provision is likely to include:

- a cost to access the facilities
- a higher quality level of experience for members
- exclusive use of facilities
- access to personalised trainers/coaches, often for an additional cost
- 24-hour access to some facilities.

The **voluntary sector** consists of non-profit organisations. Volunteers give up their time to run these. The voluntary sector is likely to include:

- access for all
- a lower quality of experience
- a request for donations or contributions towards the hiring of facilities and equipment

---

AO3

You may need an understanding of different campaigns that are aimed at promoting participation in sport.

Top Tip

Provision for sport is how the public, private and voluntary sector provide opportunities for sporting activities.

Quick Check

What provision does your local leisure centre provide for school pupils during the holidays? **AO1**

5A Participation and Provision in Sport...

> use of local community centres, which provide a sense of belonging
> limited times of access.

Making use of these provisions also depends on the individual. Some of the key factors might be:

Income	Private sector facilities might be too expensive for some. Public and voluntary sector provisions are likely to be more affordable. Public sector facilities vary but some are just as good as the private sector
Time	Access to facilities may be restricted within the voluntary sector due to limited opening times and availability of volunteers. Public and private sector facilities will have longer opening times with some private sector facilities having 24-hour opening
Motivation	People who lead a sedentary lifestyle may struggle to feel motivated to access facilities. The private sector may feel intimidating, whereas public and voluntary sectors may feel more welcoming, giving a sense of belonging to help with motivation
Accessibility	These provisions may be limited in certain areas of the country. Voluntary sector facilities depend on the availability of volunteers who are willing to give up their free time (these are usually found in close-knit community areas). Private and public sector facilities may be more common in larger towns or cities where there are more people who are willing to pay. Rural areas may have limited access

Quick Check

Outline the advantages and disadvantages of public sector sports provision. **AO1**

The Influence of School Physical Education Programmes: Extra-curricular activities and the Wider Curriculum

Children up to the age of 16 participate in physical education (PE) as a compulsory part of schooling. PE helps children to grow physically, mentally and socially as well as developing **physical literacy**.

Physical literacy is the set of capabilities that people acquire as a result of PE, including their knowledge, physical abilities, confidence and motivation. The International Physical Literacy Association define physical literacy as 'the motivation, confidence, physical competence, knowledge and understanding to value and take responsibility for engagement in physical activities for life' (2014).

▶ A compulsory PE lesson in a primary school.

When children leave school, there is a high drop-out rate of physical activity and sport. The delivery of PE should be positive, engaging and supportive to develop self-confidence and self-esteem at an early age so children love sport and physical activity and will carry on after leaving school.

Experiences at school can play an important part in influencing children's decisions about what to take part in. A school that offers a broad range of activities is more likely to encourage children to continue being active after leaving school. The provision in school is often determined under three headings:

› curriculum PE
› extra-curricular PE
› wider curriculum.

Provision	Explanation	Influences
Curriculum PE	This is a compulsory programme that all children follow	Experience a range of activities delivered by professionally qualified teachers
Extra-curricular PE	Extra-curricular clubs and activities that are offered outside PE times (break/lunch times and after school)	Encourage children to pursue their chosen activity and develop within it. Schools that offer a broad extra-curricular programme provide a range of opportunities for children to experience
Wider curriculum	These are all other opportunities with cross-curricular links to PE. For example, skills developed in sport might link to drama, dance and music	Encourage active, healthy lifestyles. Skills and attributes developed in PE can be transferred across other areas of learning

Top Tip

Reflect on your journey through school and the opportunities that have been provided for you through the PE curriculum, extra-curricular activities and the wider school curriculum.

Quick Check

Discuss how your experiences at school have influenced your participation in sport.
AO3

◂ Extra-curricular PE lessons take place during lunch times or after school.

5A Participation and Provision in Sport...

Practical Investigation

Quick Check

What is meant by the term participation?
A01

Describe how each of the factors we have discussed have had an influence on your participation in sport and physical activity.

Method

1. Use a copy of Appendix 5.1 and list the influences on your participation in sport and physical activity.

Appendix 5.1 Factors Affecting Participation – A Practical Investigation

Using the spider diagram below, describe how each of the factors have or had an influence on your participation in sport and physical activity.

Factors affecting participation: Gender, Ethnicity, Disability, Society, Cost, Access, Role models, Peers, Family, Age

Influences on my participation in sport and physical activity:

_____
_____
_____
_____
_____
_____
_____
_____

---

2. Now think about the factors you have recorded and how your journey through school has influenced them. Copy and complete the following table and make a list of:

   › the opportunities that you have had
   › the positive experiences you have had
   › any negative experiences you have had.

3. Provide a description/explanation for each point that you have identified.

Top Tip

Remember:

Curriculum

C = **C**ompulsory,

Extra-curricular

E = **E**xtra to the curriculum,

Wider

W = **W**hole school (or wider parts of school)

Influence of School Physical Education Programmes

	Your opportunities	Positive experiences	Negative experiences
Curriculum PE			
Extra-curricular PE			
Wider curriculum			

Extension Activity

Evaluate the benefits of extra-curricular PE and its use in encouraging children to take part in activities for life.

Below are some ideas of why children take part in extracurricular activities. Can you think of any more that might help you with your answer?

- Having fun
- Learning new skills
- Experiencing new activities
- Meeting new friends

171

5A Participation and Provision in Sport...

Topic Test ✓

Describe two reasons why some children are missing out on developing **physical literacy** in their **early childhood**. `2 marks`

When reading the question, look at what the key words and phrases are asking you to do:

- **Command word:** This is based on the assessment objective (AO). The assessment objective for this question is AO1: you need to demonstrate your knowledge and understanding.
- **Topic:** This is the key area of study the question is about.
- **Qualifying words or phrases:** This is the specific area you need to focus on in your answer.

Doing this will help you to build your answer so that you can access the AO for each question.

Demonstrate your knowledge (AO1)

You need to **demonstrate your knowledge and understanding** of physical literacy by describing relevant factors that prevent some children from developing it.

_____
_____
_____

You need to understand that this is an AO1 question, which means knowledge and understanding. Think about how children can develop their knowledge about physical activities, their physical abilities, confidence and motivation. Why might children not have the opportunities to develop these skills? Think about how their opportunities might be limited and what possible obstacles they might encounter.

> Remember physical literacy is: Physical skills + Confidence + Motivation

Chapter 5 Socio-Cultural Issues in Sport...

THE BIG QUESTION

RECAP

A You are starting to build the knowledge and understanding you need to answer the Big Question. Use what you have learned so far and apply your knowledge and understanding of socio-cultural issues in sport.

> 1. Statistics show that boys are more likely to participate in sports than girls. Discuss strategies that have been used to increase the involvement of girls in sport. (6 marks)

Discuss is the command word in this question. You can address this by exploring the **advantages** and **disadvantages** first and then going on to form a conclusion.

How have they been used to increase involvement in sport?

What strategies have you heard of that are aimed at encouraging females to take part in sport?

Can you think of advantages and disadvantages of the strategies you have identified?

After considering each advantage and disadvantage what are your final conclusions?

173

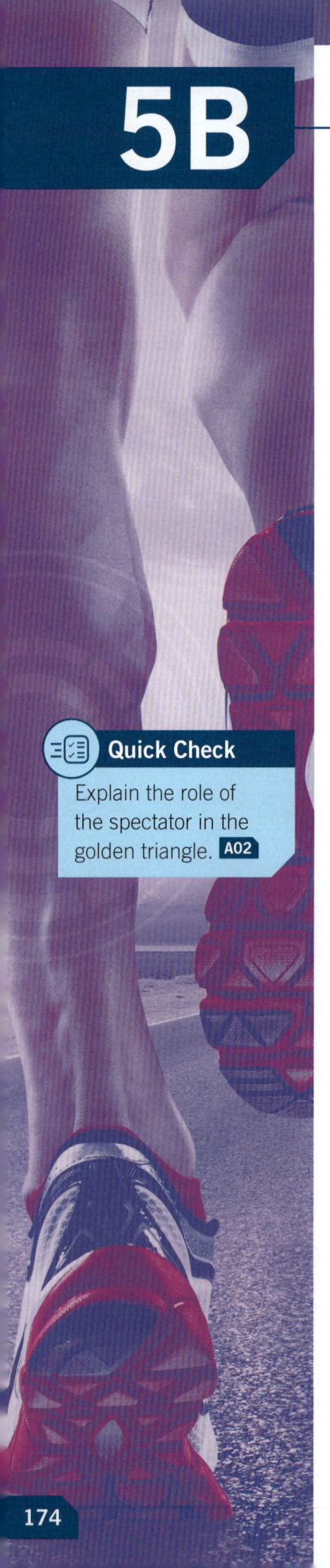

5B Commercialisation in Sport

This is the question we're going to be working towards answering at the end of this section.

> 2. Explain two positive impacts of commercialisation in sport.
>
> AO2 – 4 marks

Commercialisation

Sport is a huge industry. Not only sport itself, but sports performers are also often seen as a **commodity** than can be bought and sold.

Through sponsors and the media, the business world has taken advantage of this and, increasingly, every possible avenue is exploited for profit. Equipment, clothing, technology, merchandise, ticket sales and pay-per-view events are popular commodities among sporting spectators. Media has had a massive impact on the rise of **commercialisation**, playing its role in influencing the behaviour of spectators.

Below is 'the golden triangle'. This is a continuous cycle where each element contributes to the effectiveness of the others. In simple terms it is the financial relationship between the sport, media and the spectators.

Quick Check

Explain the role of the spectator in the golden triangle. **AO2**

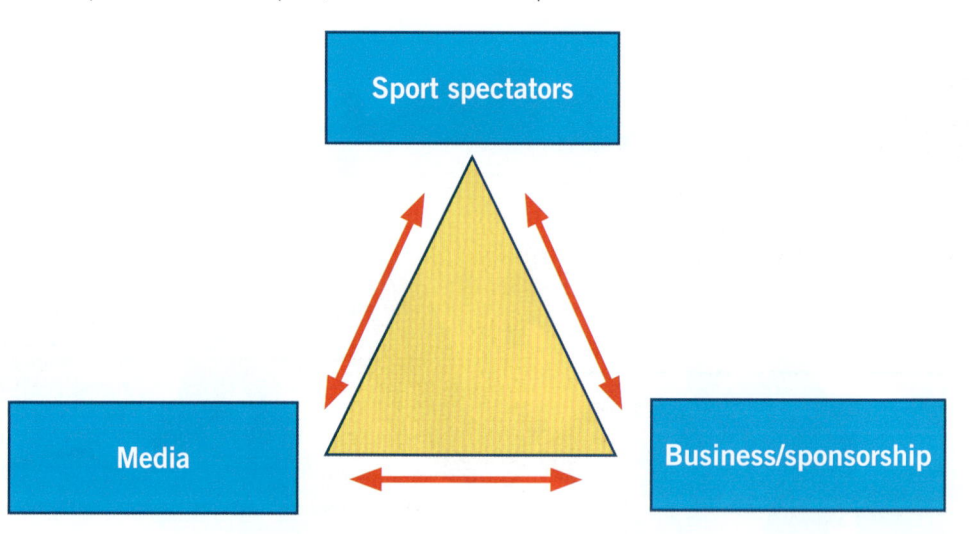

Sport spectators

Media

Business/sponsorship

For a sport to be a successful commercial product, it requires the involvement of three main parties: the sport spectators, sponsors and media. The golden triangle shows that all three parties are directly linked.

For example, a business may provide **sponsorship** for an event or team, and promotion will raise the profile of the business's product as well as the sport through a variety of media. The sports spectator, for example a fan watching a game on TV or online, may then decide to buy the product or merchandise associated with the team.

Sponsorship brings vast amounts of money to sport. In return, businesses that provide sponsorship benefit from increased media coverage. High-profile athletes and sports attract large audiences, so sport offers plenty of **brand exposure** from a variety of media streams.

174

Impact of Commercialisation

One positive impact of commercialisation is the large amount of money it allows teams to make, which enables facilities to be improved and recruitment of high-profile performers and coaches. This then increases the audience and fan base, creating more revenue. The availability of sporting events on different media platforms contributes to the **globalisation** of sport. This can mean that a few top performers gain far more worldwide attention and much more sponsorship than less prominent athletes or teams.

The role the media plays, and the extensive coverage given, means that seasons are extended, and games and events are shown at unusual times. This can have a negative impact on performers by causing injury and increasing the pressure to perform.

Commercialisation also affects some performers by raising their profile and making them celebrities, and role models, within their sport. The rise in profile brings financial gain and idolisation by fans. The increase in **social media** means that these high-profile stars are more accessible to fans than ever before. Therefore, the price of fame leads to a lack of privacy and the need to maintain a high level of performance, which in turn puts extensive pressure on the athlete.

Think about the sponsorship a racing car and its driver will have.

Think about how accessible the media has made sport and sporting performers.

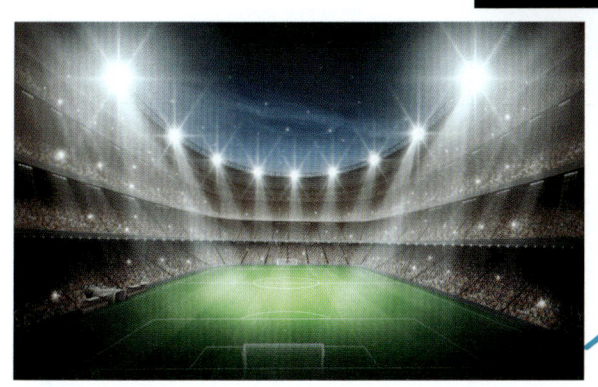

Stadiums have been developed for improved sporting performance, the supporters' experience and to provide opportunities for sponsorship.

Top Tip

Media plays a big part in the promotion of sport. It is important to remember that media is not just television – it can also be newspapers, radio stations and social media channels.

Quick Check

What is social media?
AO1

Quick Check

What is commercialisation?
AO1

5B Commercialisation in Sport

Practical Investigation

You will be carrying out some research into how commercialisation has an impact on sponsorship, media and spectators.

Method

› Identify a sport or team of your choice and then carry out research to investigate how commercialisation has had an impact on these three areas:

1. Spectators: What is the role of spectators associated with this sport in the golden triangle?

2. Media: What are the types of media and how can they influence commercialisation?

3. Sponsorship: Who are the sponsors and how do they link with the other two areas?

› Record your findings around the golden triangle in Appendix 5.2.

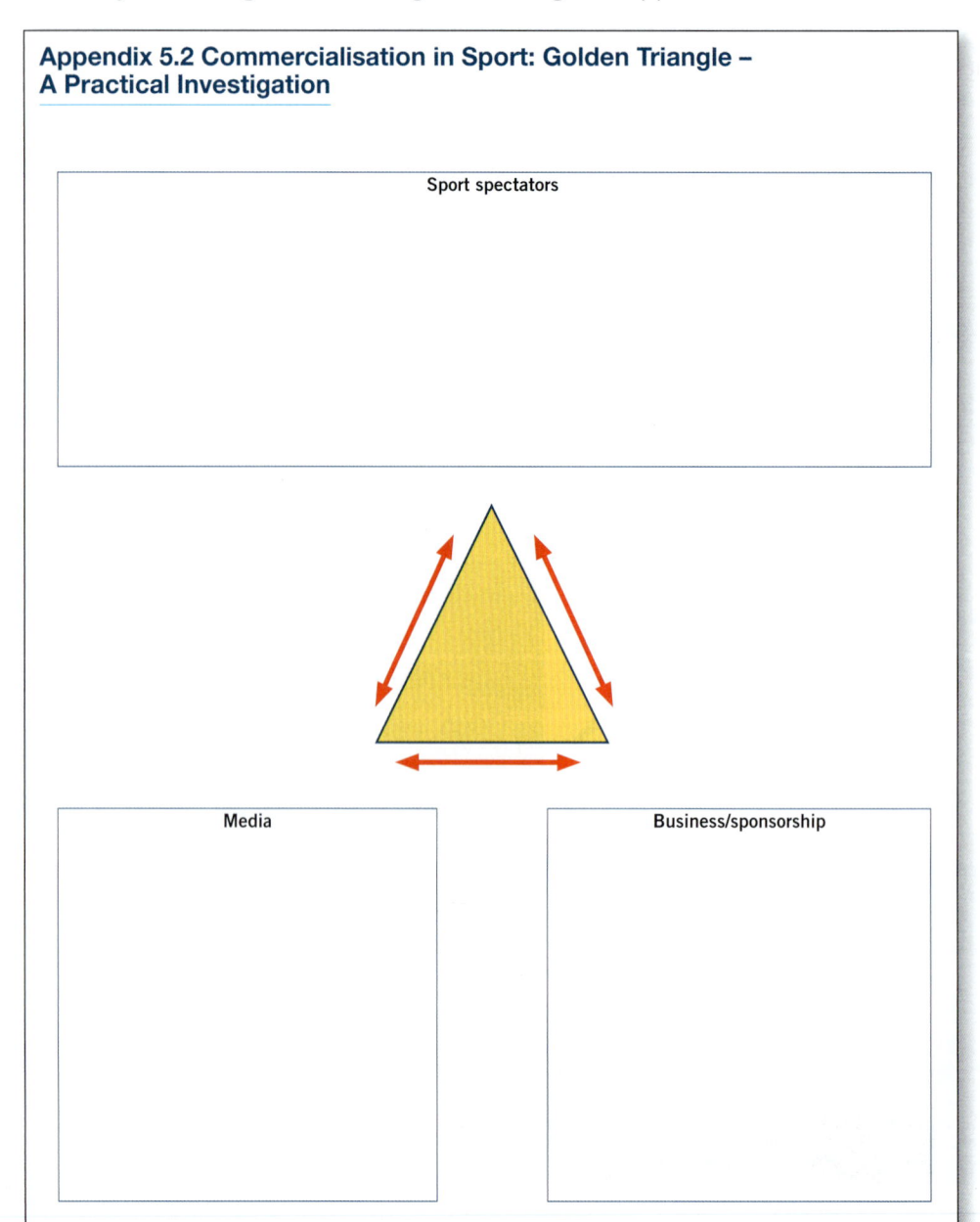

Appendix 5.2 Commercialisation in Sport: Golden Triangle – A Practical Investigation

Sport spectators

Media

Business/sponsorship

> **Top Tip**
> Think carefully about the three points of the triangle and consider how they influence each other.

Chapter 5 Socio-Cultural Issues in Sport…

Use some of the information below to help you in your planning.

Sport spectators

- What different competitions are there in my sport?
- How can I watch my team play?
- What will it cost?
- What merchandise can I buy?

Media

- What are the different types of media?
- What advertisements do I see?
- How can I find information about my team?
- How can I find information about my favourite player?

Business/sponsorship

- My favourite player has equipment made by…
- Who sponsors my team?
- Can you think of a major sponsor of a competition?

Extension

Discuss with a partner how each of the three points of the triangle will work together to provide the positive and negative effects of commercialisation for your chosen sport or team.

177

5B Commercialisation in Sport

Topic Test

Explain the **links between media** and **commercialisation** in **sport.** `4 marks`

When reading the question, look at what the key words and phrases are asking you to do:

- **Command word:** This is based on the assessment objective (AO). The assessment objective for this question is AO2: you need to apply your knowledge and understanding.
- **Topic:** This is the key area of study the question is about.
- **Qualifying words or phrases:** This is the specific area you need to focus on in your answer.

Doing this will help you to build your answer so that you can access the AO for each question.

Step 1 Demonstrate your knowledge (AO1)

You need to **demonstrate your knowledge and understanding** of commercialisation in sport.

_____
_____
_____

Use the terms in the tick list of terminology to help you plan your answer to meet AO1. Look at how many marks are available to help you decide how much detail to include:

- ☐ Spectators
- ☐ Business
- ☐ Sponsorship
- ☐ Media
- ☐ Sport

Step 2 Apply your knowledge and understanding (AO2)

You need to **apply your knowledge and understanding** of commercialisation in order to **explain** how it is linked with the media.

_____
_____
_____
_____

Hints: Think about the meaning of commercialisation and the meaning of media. How do they both work together to make financial gain?

Use the terms in the tick list of terminology to help you plan your answer to meet AO2. Look at how many marks are available to help you decide how much detail to include:

- ☐ Sponsorship
- ☐ Globalisation
- ☐ Brand exposure
- ☐ Business
- ☐ Social media

178

Chapter 5 Socio-Cultural Issues in Sport...

THE BIG QUESTION

RECAP

B You are starting to build the knowledge and understanding you need to answer the Big Question. You have already answered part 1 at the end of the last topic. So now it's time to answer part 2 and apply your knowledge and understanding of commercialisation in sport.

2. Explain two positive impacts of commercialisation in sport. (4 marks)

Sports facilities:

- Think about the experience for fans in new stadiums.
- Think about the playing experience for the performer.
- Think about the protection that some facilities offer from the weather and the impact this has on sporting events.

- How can I keep up to date with my team's performance?
- How can I find the up-to-date score?
- How can I watch them play?
- Can I watch highlights?
- What is happening with my favorite athlete?

179

5C Ethical Issues in Sport

This is the question we're going to be working towards answering at the end of this section.

> 3. Discuss whether performance-enhancing drugs should be legalised in sport.
>
> AO1 & AO3 – *6 marks*

Ethical Issues in Sport

As the pressure of sport increases at higher levels, performers start to challenge themselves to the ultimate physical and mental limits. This can be due partly to the increased pressures caused by the commercialisation of sport and the desire for profit or fame. This pressure and the desire for profit can lead to a point where athletes become vulnerable to corruption through things like cheating, bribery, match fixing or illegal betting.

When playing sports, it is expected that certain behavioural standards are met and performers behave in an appropriate 'sporting' way by performing within laws, conventions and expectations. This is known as **sportsmanship**.

Examples of sportsmanship may include:

- shaking hands with opponents before and after a game
- creating a tunnel after a game of rugby and clapping your opponents through
- a batter in cricket walking when they know they are out even before the umpire signals
- an athlete moving to one side if they are being lapped during a track race.

In some cases there is a shift from sportsmanship to **gamesmanship**. Gamesmanship is using whatever means necessary to overcome your opponent. Some reasons for gamesmanship include pressure to win, the importance of a high-profile game, rivalry (such as a derby game), and a win-at-all-costs attitude.

Examples of gamesmanship may include:

- time-wasting in football: kicking the ball away
- hitting the shuttlecock directly at an opponent in badminton: forcing them to lose the point by 'touching' it
- taking a long time to serve in tennis: slowing the game down to put your opponent off
- sledging: a wicketkeeper in cricket may talk to the batter to try to put them off.

Deviance in Sport

Deviant behaviours are those when a player, manager, spectator or anyone else involved knowingly breaks the rules of the sport. These behaviours take many forms, such as cheating, violence, bribery of officials and **doping**.

There are many types of cheating and sometimes they are not easy to detect. Match fixing or illegal betting may be carried out in private and so be difficult to spot.

Quick Check

Identify two different examples of sportsmanship shown in sport. **AO1**

Top Tip

Make sure you know the difference between gamesmanship and deviance. Gamesmanship is pushing the boundaries to gain an advantage or win. Deviance is playing outside the rules.

Detection of doping requires specialist testing to determine if any illegal substances have been taken. Doping is a major problem in all sports and millions of pounds are spent on testing, as well as on campaigns to eradicate it.

Other deliberate acts of **deviance** may be more easily detected, such as ball tampering in cricket or deliberately fouling a player in football.

> **Quick Check**
> Describe why a performer would use deviant behaviour in sport. **A02**

◀ It is important to behave ethically in sport and understand the boundaries of the rules.

Doping

'Doping' is the term used when athletes take substances that enhance their performance and are illegal to use within their sport. Substances are usually classed as banned when they have the following effects:

> enhance performance
> threaten the health or safety of the athlete
> go outside the rules and spirit of the sport.

Anabolic steroids are the most commonly used method of doping. These anabolic agents allow athletes to train harder, build muscle faster and recover from training much quicker. Anabolic steroids have many side effects, for example increased aggression and damage of internal organs such as the kidneys.

? Knowledge Check

Explain the difference between sportsmanship and gamesmanship.
Use these terms below to help you to explain your answer:

| winning at all costs | shaking hands |
| congratulating your opponents | time-wasting |

Sportsmanship is:
_____
_____

Gamesmanship is:
_____
_____

5C Ethical Issues in Sport

Practical Investigation

Performance-enhancing drugs are taken to augment a person's performance in sport, training or everyday lifestyle.

Method

Complete a copy of the table below by researching and highlighting the effect each drug can have.

Name of drug	Effect on performance	Side effects	Who might take it?
Anabolic steroids			
Beta blockers			
Diuretics			
Narcotic analgesics			
Stimulants			

To help you with the task, here are some examples:

> **Effect on performance:** Each drug will have its own effect on performance and will be specific to the needs of the performer taking it.

> **Side effects:** There will be both positive and negative side effects to taking drugs. The positive effects might be short-term improvements in performance but the negative effects may have a lifelong impact on the individual's health.

> **Who might take it?** Different drugs will have different effects on sporting performance, e.g., a performer involved in a sport that needs power and aggression may turn to anabolic steroids.

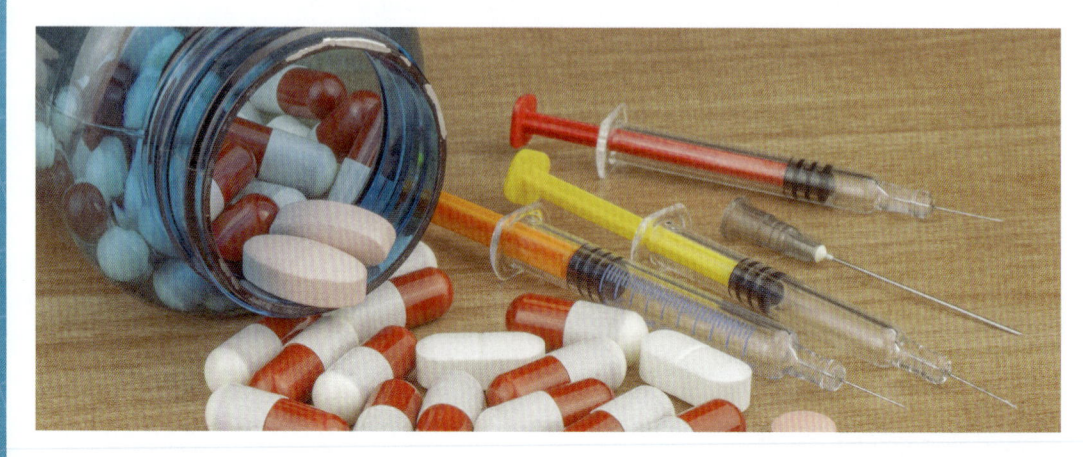

Extension

Why do you think athletes take performance-enhancing drugs?

What is the consequence for the athlete if they are caught taking performance-enhancing drugs?

▶ Drugs used to enhance performance in sport.

Chapter 5 Socio-cultural Issues in Sport...

Topic Test

Commercialisation in sport can increase deviance by putting performers under more pressure to be successful.

Identify one example of **deviance in sport.** `1 mark`

When reading the question, look at what the key words and phrases are asking you to do:

- **Command word:** This is based on the assessment objective (AO). The assessment objective for this question is AO1: you need to demonstrate your knowledge and understanding.
- **Topic:** This is the key area of study the question is about.
- **Qualifying words or phrases:** This is the specific area you need to focus on in your answer.

Doing this will help you to build your answer so that you can access the AO for each question.

Demonstrate your knowledge (AO1)

You need to **demonstrate your knowledge and understanding** of deviance in sport.

_____

_____

The pressure of winning and being successful may produce deviant behaviours in performers. Some forms of deviance are visible and easily detected but others can be difficult to identify.

THE BIG QUESTION

RECAP

C You are starting to build the knowledge and understanding you need to answer the Big Question. You have already answered parts 1 and 2; now it's time to answer part 3 and apply your knowledge and understanding of commercialisation in sport.

3. Discuss whether performance-enhancing drugs should be legalised in sport. (6 marks)

A discuss question is looking for you to explore the subject and consider advantages and disadvantages.

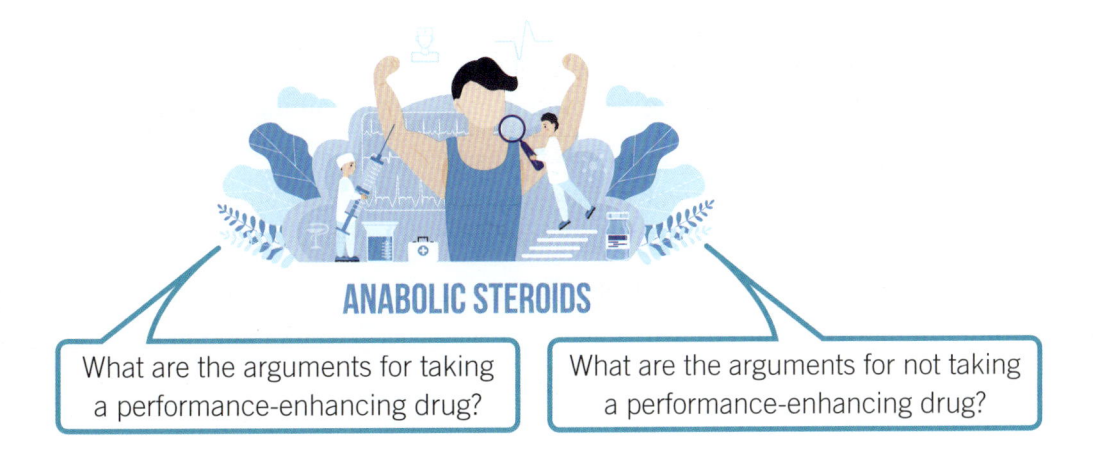

ANABOLIC STEROIDS

What are the arguments for taking a performance-enhancing drug?

What are the arguments for not taking a performance-enhancing drug?

183

Glossary

Abduction Movement away from the midline of the body. In a star jump abduction occurs when the arms are lifted out to the side.

Adduction Movement towards the midline of the body. An example is the arms returning to the side of the body when performing star jumps.

Adherence Continued participation in physical activity, without giving up.

Aerobic energy system Using oxygen in the production of energy, low- to moderate-intensity exercise.

Aerobic exercise Exercise with the use of oxygen.

Aerobic training zone The intensity of work in the aerobic zone is 60–80% of your maximum heart rate.

Agonist (prime mover) The muscle controlling the movement.

Anabolic steroids An artificial hormone that promotes muscle growth.

Anaerobic energy system The production of energy from carbohydrates without oxygen during high-intensity exercise.

Anaerobic exercise Exercise without the use of oxygen.

Anaerobic threshold The point in exercise where lactic acid is built up quicker than it can be removed.

Anaerobic training zone The intensity of work in the anaerobic zone is 80% or more of your maximum heart rate.

Antagonist The muscle that is relaxing while the agonist contracts.

Antagonistic muscle action This muscle relaxes while the agonist contracts. The opposite muscle to the agonist.

Anxiety A negative mental state, which can cause a lack of focus, nervousness and tension.

Arousal An alert mental state that increases adrenaline and concentration.

Associative stage of learning (intermediate) A performer at this stage understands the movement and is becoming more consistent, fluent and moving towards skills that are more complex.

Atherosclerosis A disease where fatty deposits build up in the arteries.

Atria The upper chambers of the heart.

Autonomous stage of learning (expert) A performer at this stage is consistent, effective, fluent and aesthetic in their movements.

Axis (plural axes) Imaginary rod which runs through the body. The body rotates around an axis.

Basic skill A simple skill requiring few decisions to be made.

Brand exposure Promoting the brand of a product or company to expose it to more people.

Breathing frequency The number of breaths taken per minute.

Calorie A unit of energy found in food or drink.

Cardiac hypertrophy The thickening of the heart muscles.

Cardiac muscle Muscle found in the walls of the heart.

Cardio-respiratory system The heart and lungs working together to supply the body with oxygen.

Cardiovascular system The heart, blood vessels and blood.

Circumduction A movement in which a joint moves in a circle. The shoulder joint of a bowler in cricket would perform circumduction when bowling the ball.

Closed skill A skill not strongly affected by the environment, performed in controlled conditions.

Cognitive stage of learning (beginner) A performer at this stage is inconsistent in their performance, making many mistakes and lacking fluency.

Commercialisation Working mostly in order to make a profit.

Commodity Something that can be bought and sold.

Complex skill A skill requiring lots of decisions to be made.

Component of fitness Fitness can be broken down into different elements specific to the needs of the individual and the demands of the activity.

Concentric contraction Isotonic muscle contraction where the muscle gets shorter under tension.

Continuous training A method of training involving continuous work for at least 20 minutes.

Contract Shortening of a muscle or reducing an angle at a joint.

Creatine phosphate system (ATP-CP system) The first anaerobic energy system, based on stores of CP in the cells, which lasts for 10 seconds.

Dehydration Having insufficient water in the body to carry out daily functioning.

Deoxygenated blood Blood carrying low levels of oxygen.

Deviance Behaviour that is well outside social, legal or sporting norms, such as cheating or breaking the rules of a sport.

Diabetes A condition that causes higher than normal blood sugar levels within the body.

Diffusion The movement of molecules from an area of high concentration to an area of low concentration.

Disability A mental or physical condition that limits the activities a person is able to perform.

Doping Using a prohibited medication, drug or treatment with the intention of improving athletic performance.

Duration How long an activity lasts.

Eccentric contraction Isotonic muscle contraction where the muscle lengthens under tension.

Effort Force applied to move a load, e.g. the working muscle.

Effort arm In a lever, the effort arm is the distance between the fulcrum (joint) and the effort (exerted by muscle).

Ethnicity A social grouping linked, for example, by a common nation, tradition or culture.

Exercise Physical activity.

Exhale Breathe out.

Expiration The act of breathing out.

Extension This is the straightening movement when a joint opens. An example of this is extension of the elbow or shoulder when a tennis player throws the ball in the air during a serve.

Glossary

Externally paced skill A skill controlled by external factors such as the opposition or a starting pistol.

Extrinsic feedback Feedback that comes from external sources, such as coaches or spectators.

Feedback Information about whether or not an action has been successful.

Fitness The ability to meet the demands of your environment.

Fitness test A way of measuring a component of fitness.

Fixed practice This involves repeatedly practising a skill.

Flexion This is the bending movement when a joint closes. An example is flexion at the elbow when performing a biceps curl.

Force Strength or energy that is used to perform an action.

Frontal axis Imaginary line the body rotates around, running through the hips from left to right.

Frontal plane Imaginary flat surface that the body moves through, dividing into back and front.

Fulcrum A fixed pivot point, e.g. a joint in the body.

Gamesmanship Bending or breaking the rules using controversial methods.

Globalisation The development or operation of something on an international scale.

Glycolysis The breakdown of carbohydrates to produce energy.

Goal-setting Deciding on targets to aim for.

Hawk-Eye Technology used to help make informed decisions, e.g. in tennis informing the umpire if the ball was in or out.

Health Physical, social and mental wellbeing, free from disease.

Hydration The process of taking in water to help carry out daily functions.

Hypertension High blood pressure above the recommended levels.

Inhale Breathe in.

Input Information taken in by the senses.

Insomnia The inability to sleep.

Inspiration The act of breathing in.

Intensity How hard an activity is or how much effort is needed to perform it.

Interval training A method of training that involves periods of high-intensity work alternating with periods of rest.

Intrinsic feedback Feedback that comes from inside the performer – it is what the performance has felt like.

Involuntary muscles Muscles that contract automatically without conscious control.

Isometric contraction The muscle is under tension but there is no movement.

Isotonic contraction The muscle under tension either shortens or lengthens.

Lactic acid A compound produced during the breakdown of glycogen when there is not enough oxygen present. A build-up of lactic acid causes fatigue.

Lactic acid system The anaerobic energy system used for high-intensity exercise for a longer duration than the ATP-CP system. It lasts for 90 seconds but produces lactic acid as a waste product.

Left atrium The upper chamber of the heart which receives oxygenated blood from the lungs.

Left ventricle The lower chamber of the heart which pumps oxygenated blood to the body.

Lever arm A rigid bar or object that produces the movement at the fulcrum of a lever, e.g. the bones of the skeletal system.

Glossary

Ligament A band of connective tissue attaching bone to bone.

Load The resistance (weight/mass) moved by a lever, e.g. the body or a dumb-bell.

Load arm In a lever, the load arm is the distance between the fulcrum and the load.

Long-term memory The part of the memory in which previous experiences are stored.

Manual guidance Guidance provided by taking a learner physically through a movement.

Mechanical advantage A lever with mechanical advantage can move a large load with relatively little effort. The effort arm is longer than the load arm.

Mechanical disadvantage A lever with mechanical disadvantage requires a relatively large effort to move a load. The effort arm is shorter than the load arm.

Mechanical guidance The use of equipment to help learners perform. Can be used as a safety measure to develop confidence and help learners get the 'feel' of the movement.

Media Means of communication including social media, television, radio, newspapers, podcasts.

Mental wellbeing Feeling well enough in one's mind to maintain a high quality of life: having a sense of purpose, living and working productively to cope with the normal stresses of day-to-day life.

Minute ventilation Volume of air breathed in or out per minute. Minute ventilation = breathing frequency × tidal volume.

Motivation The driving force that compels you to do something.

Muscle contractions The shortening of a muscle.

Notational analysis The study of tactics, strategy and movement patterns in team sports.

Open skill A skill affected by the environment, such as the opposition, weather and spectators.

Outcome goal An outcome goal relates to a specific desired outcome, for example to win a specific race or competition.

Output The result of a process, such as the action performed by an athlete after they have received an input and made a decision.

Oxygen debt The lack of sufficient oxygen after anaerobic respiration which must be repaid to restore all systems to their normal state.

Oxygenated blood Blood carrying oxygen.

Part practice This involves breaking a skill up into parts.

Participation The act of taking part in something.

Performance goal A performance goal relates to an area of performance. For example, a 100 m sprinter may focus on the sprint start.

Perpendicular Meeting at right angles.

Physical adaptations Changes to the body after following an exercise programme.

Physical literacy The set of capabilities that people acquire as a result of physical exercise, including their knowledge, physical abilities, confidence and motivation.

Physical wellbeing Being well enough to engage in physical activities, be physically healthy and maintain a high quality of life, e.g. maintenance of a healthy weight through regular exercise and a balanced diet.

Glossary

Plane An imaginary surface which runs through the body. The body moves through a plane.

Plateauing Reaching a point in training where no improvement is taking place.

Pulmonary circulatory system The system in which deoxygenated blood travels from the heart to the lungs and oxygenated blood travels from the lungs to the heart.

Qualitative data Data that gives information that can't be measured or counted, like thoughts and opinions.

Quantitative data Data that gives numerical Information (quantities).

Reliable Consistent and trustworthy. For example, the results of a reliable test are accurate and dependable.

Rep One of the times you carry out an exercise during a set.

Respiration The process of taking oxygen from the environment, creating carbon dioxide and removing carbon dioxide from the body.

Reversibility The fact that training gains can be lost if training is stopped.

Right atrium The upper chamber of the heart which receives deoxygenated blood from the body.

Right ventricle The lower chamber of the heart which pumps deoxygenated blood to the lungs.

Rotation A twisting movement at a joint. For example, a golfer will rotate the hips to perform a drive to the fairway.

Sagittal axis Imaginary line the body rotates around, running from back to front.

Sagittal plane Imaginary flat surface that the body moves through, dividing the body into left and right sides.

Sedentary A sedentary lifestyle is one that involves little or no physical activity.

Self-paced skill A skills controlled by the performer from start to finish.

Set One of the short periods of exercise you carry out between breaks during interval training.

Short-term memory The part of the memory that stores small amounts of information for a short period of time.

Skeletal muscles Muscles that are connected to the skeleton.

SMART target A target that is specific, measurable, agreed, realistic and time phased.

Smooth muscle Muscle found in the walls of internal organs that helps to maintain bodily functions.

Social media Computer-based technology allowing the sharing of social information, e.g. Twitter, Facebook, Instagram.

Social wellbeing Having a sense of belonging, including being able to interact with a range of people.

Sponsorship Providing money to an event or person in exchange for the ability to attach your business' brand name to them and gain brand exposure.

Sportsmanship Performing within the laws, conventions and expectations of the activity.

Stereotyping Making assumptions about what people with certain traits are like, or what they can or should do, for example believing that girls shouldn't play rugby.

Synovial joint A type of joint that is found between bones that move against each other.

Systemic circulatory system The system in which oxygenated blood travels from the heart to the body and deoxygenated blood travels from the body to the heart.

Technology Technology in sport refers to equipment and methods that have been developed to support or improve performance.

Tedium Boredom due to a lack of variety.

Tendon A band of connective tissue connecting muscle to bone.

Test protocol Clear instructions on how a test should be completed.

Tidal volume The amount of air that is breathed in or out during a breath.

TMO Television Match Official.

Transverse plane Imaginary flat surface that the body moves through, dividing into top and bottom.

Valid Suitable for the purpose. For example, a valid test will measure what it is supposed to measure, e.g. a 30 m sprint test will measure speed.

VAR Video Assistant Referee.

Varied practice This involves changing the practice so the performer is challenged in a variety of situations.

Vascular system A large, complex system of blood vessels.

Vasoconstriction Decrease in diameter of a blood vessel, causing a decrease in blood flow.

Vasodilation Increase in diameter of a blood vessel, causing an increase in blood flow.

Verbal guidance Guidance provided through oral instruction.

Vertical axis Imaginary line the body rotates around, running from head to feet.

Viscosity The thickness of blood.

Visual guidance Guidance using images and videos to demonstrate and analyse performance.

Vital capacity The maximum amount of air that someone can breathe out after breathing in as far as they can.

Voluntary muscle Muscle that you choose to move.

Whole practice This involves practising a skill as a whole.

Mark Scheme

Chapter 1

These mark schemes can be downloaded from https://www.illuminatepublishing.com/product/wjec-eduqas-gcse-pe

Question number	Question	Answer guidance	Marks
1.	Describe **one** possible impact of a sedentary lifestyle	Award 1 mark for identifying a possible impact of a sedentary lifestyle and a further mark for a description of the impact identified	(AO1 – 2 marks)
2.	Compare the diets of a typical marathon runner and a typical 100 m sprinter during the build-up to a race	Carbohydrates: › Marathon runner – will need a high level due to intensity and duration › Predominantly starchy carbohydrates › Carbohydrate-loading Proteins: › 100 m sprinter – will need protein for muscle growth and repair › Will need to build muscle for power and speed Fats: › Low for both so as not to carry excess weight	(AO2 – 4 marks)
3.	A downhill mountain biker needs to contract her leg muscles quickly and apply force to the pedal in an explosive act to generate speed and complete the course in the fastest time possible		
a)	Other than speed, identify **one** component of fitness the mountain biker requires	Any suitable component of fitness related to riding a bike (other than speed), e.g. muscle endurance is used when continually using the leg muscle to pedal the bike	(AO1 – 1 mark)
b)	Outline a definition of the component of fitness you identified in part a)	Accurate definition of the component of fitness identified in part a)	(AO1 – 1 mark)
c)	Identify a fitness test that can be used to test the component of fitness you named in part a)	Suitable test for the component of fitness named in part a)	(AO1 – 1 mark)

Chapter 1 Mark Scheme

Question number	Question	Answer guidance	Marks
4.	Football players need to develop speed to help them cover the pitch		
a)	Identify a method of training that a centre forward in football could use to develop their speed	Accept interval or plyometric training	(AO1 – 1 mark)
b)	Speed relies on the anaerobic energy system. What percentage of a player's maximum heart rate are they likely to be working at when sprinting down the pitch?	80% of maximum heart rate or more	(AO1 – 1 mark)
5.	Explain how an athlete can use the principles of training to improve their performance	Answer must refer to the principles of training (SPOV). S – Specificity. The training must be relevant to the component of fitness/individual/activity P – Progression. Training becomes progressively more difficult O – Overload. Pitch activities slightly above the performer's comfort zone/increase frequency, intensity and duration V – Variance. Changes in training to maintain motivation and interest	(AO2 – 4 marks)
6.	Describe one benefit of cooling down after completing a training session	Award 1 mark for: › Reduces recovery time/returns body to pre-competition levels Award 1 additional mark for the amplification: › Gradually cools body temperature › Returns muscles to their optimal length–tension relationships › Prevents venous pooling of blood in the lower extremities › Removes waste products › Replenishes nutrients/hydration levels › Reduces effects of DOMS › Repays oxygen debt Award a maximum of 1 mark for two amplifications.	(AO1 – 2 marks)

Mark Scheme

Chapter 2

Question number	Question	Answer guidance	Marks
1.	A javelin thrower needs to generate speed and power to throw the javelin in a competition		
a)	Identify the bones that articulate at the elbow joint as the thrower prepares to release the javelin	Award 1 mark for one or two correctly identified. Award 2 marks for all three: › Humerus › Radius › Ulna	(AO1 – 2 marks)
b)	Identify and explain which muscle fibre type is most likely to be used in the run-up	Muscle fibre type: Fast twitch/Type II (1 mark) Award additional 1 mark for explanation (one of the following): › Generate explosive movement › Generate speed/power › Short explosive movement › Use no oxygen/anaerobic	(AO1 – 2 marks)
2. a)	Complete the diagram of the heart by writing the letters from the diagram in the table next to the correct chamber	Award 2 marks if all four are correct. Award 1 mark if three or fewer are correct: Right atrium A Left atrium C Right ventricle B Left ventricle D	(AO1 – 2 marks)
b)	Explain how the alveoli enable gaseous exchange to take place	Award 1 mark for any of the following points made (to a maximum of three): › Alveoli have thin, moist walls which allow diffusion to take place › Capillaries are wrapped around alveoli walls, which increases efficiency of diffusion › Oxygen enters blood stream through the thin wall of capillaries › Oxygen attaches to haemoglobin in red blood cells	(AO2 – 3 marks)

Chapter 2 Mark Scheme

Question number	Question	Answer guidance	Marks
		› Oxygen leaves the alveoli and enters the blood stream to be used in the body › Carbon dioxide leaves the blood stream and enters the alveoli to be exhaled	
3.	Look at the image of a 100m race		
a)	Identify the dominant energy system used in this event	Anaerobic energy system/lactic acid system/anaerobic glycolysis system	(AO1 – 1 mark)
b)	Identify three characteristics of the energy system identified above	Award 1 mark for any of the following points made (to a maximum of three): › No oxygen required › A fast supply of energy › Creatine phosphate is the fuel used › Used for high-intensity activities › Used in short duration activities › Leads to oxygen debt/lactic acid build-up › Limited amount of creatine phosphate/CP stored in the muscles	(AO1 – 3 marks)
4.	Explain the long-term adaptations to the cardiovascular system after following an eight-week training programme	Award 1 mark for any of the following points made (to a maximum of three): › Increase in size of the heart (cardiac hypertrophy) › Decrease resting stroke volume › Increase in cardiac output › Increase in the number of red blood cells › Reduction of resting heart rate › Increase in number of capillaries	(AO2 – 3 marks)

Mark Scheme

Chapter 3

Question number	Question	Answer guidance	Marks
1.	Athletes preparing for major competitions require a range of movements to compete fluently		
a)	A gymnast performs a handstand during a routine. Explain which muscle contraction takes place to hold a balance	Award 1 mark for: › Isometric contraction Award 3 additional marks for amplification: › No lengthening or shortening of the muscle › Static movement › Holding a balance	(AO2 – 4 marks)
b)	In order to perform a split leap, a gymnast pushes off the floor with one foot. (i) Identify the class of lever shown in the image	Second class lever	(AO2 – 1 mark)
	(ii) Explain the mechanical advantages and disadvantages of the class of lever shown in the image	Award 1 mark for any two of the following points made: › Can lift heavy loads › More efficient › Load is closer to the fulcrum › Shorter load arm › Longer effort arm	(AO1 – 2 marks)
c)	A gymnast performs a routine that includes a somersault and a cartwheel (i) The gymnast runs forwards to gain speed in preparation for the somersault. Identify the plane of movement she moves through.	Sagittal plane	(AO1 – 1 mark)
	(ii) Identify the axis of movement that the gymnast's body rotates around while she performs a cartwheel	Sagittal axis	(AO1 – 1 mark)

Chapter 3 Mark Scheme

Question number	Question	Answer guidance	Marks
d)	Explain, using appropriate examples, how a gymnast and a coach may use technology to help improve the gymnast's performance	Award 4 marks for identifying any two of the following along with corresponding amplification: › Develop technique › Identify strength and weakness › Identify tactics › Monitoring progress Amplification points: › Develop technique through video analysis by refining performance › The use of data to provide effective feedback › The use of data, video replay for motivation › Data analysis to identify training focus › Monitoring progress through use of data analysis from GPS or heart rate monitors › Use of technology to identify strategies and tactics › Use of technology to identify strength and weakness of the opposition	(AO2 – 4 marks)

Mark Scheme

Chapter 4

Question number	Question	Answer guidance	Marks
1.	Before you start to plan a personal fitness programme, it is important to know what you want to improve Discuss how goal-setting can help you plan a personal fitness programme	› Ensures/gives/enables success › Recognises progress/progress made obvious/measurable/recorded › Encouraging and exciting › Gives evidence that you have become faster/stronger/fitter › Motivating › Control over what happens › Identifies challenges › Encourages adherence	(AO3 – 6 marks)
2.	Feedback is an important component of information processing during sport Using examples from sport, explain why feedback is important when learning a new skill	Award a maximum of 2 marks for effects of feedback. Award a maximum of 2 marks for examples. › Motivates you to try harder › Reinforces good performance › Helps you to improve › Helps you to realise your errors › Increases confidence › Increases adherence levels	(AO2 – 4 marks)
3.	Compare how coaches use guidance for performers in the cognitive and autonomous stages of learning	Award a maximum of 2 marks per stage of learning. › Mechanical guidance involves the use of equipment to help support the learner/shape the skill › Mechanical guidance is best used during the cognitive stage of learning as it helps the performer learn a movement while building confidence and getting a sense of how it should feel › Manual guidance is useful for all stages of learning. Uses physical support, which develops a kinaesthetic awareness and gives confidence to the learner	(AO2 – 4 marks)

Question number	Question	Answer guidance	Marks
		› Verbal guidance should be simple and generic for learners at the cognitive stage › Verbal guidance should be technical and specific for learners at the autonomous stage › Visual guidance can be used to introduce learners at the cognitive stage to movements they have never seen › Visual guidance can be used to aid analysis of movement at the autonomous stage	
4.	Evaluate two mental preparation techniques a cyclist might use before a race	Answer must include evaluation to gain full marks. Relevant points include: **Imagery/visualisation** › Imagining cycling the route/map › Imagining the race using different senses, e.g. 'seeing' yourself overtaking an opponent › Picturing a successful outcome, e.g. lifting the trophy, winning the race **Mental rehearsal** › Picturing the component parts of the race › Imagining what to do to be successful, e.g. when to accelerate › Imagining using different senses, e.g. persevering as you 'feel' the fatigue in your legs **Impact of techniques** › Confidence › Control › Challenge › Commitment › Arousal › Anxiety › Motivation › Performance	(AO3 – 5 marks)

Chapter 4 Mark Scheme

Question number	Question	Answer guidance	Marks
5.	BMX freestylers are regarded as having a high level of skill Explain two characteristics of a skilful performance using sporting examples	Award a maximum of 2 marks per characteristic for an explanation and an example. Answers do not have to relate to BMX freestyling. Answers should refer to characteristics of a skilful performance, with relevant explanations, for example: › Effectiveness (producing the desired result) › Accuracy (performing with precision) › Consistency (performing to the same standard each time) › Control (executing a skill with a high degree of control) › Confidence (self-belief when executing a skill) › Efficiency (using less energy and executing the skill relatively effortlessly) › Technique (including fluency, preparation, action and recovery) › Aesthetics (executing the skill in a way that is pleasing to watch) Accept explanations in the form of relevant examples from sport, for example a skilful centre in hockey should: › move around the whole pitch, be well balanced with fluent movements, footwork and stick control. Show good posture, speed and reactions › select the correct pass at the correct moment and time. Passes will also be refined, precise and effortless	(AO2 – 4 marks)

Question number	Question	Answer guidance	Marks
		<ul><li>have the ability to read the game, by watching opponents' actions</li><li>play to own strengths and opponent's weaknesses (tactics)</li><li>appear to move effortlessly and carry out actions with ease and without thinking</li><li>perform a wide variety of skills, shots and passes</li></ul>	

Mark Scheme

Chapter 5

Question number	Question	Answer guidance	Marks
1.	Statistics show that boys are more likely to participate in sports than girls. Discuss strategies that have been used to increase the involvement of girls in sport	Any suitable strategies with valid discussion. Strategies could include: > campaigns like 'This Girl Can' > female-only activities such as swimming and exercise classes > girls' clubs and teams Discussion should include relevant points, e.g.: > increase self-esteem > raise awareness of opportunities > combat stereotypes > Some girls may feel more comfortable in female-only spaces	(AO3 – 6 marks)
2.	Explain two positive impacts of commercialisation in sport	Award a maximum of 2 marks for two valid responses and 2 marks for valid explanations, for example: > can enhance performance because sponsorship money allows better resources/more training > improves experience for spectators because of the availability of worldwide media streaming > can increase participation as it raises the profile of sports > makes money for the businesses and teams involved	(AO2 – 4 marks)
3.	Discuss whether performance-enhancing drugs should be legalised in sport	Answers should mention positive and negative points. Maximum of 2 marks for demonstrating knowledge and 4 marks for discussion.	(AO1 – 2 marks; AO3 – 4 marks)

Question number	Question	Answer guidance	Marks
		Answers could discuss the physical, moral, psychological, social implications of performance-enhancing drugs, for example: › cheating and integrity › gamesmanship and sportsmanship › the 'true spirit' of sports › fairness and unfairness in competition › role models › impacts on the health of athletes › enhancing performance makes it exciting to watch › higher records › allowing athletes greater personal achievements › showing respect and passion › giving sport a bad name	

Appendices

Chapter 1

These appendices can be downloaded from https://www.illuminatepublishing.com/product/wjec-eduqas-gcse-pe

Appendix 1.1 Revision Mat – A Practical Investigation

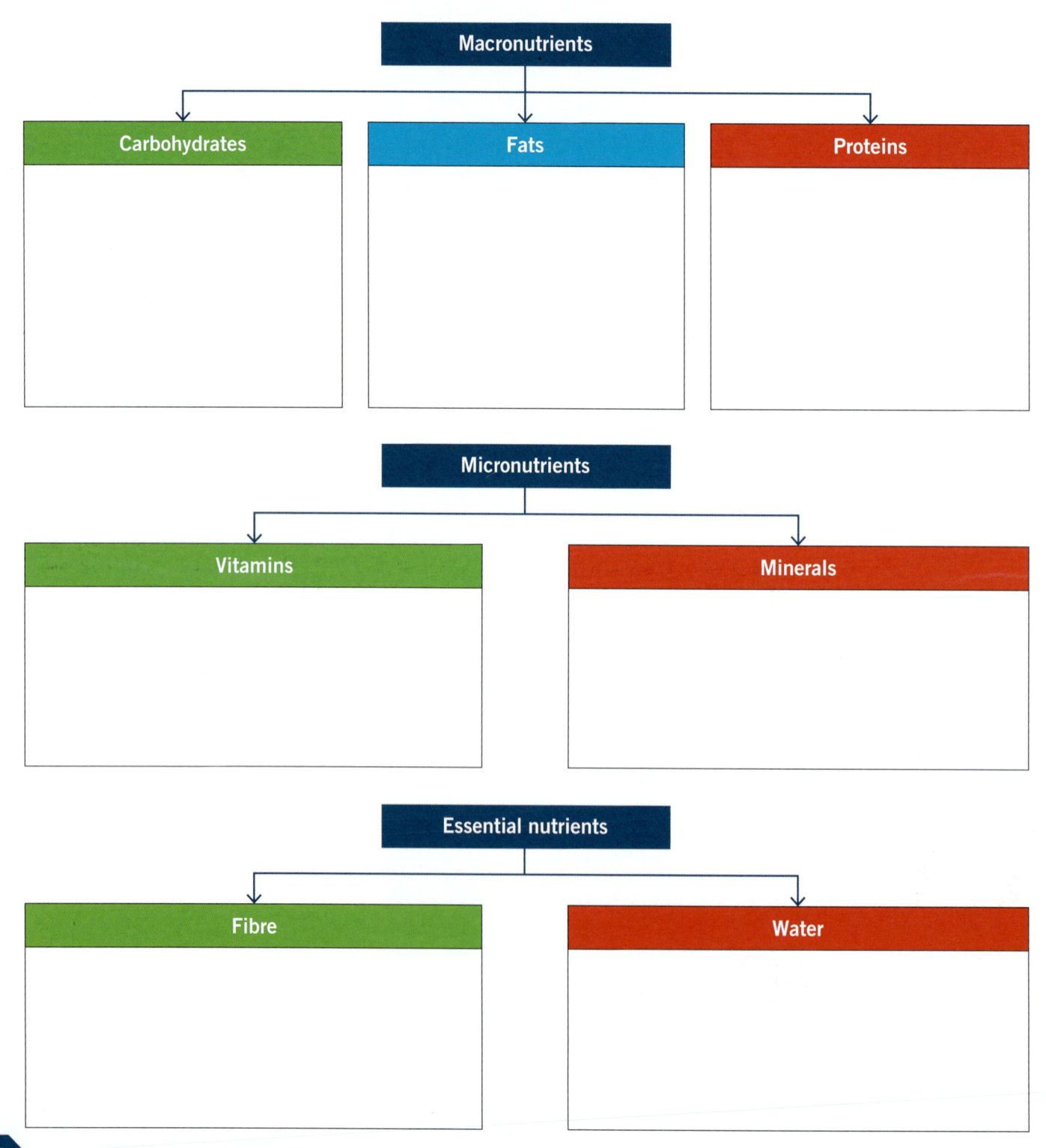

Macronutrients
- Carbohydrates
- Fats
- Proteins

Micronutrients
- Vitamins
- Minerals

Essential nutrients
- Fibre
- Water

Appendix 1.2 Revision Wheel – A Practical Investigation

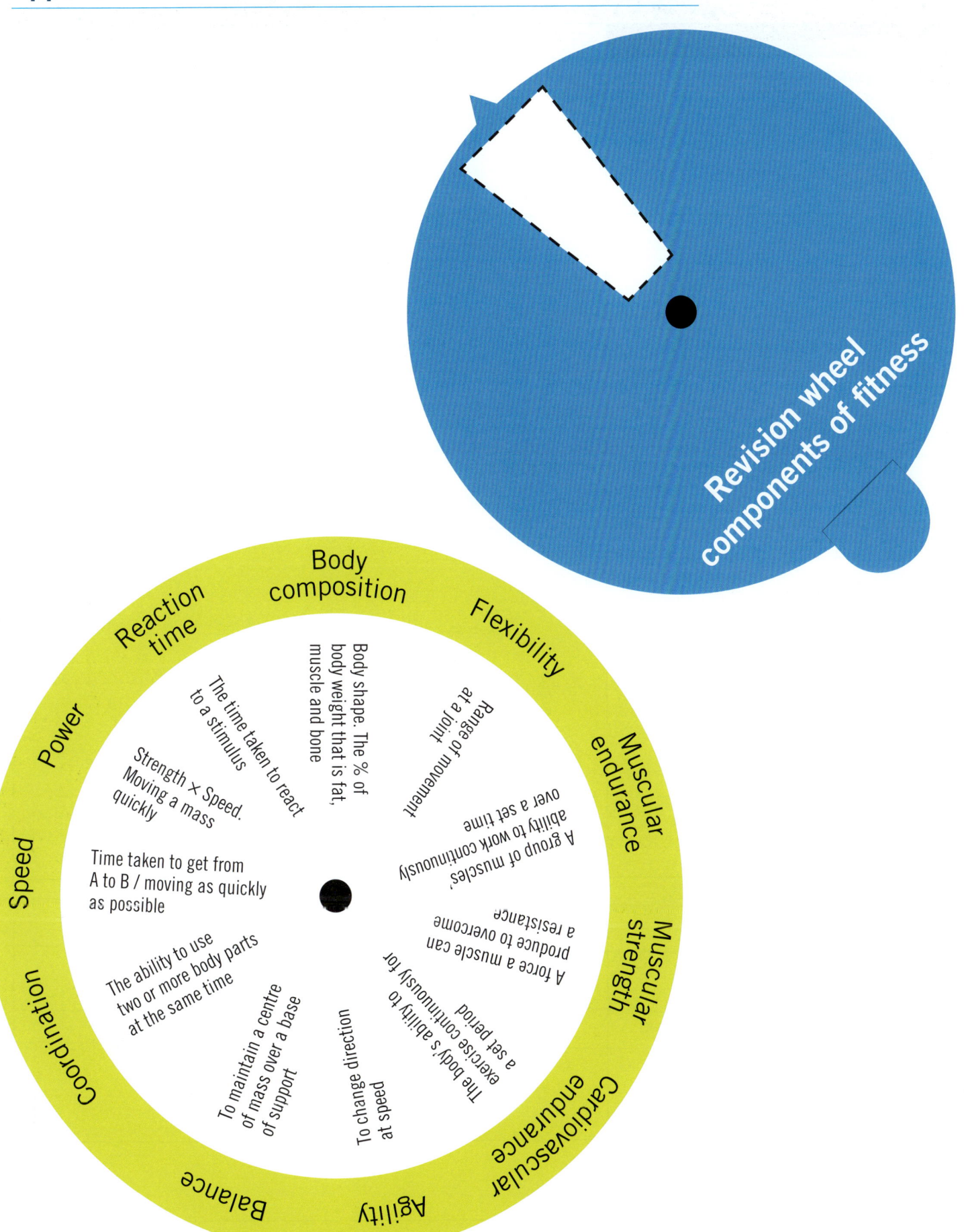

Revision wheel components of fitness

- **Body composition** — Body shape. The % of body weight that is fat, muscle and bone
- **Flexibility** — Range of movement at a joint
- **Muscular endurance** — A group of muscles' ability to work continuously over a set time
- **Muscular strength** — A force a muscle can produce to overcome a resistance
- **Cardiovascular endurance** — The body's ability to exercise continuously for a set period
- **Agility** — To change direction at speed
- **Balance** — To maintain a centre of mass over a base of support
- **Coordination** — The ability to use two or more body parts at the same time
- **Speed** — Time taken to get from A to B / moving as quickly as possible
- **Power** — Strength × Speed. Moving a mass quickly
- **Reaction time** — The time taken to react to a stimulus

203

Chapter 1

Appendix 1.3 Training Session – A Practical Investigation

Training type:	
About this training method:	
My exercise(s):	
Equipment:	
Description of session: What did you do? Was it mostly aerobic or anaerobic? Which component of fitness did you develop?	
Advantages of this training method:	
Disadvantages of this training method:	
Sport or activity this is suitable for:	

Appendix 1.4 Warm-up Plan – A Practical Investigation

Main activity _____

Phase of warm-up	Example	Why?
Heart raiser		
Mobility/stretching		
Skills-based activity		

Appendices

Chapter 2

Appendix 2.1 Skeletal System – A Practical Investigation

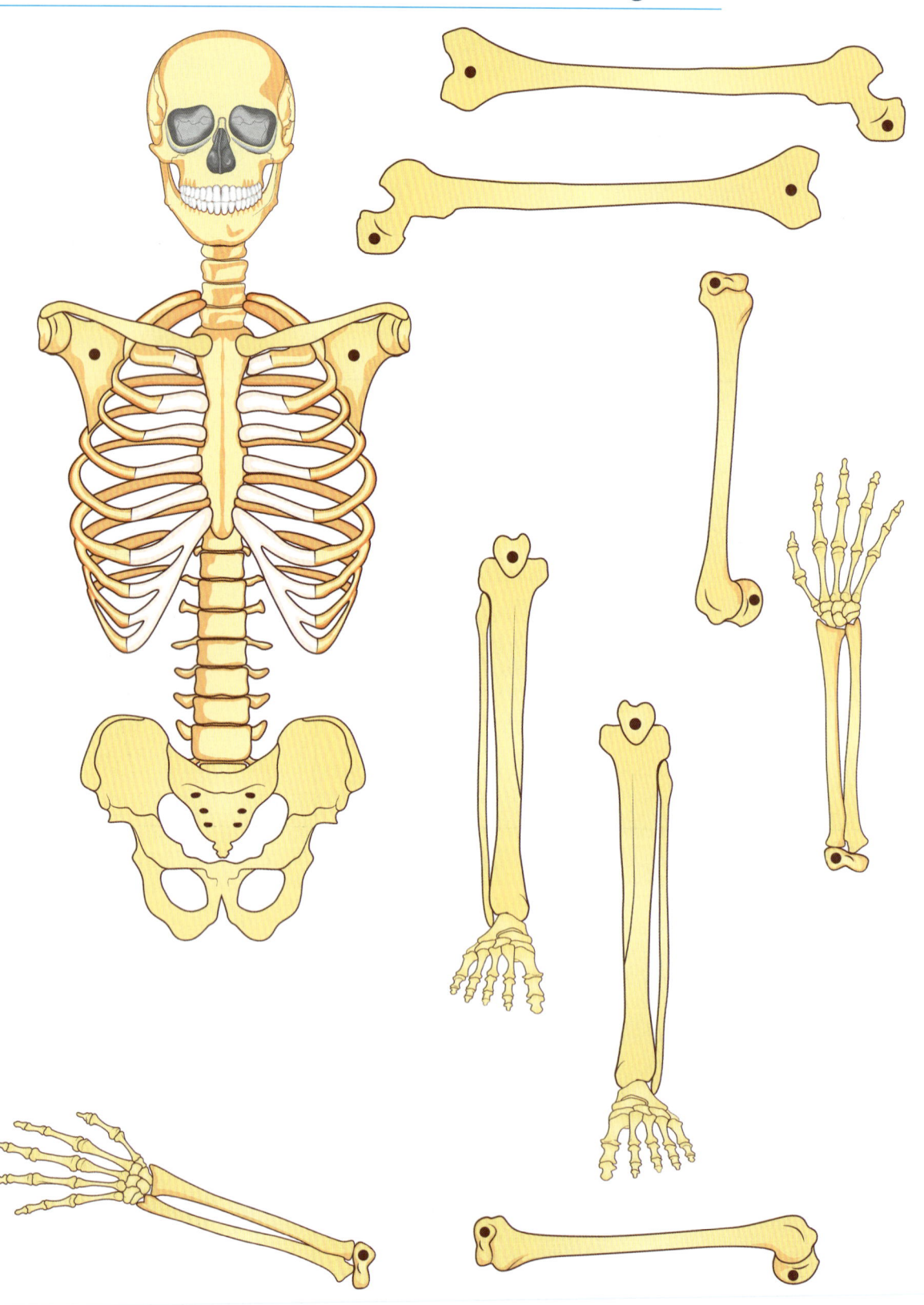

Chapter 2 Appendices

Appendix 2.2 Circulatory Systems – A Practical Investigation

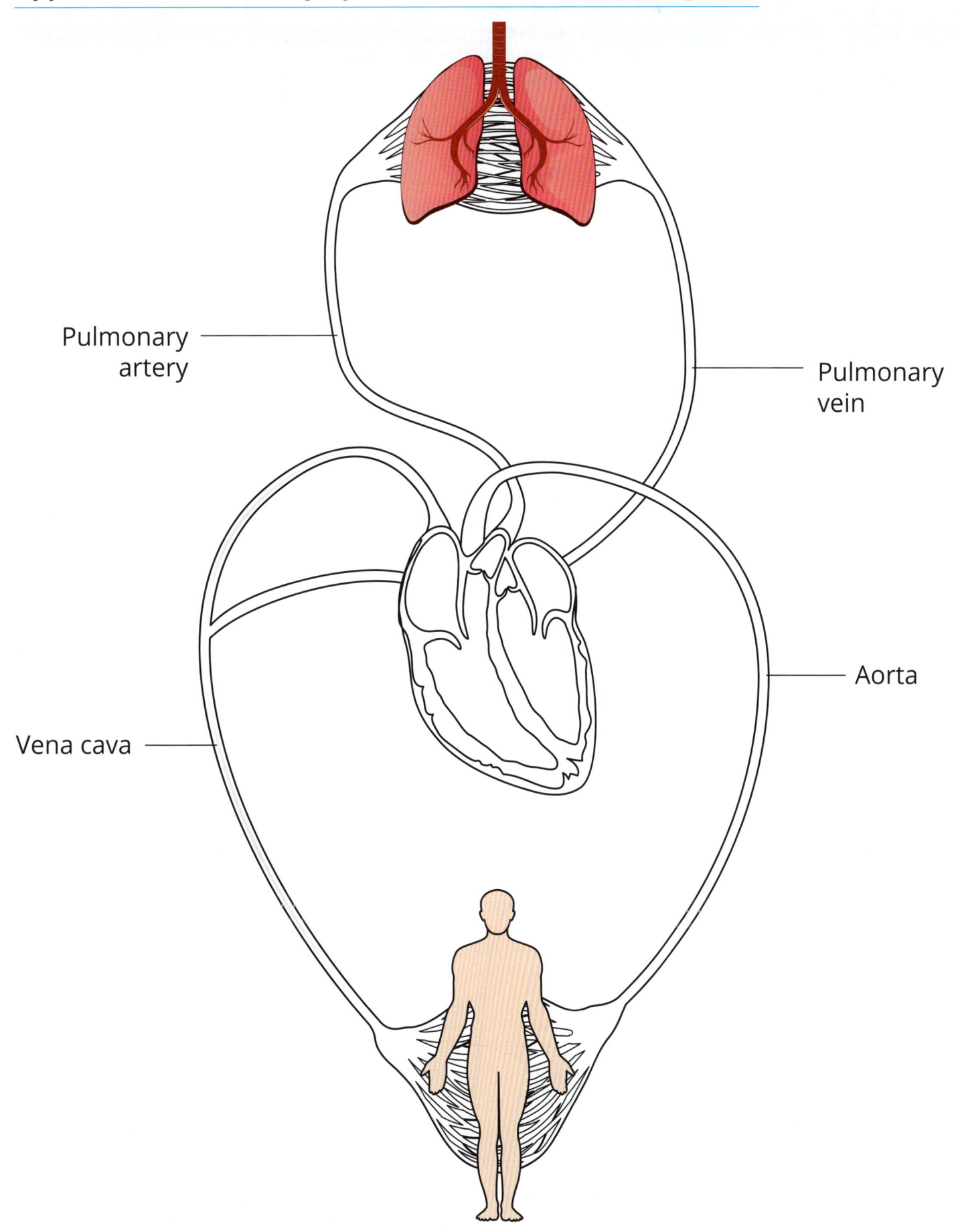

Pulmonary artery

Pulmonary vein

Aorta

Vena cava

207

Chapter 2

Appendix 2.3 Energy Continuum – A Practical Investigation

Task	Comments
Sprint for ten seconds	
Sprint for 90 seconds	
Run continuously for ten minutes	

Reflect on the practical activity and then label and highlight the following lines on the graph:

› Label the ATP-CP system and highlight in **green**.
› Label the lactic acid system and highlight in **blue**.
› Label the aerobic system and highlight in **red**.

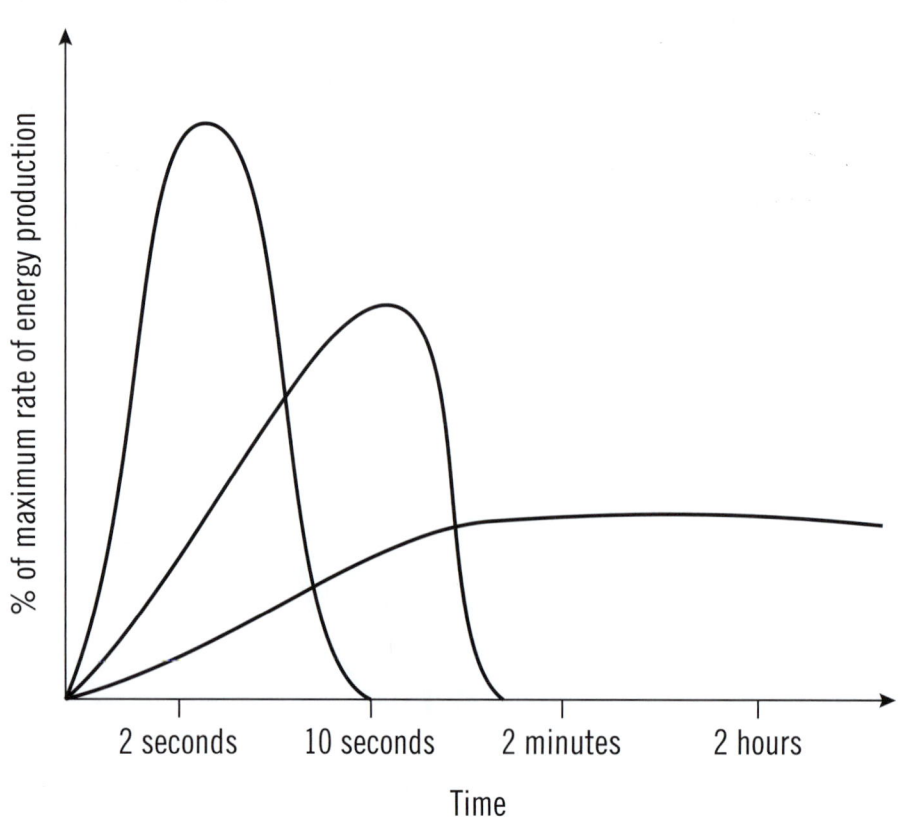

Chapter 3 Appendices

Appendix

Chapter 3

Appendix 3.1 Antagonistic Muscle Model – A Practical Investigation

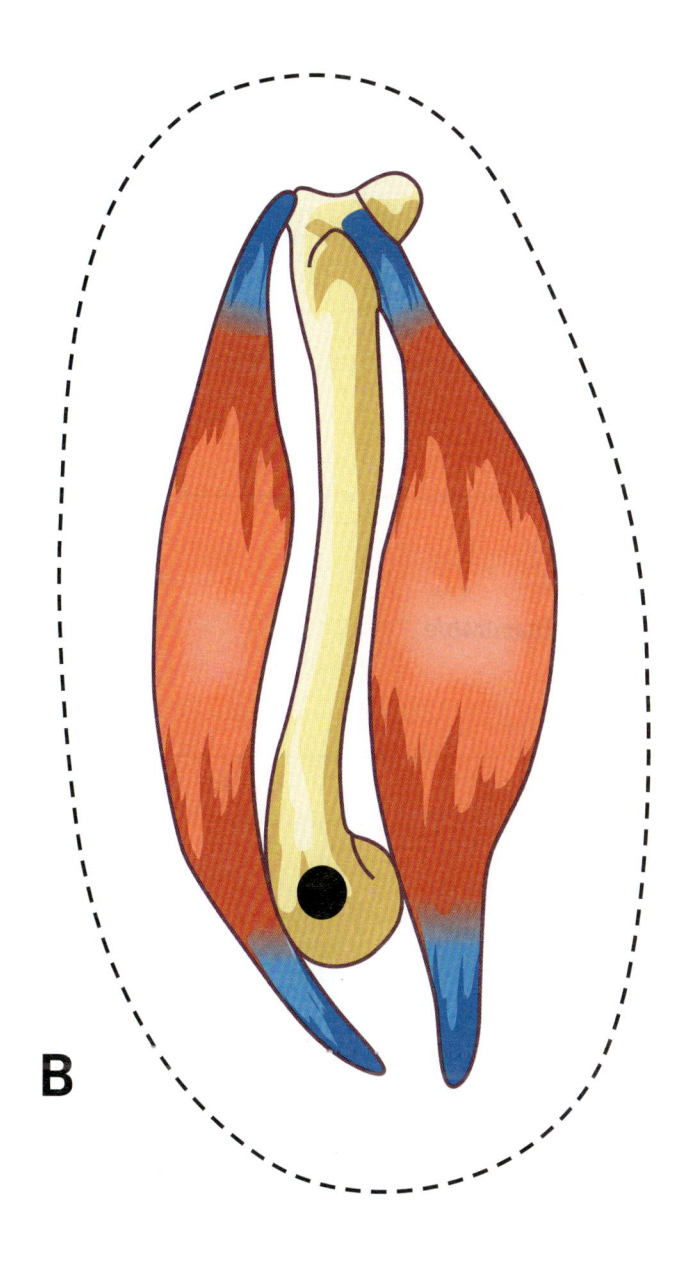

A

B

209

Appendices

Chapter 4

Appendix 4.1 SMART targets – A Practical Investigation

	Goal	
S	Specific	
M	Measurable	
A	Agreed	
R	Realistic	
T	Time phased	

Chapter 4 Appendices

Appendix 4.2 Information processing model – A Practical Investigation

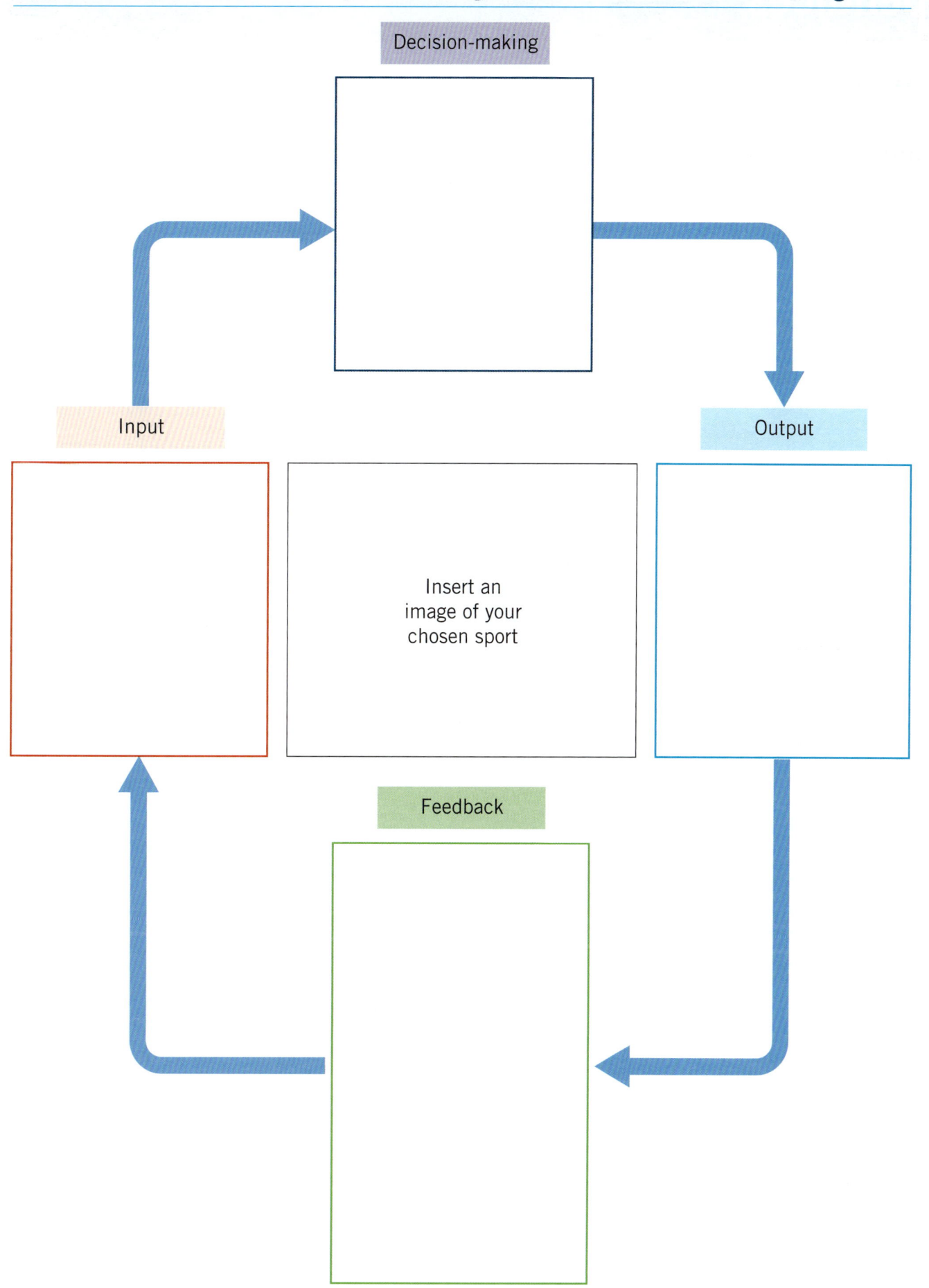

Decision-making

Input

Output

Insert an image of your chosen sport

Feedback

211

Appendices

Chapter 5

Appendix 5.1 Factors Affecting Participation – A Practical Investigation

Using the spider diagram below, describe how each of the factors have or had an influence on your participation in sport and physical activity.

Factors affecting participation:
- Gender
- Ethnicity
- Disability
- Society
- Cost
- Access
- Role models
- Peers
- Family
- Age

Influences on my participation in sport and physical activity:

_____
_____
_____
_____
_____
_____

Appendix 5.2 Commercialisation in Sport: Golden Triangle – A Practical Investigation

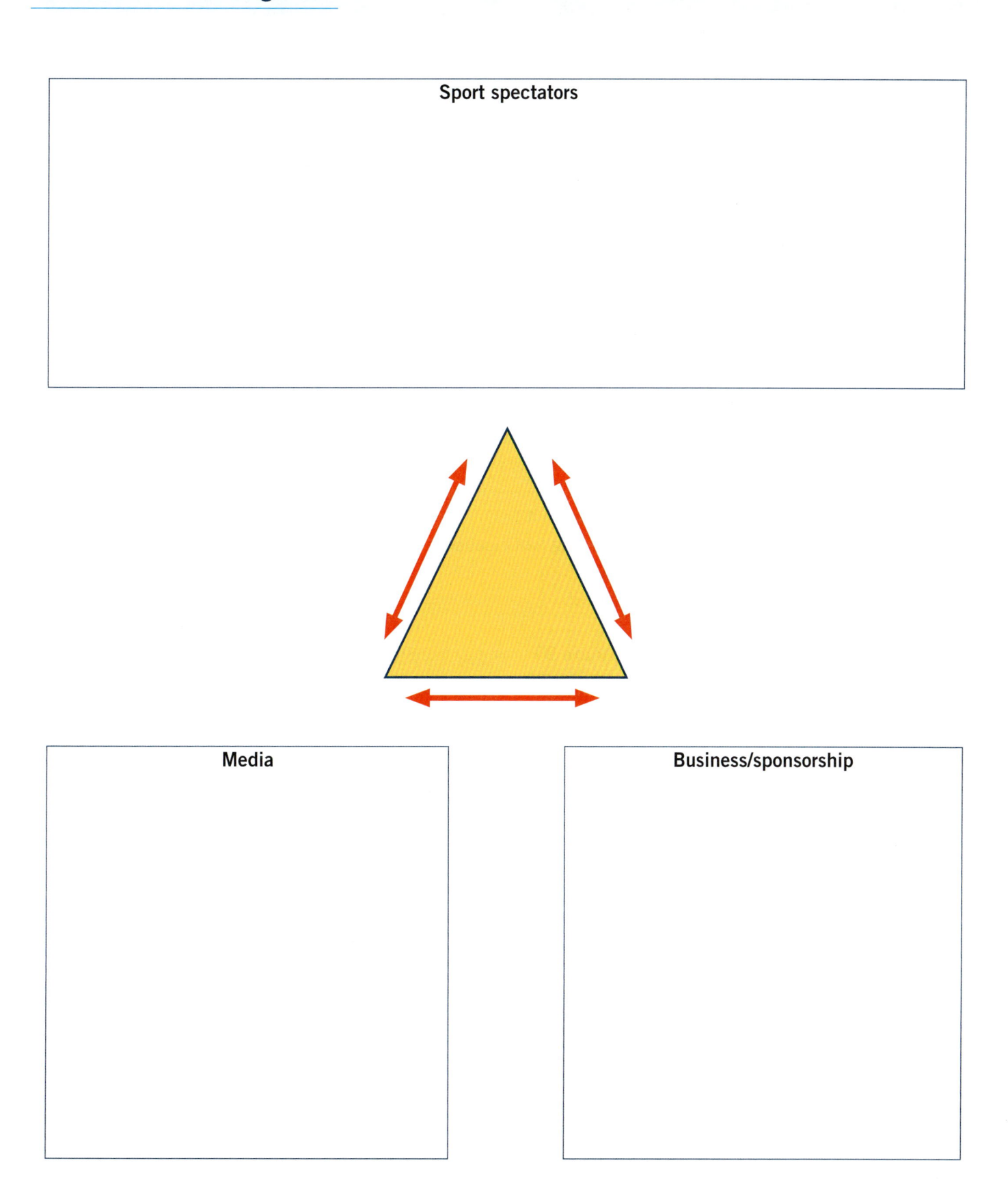

Sport spectators

Media	Business/sponsorship

Index

A
abdominal curl test 31
accessibility 43, 120, 124–125, 162–163, 165–168, 170, 175
adaptations of the body *see* physical adaptations
adherence 132, 137, 150–151
advertising 10, 125, 161, 177
aerobic
    energy system 38, 59, 76, 78–79, 81
    exercise 7, 57, 76–79, 83, 135
    fitness 41
    threshold 41
    training zone 39, 41, 43
age as factor affecting participation 162–163, 170
agility 28, 30, 34–35
agonist 95
alternate hand throw 30
alveoli 66, 68–69, 75, 86
anabolic steroids 181–182
anaerobic
    energy system 38, 45, 59, 77–79, 81
    exercise 7, 45, 57, 76–79, 83
    fitness 41
    glycolysis 76, 78
    threshold 41, 78
    training zone 39, 41, 43
anatomical position 110, 116
antagonist 95
antagonistic muscle actions 8, 91, 94–97
anxiety 150, 153
arousal 150
arteries 68, 71–72, 86
associative stage of learning 138, 144–146
atherosclerosis 18
ATP-CP system 77–78, 80–81
atria (left/right atrium) 66–67, 73, 75
autonomous stage of learning 138, 144–146, 149, 154
axes of movement/rotation 8, 91, 110, 113–115, 117, 119

B
balance 28, 30, 34–35, 92, 99
basic skills 154
biceps 31, 58–59, 92–93, 103, 111
blood pressure 18, 33, 68, 86; *also see* hypertension
blood vessels 66, 69, 71, 78, 84, 87
body composition 29, 31, 34
body fat 17, 31, 41
body image 18, 164
bones 23, 29, 34, 57–58, 60–63, 65, 85, 92, 94, 97, 100–101
    types of 61
brand exposure 174
breathing frequency 70, 86

C
calories 22–24, 33
campaigns 10, 162, 164–167, 181
capillaries 69, 71, 86
carbo-loading 24
carbohydrates 23–25, 51, 77–79
carbon dioxide 66, 69, 71, 73, 78–79, 84, 87
cardiac hypertrophy 86
cardiac output (Q) 68, 84, 86
cardiac values 7, 68
cardio-respiratory system 7, 60, 66, 84
cardiovascular endurance 29, 32, 39, 41
cardiovascular system 17, 84–86, 89
circuit training 38–39, 42

Index

circulatory system 72–73
closed skills 146, 154
coaching
    feedback 139, 143
        goal-setting 131–133, 135
        guidance 144–145, 149
        technology 8, 121–124, 126, 129
cognitive stage of learning 138, 144–146, 154
commercialisation of sport 10, 124–125, 161, 174–177, 179–180
commodity 174
concentric contraction 93–94
confidence 17–18, 50, 124, 145, 150, 154–155, 162–163, 165–166, 168–169
continuous training 38–39, 42
cool-down 6, 15, 38–39, 51, 53
Cooper's 12-minute run 32–33
coordination 28, 30, 34–35
creatine phosphate (CP) system 77; *also see* ATP-CP system
curriculum 10, 161, 167–171

D

data analysis 9–10, 33, 59, 121–124, 145, 164
decision-making 24, 79, 138, 140–141, 157
dehydration 24, 51, 79
delayed onset of muscle soreness (DOMS) 51
deviance 10, 121–122, 161, 180–181
diabetes 17–18
diaphragm 69, 86
diastolic pressure 68
diet 6, 15, 17–18, 22–25, 27; *also see* nutrition
diffusion 57, 69, 71
digital media 124–125
disability as factor affecting participation 10, 162, 165–167, 170
doping 180–181
duration of activity 7, 16, 22, 24, 27, 38, 43, 46, 68, 70, 77–78, 80, 83–85, 135

E

eccentric contraction 93–94
effort (force) 100–105, 107, 109
effort arm 104–105
energy balance 6, 22–24
essential nutrients 25
ethical issues 180–183
ethnicity as factor affecting participation 162, 164–165, 170
exercise
    frequency 43, 46, 135
        duration 7, 16, 22, 24, 27, 38, 43, 46, 68, 70, 77–78, 80, 84–85, 135
    intensity 7, 16, 22–24, 38–39, 41, 43, 45–46, 50–51, 58, 70, 76–81, 83–85
    long-term effects of 85–87
    short-term effects of 84
exhale 66, 69, 73, 84
expiration 69
externally paced skills 146, 154–155
extra-curricular activities 161, 168–171
extrinsic
    feedback 139–141, 143
    motivation 9, 151

F

fartlek 38–39, 42
fast twitch muscle fibres 59
fatigue 59, 77–78, 83–84
fats 23, 25, 78–79
feedback 121–122, 131, 138–141, 144
FID *see* progressive overload
first class lever 101–102, 104–105, 107
fitness
    aerobic 41
    anaerobic 41
    components of 15, 28–35, 38–39, 41, 43
    maintaining 47
    measuring 6, 15, 28–35, 121–122
    personal programme 9, 131–132, 135, 137

Index

relationship with health/exercise/
wellbeing 15–16
tests 28–35, 135
fixed practice 146
flexibility 29, 31, 34–35, 39, 49, 87,
163
football 15, 38, 45, 53, 107, 135,
166–167, 180–181
force 28–29, 37, 100–101, 105
frontal plane/axis 8, 113–117
fulcrum 100–104, 107, 109

G

game-specific activity 50
gamesmanship 10, 180
gaseous exchange 57, 66, 68–69, 71,
73, 75, 84, 86–87
gender as factor affecting participation
10, 162, 164, 166, 170, 173
goal-setting 9, 131–135
globalisation 10, 161, 175
golden triangle 174, 176
guidance 9, 131, 144–145

H

haemoglobin 69, 86
hamstrings 39, 59, 92, 95
hand grip dynamometer 32
handstand 28, 91–92, 99
Hawk-Eye 123
health
agenda 166
cardiac 41
definition of 6, 16, 19
factors contributing to 22–24
measuring 6, 15, 28–35, 121–122
mental 16, 18
physical 16, 18, 132
questionnaire 33
relationship with fitness/exercise/
wellbeing 15
social 16, 18
health-related components of fitness
28–29, 31–33

heart 17, 41, 57–58, 66–69, 71–73,
86; *also see* heart rate
diagram 66
heart raiser 50, 52
heart rate (HR) 33, 38–41, 43, 45,
50–52, 68, 79, 84, 86, 120–122
heart rate monitor 33, 120–122
heart reducer 51, 55
high jumper 159
hydration 23–24, 78–79
hypertension 17–18
hypertrophy 85–86

I

Illinois agility run 30
imagery 150
information processing 9, 131, 138–
141
inhale 66, 84, 86
input 138, 140–141
insomnia 18
inspiration 69
intensity of activity 7, 16, 22–24,
38–39, 41, 43, 46, 50–51, 58, 70,
76–81, 83–85
interval training 38–39
intrinsic
feedback 139–141, 143
motivation 9, 151
isometric contraction 94
isotonic contraction 93–94

J

joint
abduction 59, 62, 92, 111–112,
117
adduction 59, 62, 92, 111–112
circumduction 58, 62, 111
extension 59, 62, 92–93, 95,
111–112, 117
flexion 59, 62, 92–93, 95, 111–112,
117
rotation 8, 59, 62, 92, 110–111,
113–115, 117

L

lactic acid 41, 51, 66, 71, 76–81, 84, 87
lever arm 100–101
lever systems 8, 60–61, 91, 100–107, 109
   classification of 8, 101–103, 109
   main functions of 104
   mechanical advantage 8, 91, 100, 104–107, 109
   mechanical disadvantage 8, 91, 105–107
lifestyle choices 17–19
ligaments 7, 62
load 94, 100–105, 107, 109
load arm 104–105
long-term memory (LTM) 138, 141
lungs 7, 57, 67, 69–70, 72–73, 86–87
   volume 7, 86

M

macronutrients 25
manual guidance 145
marathon runner 15, 22, 27, 29, 59, 78
maximum heart rate 15, 38–41, 43, 45
mechanical advantage/disadvantage *see* lever systems
   guidance 144–145, 149
media coverage 165, 167, 174
media, role in commercialisation/globalisation 10, 161, 174–177
mental preparation 9, 131, 150–151
mental rehearsal 150–151
methods of training 6, 15, 38–40, 42–43, 46–47, 49
micronutrients 25
minerals 23, 25
minute ventilation 70
mobility 39, 50–51, 53, 55
motivation 9, 16–18, 30, 46, 49–50, 120, 131–133, 150–151, 153, 168
mountain biking 15, 28, 37
multi-stage fitness test (MSFT) 32, 135
muscles
   cardiac 58
   contraction 8, 28, 37, 51, 55, 58–59, 68–69, 84, 86, 91–97, 99, 104
   diagram of 59, 92
fibres 7, 57, 59, 65
growth 27
involuntary 58
smooth 58
voluntary 58
muscular endurance 29, 31, 34–35
muscular strength 29, 32, 34–35
muscular system 7, 58, 62, 84, 105
muscular-skeletal system 7, 57–63, 85

N

notational analysis 123
nutrients, function of 23
nutrition 6, 15–16, 22–25, 78–79; *also see* diet

O

obesity 17–18
officials, technology for 123–124, 126
one rep max test 32–33
open skills 146, 154
outcome goal 132
output 138–141
overload 15, 43, 46, 49
oxygen 7, 50–51, 55, 66–67, 69, 71, 73, 76 79, 83–84, 86–87
oxygen debt 77

P

part practice 146
participation in sport 10, 120, 125, 161–171
   factors affecting 161–165, 170–171
   increasing 10, 161–163, 165–168
performance 10, 24, 46, 53, 87, 91,

Index

110, 120–126, 131, 139–141, 144–145, 150, 154–156, 161, 175, 180–182
   analysing/evaluating 110, 120–125, 129, 139–141, 144–145
   characteristics of a skilled performance 131, 154–156
   equipment 120–122, 134, 145
   goal 132
   monitoring 120, 122
performance-enhancing drugs 161, 180–183
personal fitness programme *see* fitness
physical activity 6, 9–10, 13, 18, 24, 33, 131, 154, 161–163, 166, 168–170
physical activity readiness questionnaire (PAR-Q) 33
physical adaptations 47, 84–85, 89
physical education 10, 161, 168–171; *also see* curriculum
physical literacy 10, 161, 168
planes of movement 8, 91, 110–113, 117, 119
plateauing 46
plyometric training 38, 40, 42
power 28–29, 31, 34–35, 39–41, 49, 57–58, 65, 78, 182
practice 9, 131, 141, 144–147
   types 146–147
press-up test 31
principles of training (SPOV) 6, 15, 46
progression 46
progressive overload (FID) 6, 46
proteins 23–25, 51, 78
provision for sport 10, 161, 167–169
pulmonary circulatory system 72–73

Q

quadriceps 39, 59, 92, 95
qualitative data 122–123
quantitative data 122–123
questionnaire 33

R

race as factor affecting participation 10, 164–165
racism 165, 167
range of movement 29, 34–35, 39, 50, 91–92, 99–100, 109–110, 119–120, 129
reaction time 29, 31, 34–35
recovery 47, 51, 55, 80, 87, 120–121, 181
refuelling 51, 55
reliability 30, 33, 124
rep 32–33, 39–40
respiration 66
respiratory system 7, 17, 69, 84–86
respiratory values 70
reversibility 47
revision wheel 34–35
role models 125, 162–164, 167, 170, 175
ruler 31

S

sagittal plane/axis 8, 112–117
second class lever 101–105
sedentary 6, 15–19, 21, 41, 168
self-confidence 16–18, 163, 169
self-esteem 18, 87, 163, 166, 169
self-paced skills 154–155
short-term memory (STM) 138, 141, 182
sit and reach 31
skeletal muscles 58–59, 79, 92, 95
skeletal system 7–8, 57–58, 60, 62–63, 92, 100, 102, 105
   functions of 60
skeleton 60–61, 63, 85
skill classification 9, 131, 154–157
skill-related components of fitness 28–31
skinfold callipers test 31
slow twitch muscle fibres 59
SMART targets 9, 132–135, 137

218

Index

social media 124–125, 175
society as factor affecting participation 162, 170
socio-cultural issues 10, 160–183
specification for exam 4–5, 10, 13
specificity of goals/training 39, 41, 46, 49–50, 52, 92, 122, 133–135
speed of athletes 29, 31, 33–35, 37–39, 41, 45, 49, 57–58, 65, 91, 110, 119
speed of lever movement 104–105
speed of muscle contraction 59, 93
sponsorship 125, 174–177
sports technology 8, 91, 120–127, 129
sportsmanship 10, 161, 180
sprint test 31, 33
sprinting 15, 22, 27, 29, 31, 33, 38–39, 45, 59, 77–78, 132
SPOV *see* principles of training
starches 23–24, 79
stereotyping 162–165
stork balance test 30
stress 16–18
stretching 39–40, 50–51, 55
stroke volume 68, 84, 86
success 17, 30, 135, 139, 141, 150–151, 174
sugars 23
supporters, technology for 124–126
synovial joints 62
systemic circulatory system 72–73
systolic pressure 68

T

tedium 46
tendons 7, 60, 62, 85, 92, 97
test protocols 6, 28, 30–33
thermoregulation 71, 84
third class lever 101, 103, 105
tidal volume 70, 84, 86
TMO 123

training
    methods *see* methods of training
    zones 6, 15, 39, 41, 43
transport of nutrients/oxygen/waste products 7, 66, 71, 73, 87
transverse plane 8, 113–114, 117

V

validity 30, 33
VAR 123
variance 46
varied practice 146
vascular system 7, 57, 66, 71, 86
vasoconstriction 71, 84
vasodilation 71, 84
veins 71–72
ventricles 66–67, 73, 75, 86
verbal guidance 144–145
vertical axis 8, 113–117
vertical jump 31
viscosity 78
visual guidance 144–145
visualisation 150–151
vital capacity 70, 86
vitamins 23, 25

W

warm-up 6, 15, 32, 38–39, 50, 52–53, 80
water 23–25, 47, 55, 78–79
weight training 38, 40, 42, 46
wellbeing 6, 11, 15–19, 121–122, 131–132, 161, 166
    definition of 6, 16–17
    mental 16–17, 19, 166
    physical 16–17, 19, 132, 161, 166
    social 16–17, 19, 166
    relationship with fitness/health/exercise 15–16
whole practice 146
written assessment 4

Acknowledgements

(WJEC GCSE PE specification) Welsh Joint Education Committee (v.2 2019) 'WJEC GCSE in Physical Education' Cardiff, WJEC CBAC Ltd. pp. 3–10, 13, 14, 56, 90, 130, 160. Available at https://www.wjec.co.uk/qualifications/physical-education-gcse/; (Eduqas GCSE PE specification) WJEC Eduqas (v.3 2020) 'WJEC Eduqas GCSE in Physical Education' Cardiff, WJEC CBAC Ltd. pp. 3–10, 13, 14, 56, 90, 130, 160. Available at https://www.eduqas.co.uk/qualifications/physical-education-gcse/; M. Malsom 'Benefits of a Healthy Lifestyle poster' p.19.

Please note: The specification information in this book is correct at the time of going to press. It is, however, important to check with your examination board (WJEC or Eduqas) to view their current specification and assessment information.

Photographs

p.4 (PE lesson) Juice Flair / Shutterstock.com; p.5 (Sports bag with equipment) Africa Studio / Shutterstock.com; p.6 (Health, training and exercise) Syda Productions / Shutterstock.com; p.7 (Physiology) ForeverLee / Shutterstock.com; p.8 (Movement analysis) Gino Santa Maria / Shutterstock.com; p.9 (Psychology of sport and physical activity) Syda Productions / Shutterstock.com; p.10 (Participation) wavebreakmedia / Shutterstock.com; p.12 (Football equipment) koonsiri boonnak / Shutterstock.com; p.14 (Chapter 1 background) Jacob Lund / Shutterstock.com; p.18 (Unhealthy choices) Opat Suvi / Shutterstock.com; p.19 (Benefits of a Healthy Lifestyle poster) Millie Malsom; p.20 (Health symbols) Tefi / Shutterstock.com; p.21 (Man sitting on sofa) EvMedvedeva / Shutterstock.com; p.24 (Health food) Nok Lek / Shutterstock.com; p.27 (Marathon runners) lzf / Shutterstock.com; p.27 (Sprinters) Juice Dash / Shutterstock.com; p.33 (Heart rate monitoring) Andrey_Popov / Shutterstock.com; p.36 (Netball players) Image Source Trading Ltd / Shutterstock.com; p.37 (Mountain biker) Maciej Kopaniecki / Shutterstock.com; p.39 (Fartlek training) David Pereiras / Shutterstock.com; p.39 (Circuit training) TWStock / Shutterstock.com; p.40 (Plyometric training) Daxiao Productions / Shutterstock.com; p.40 (Weight training) Hananeko_Studio / Shutterstock.com; p.45 (Footballer) matimix / Shutterstock.com; p.47 (Taking a rest) Photo Smoothies / Shutterstock.com; p.47 (Training whilst injured) BalanceFormCreative / Shutterstock.com; p.49 (Long jumper) Pavel1964 / Shutterstock.com; p.50 (Warming-up) bbernard / Shutterstock.com; p.51 (Cooling- down) Julia Albul / Shutterstock.com; p.53 (Warm-up) Rawpixel.com / Shutterstock.com; p.55 (Cool-down) Dean Drobot / Shutterstock.com; p.56 (Chapter 2 background) Maridav / Shutterstock.com; p.59 (Muscle anatomy) newart-graphics / Shutterstock.com; p.64 (Shot put) wavebreakmedia / Shutterstock.com; p.65 (Javelin) sportpoint / Shutterstock.com; p.76 (Sprinters) sportpoint / Shutterstock.com; p.76 (Aerobic exercise) Maridav / Shutterstock.com; p.77 (Anaerobic exercise) dotshock / Shutterstock.com; p.79 (Water bottle) Stefanovic Mina / Shutterstock.com; p.79 (Aerobic exercise) sebastienlemyre / Shutterstock.com; p.79 (Anaerobic exercise) Flamingo Images / Shutterstock.com; p.83 (Sprinters) sportpoint / Shutterstock.com; p.85 (Runner) lzf / Shutterstock.com; p.86 (Cardiovascular system) Shot4Sell / Shutterstock.com; p.87 (Sport injury) AstroStar / Shutterstock.com; p.89 (Cardiovascular system) Lightspring / Shutterstock.com; p.90 (Chapter 3 background) wavebreakmedia / Shutterstock.com; p.93 (Concentric/eccentric contraction) EreborMountain / Shutterstock.com; p.94 (Plank (isometric contraction)) Prostock-studio / Shutterstock.com; p.95 (Leg extension (quadriceps)) Makatserchyk / Shutterstock.com; p.95 (Leg curl (hamstring)) Makatserchyk / Shutterstock.com; p.96 (Photo of scissors, glue and split pin) Dominique Wade; p.97 (Diagram of elbow) BlueRingMedia / Shutterstock.com; p.98 (Gymnast running) sportpoint / Shutterstock.com; p.99 (Gymnast doing handstand) I T A L O / Shutterstock.com; p.100 (Gymnast on tiptoes) I T A L O / Shutterstock.

Index

com; p.102 (Lever neck) udaix / Shutterstock.com; p.102 (Lever ankle) udaix / Shutterstock.com; p.102 (Football header) wavebreakmedia / Shutterstock.com; p.102 (Runner) OSTILL is Franck Camhi / Shutterstock.com; p.103 (Lever elbow) udaix / Shutterstock.com; p.103 (Biceps curls) YAKOBCHUK VIACHESLAV / Shutterstock.com; p.104 (Basketball) imtmphoto / Shutterstock.com; p.106 (Football equipment) koonsiri boonnak / Shutterstock.com; p.107 (Football header) wavebreakmedia / Shutterstock.com; p.108 (Male gymnast running) Master1305 / Shutterstock.com; p.109 (Gymnast on tiptoes) I T A L O / Shutterstock.com; p.112 (Runner) Studio Romantic / Shutterstock.com; p.112 (Weightlifting) UfaBizPhoto / Shutterstock.com; p.112 (Throwing a javelin) Master1305 / Shutterstock.com; p.112 (Standing figure (medial plane)) SciePro / Shutterstock.com; p.112 (Diver) Maxisport / Shutterstock.com; p.112 (Star jumps) Syda Productions / Shutterstock.com; p.112 (Standing figure (frontal plane)) SciePro / Shutterstock.com; p.112 (Lateral raises) MDV Edwards / Shutterstock.com; p.112 (Cartwheel) Dusan Petkovic / Shutterstock.com; p.112 (Speed skating) Coolakov_com / Shutterstock.com; p.113 (Discus) wavebreakmedia / Shutterstock.com; p.113 (Standing figure (transverse plane)) SciePro / Shutterstock.com; p.113 (Gymnast) sportpoint / Shutterstock.com; p.113 (Ice skater) Artur Didyk / Shutterstock.com; p.113 (Basketball players) Alex Kravtsov / Shutterstock.com; p.114 (Sagittal axis (gymnast)) Dusan Petkovic / Shutterstock.com; p.114 (Frontal axis (diver)) Maxisport / Shutterstock.com; p.115 (Vertical axis (ice skater)) Artur Didyk / Shutterstock.com; p.116 & 117 (Jelly babies photos) Dominique Wade; p.117 (Star jumps) Syda Productions / Shutterstock.com; p.119 (Cartwheel) Microgen / Shutterstock.com; p.120 (Runner with smart watch) SeventyFour / Shutterstock.com; p.122 (Coach with ipad) Thx4Stock / Shutterstock.com; p.123 (VAR) Kris Petkong / Shutterstock.com; p.124 (Phone) Piotr Piatrouski / Shutterstock.com; p.125 (Stadium) Vladimir_Vinogradov / Shutterstock.com; p.127 (Phone technology) Rawpixel.com / Shutterstock.com; p.129 (Gymnast and video camera) muratart / Shutterstock.com; p.130 (Chapter 4 background) santypan / Shutterstock.com; p.132 (Personal trainer) Ojan Milinkov / Shutterstock.com; p.133 (Time-focused targets) RomanR / Shutterstock.com; p.136 (Basketball team and coach) Monkey Business Images / Shutterstock.com; p.136 (Tennis player and coach) Microgen / Shutterstock.com; p.137 (Woman writing) Starstuff / Shutterstock.com; p.139 (Happy footballer) DoublePHOTO studio / Shutterstock.com; p.139 (High five) Rawpixel.com / Shutterstock.com; p.141 (Cricketer) vectorfusionart / Shutterstock.com; p.142 (Rugby players) wavebreakmedia / Shutterstock.com; p.143 (Bowler) wavebreakmedia / Shutterstock.com; p.143 (Football training) matimix / Shutterstock.com; p.147 (Golfer) Freebird7977 / Shutterstock.com; p.147 (Footballer) Fotokostic / Shutterstock.com; p.147 (Tennis serve) dotshock / Shutterstock.com; p.147 (Swimming exercises) Odua Images / Shutterstock.com; p.149 (Coach) Chalermpon Poungpeth / Shutterstock.com; p.149 (Tennis coach) Olena Yakobchuk / Shutterstock.com; p.149 (Swimming coach) dotshock / Shutterstock.com; p.151 (Trophy) wavebreakmedia / Shutterstock.com; p.153 (Cyclist) Maciej Kopaniecki / Shutterstock.com; p.155 (Golfer) Maatman / Shutterstock.com; p.156 (Hockey) Skumer / Shutterstock.com; p.157 (Wheelchair tennis player) Nejron Photo / Shutterstock.com; p.159 (BMX) 4 PM production / Shutterstock.com; p.159 (High jumper) sportpoint / Shutterstock.com; p.160 (Chapter 5 background) Rocksweeper / Shutterstock.com; p.163 (Age) Rido / Shutterstock.com; p.164 (Gender) Fotokostic / Shutterstock.com, p.165 (Ethnicity) Monkey Business Images / Shutterstock.com; p.165 (Disability) mezzotint / Shutterstock.com; p.166 (Wheelchair tennis player) 101akarca / Shutterstock.com; p.168 (Relay race) Robert Kneschke / Shutterstock.com; p.169 (Football) Steve Scott / Shutterstock.com; p.171 (Children playing football) Photographee.eu / Shutterstock.com; p.172 (Climbing apparatus) Air Images / Shutterstock.com; p.173 (Rugby players) Rawpixel.com / Shutterstock.com; p.175 (Racing car) Digital Storm / Shutterstock.com; p.175 (Screen) Sergey Nivens / Shutterstock.com; p.175 (Stadium) EFKS / Shutterstock.com; p.177 (Live streaming) McLittle Stock / Shutterstock.com; p.177 (Screen) Sergey Nivens / Shutterstock.com; p.177 (Business/sponsorship) Matej Kastelic / Shutterstock.com; p.179 (Stadium) hlopex / Shutterstock.com; p.179 (Smiling athlete) GaudiLab / Shutterstock.com; p.181 (Weights) Georgios Tsichlis / Shutterstock.com; p.181 (Gamesmanship) JoeSAPhotos / Shutterstock.com; p.182 (Steroids) Marsan / Shutterstock.com; p.183 (Performance enhancing drugs) BestStockVector / Shutterstock.com.